Culture and Development

Culture and Development
A Critical Introduction

Susanne Schech and Jane Haggis
Flinders University of South Australia

BLACKWELL
Publishers

Copyright © Susanne Schech and Jane Haggis 2000

The right of Susanne Schech and Jane Haggis to be identified as authors of this work has been asserted in accordance with the Copyright, Designs and Patents Act 1988.

First published 2000

2 4 6 8 10 9 7 5 3 1

Blackwell Publishers Ltd
108 Cowley Road
Oxford OX4 1JF
UK

Blackwell Publishers Inc.
350 Main Street
Malden, Massachusetts 02148
USA

British Library Cataloguing in Publication Data

A CIP catalogue record for this book is available from the British Library.

Library of Congress Cataloging-in-Publication Data has been applied for.

ISBN 0-631-20950-6 (hbk)
ISBN 0-631-20951-4 (pbk)

Typeset in 10½ on 12½ pt Palatino
by Ace Filmsetting Ltd, Frome, Somerset
Printed in Great Britain by TJ International Ltd, Padstow, Cornwall

This book is printed on acid-free paper.

Contents

Figures and Tables

Figures

Tables

Preface: The Cross-overs of Culture and Development

What has culture to do with development? Here is one example, set in the context of the Asian economic crisis which descended on countries previously celebrated as "Asian tigers" for their high economic growth rate and fast rate of social development (Jomo 1998). A newspaper article featured in the business section of a respected Australian daily newspaper (Macleay 1998: 25) shows how Western perceptions of this crisis are steeped in cultural assumptions about Asia, and at the same time, how strongly economic flows of capital are affected by what appear to be irrational trends in investment culture (figure 0.1).

1   Investing in the Asian snake pit

The article discusses the decision by property and financial services giant Lend Lease not to invest in new projects in Asia "because of the region's financial meltdown." This opinion ignores the way in which it is precisely decisions such as this which have contributed to Asia's financial meltdown, turning it into a deep economic crisis. As one foreign investor after another pulls out of the region, we are left unsure whether it is for "sound economic reasons," or because investors have persuaded each other, by sharing their perceptions and copying each other's behavior, that "[p]eople just aren't investing in Asia at the moment" (Lend Lease managing director David Higgins, quoted in Macleay 1998: 25). A cultural process or an economic process, or both?

What pulls the reader's eye to the article, however, is the image which accompanies it. Entitled "Asian snake pit," it features an Asian-looking woman reclining in the midst of an entangled mass of snakes. With the snakes winding around her body, the woman looks alluring and mysterious, but perhaps too dangerous to handle. In the context of the article, the image can be interpreted as a representation of Asia in its present crisis – attractive and enticing, but fraught with danger. It draws on a long tradition of perceptions of Asia as

BUSINESS

Lend Lease puts the brakes on Asia

Asia fallout

John Marley

PROPERTY and financial services giant Lend Lease has dramatically curtailed its push into Asia because of the region's financial meltdown, conceding yesterday it did not expect to commit itself to any new projects for up to five years.

Managing director David Higgins said although Lend Lease would defer new opportunities in Asia, it remained confident the slowdown would have a minimal effect on existing assets in the region.

Nevertheless, Lend Lease has made provisions of $25 million to cover potential losses in the region.

"People just aren't investing in Asia at the moment," Mr Higgins said.

"The sales on our development projects have effectively stopped ... our project management business has been significantly curtailed.

Provisions of $17 million —

out of a book value of Asian assets of $203 million — have been made against projects in Indonesia, Thailand and China. Also, the company's funds

management joint venture with Sinar Mas in Indonesia has experienced a sharp outflow of funds, from $600 million to $145 million.

ASIAN SNAKE PIT

ASIAN ASSETS							
($million)	Jun 97	31 Dec 97	Jun 97	Dec 97	Dec 97	Jun 97	Dec 97
Singapore	69.6	(4.0)	115.8	118.4			
Indonesia	92.8	(11.0)	73.4	16.4			
Thailand	22.0	(6.0)	13.7	9.9			
China	6.7	(4.0)	2.7	3.8			
Total	221.4	(25.0)	203.3	146.4			

TOTAL ASSETS				
($million)	Dec 96	Jun 97	Dec 97	
Aust and Pacific	77.5%	69.5%	61.5%	
Asia	9.0%	7.0%	6.5%	
Europe	6.5%	6.5%	9.5%	
North America	7.0%	21.5%	22.4%	

LEND LEASE HOLDINGS LTD		
Half year	1997	1996
Total revenue ($bn)	1.37	1.03
Net profit ($m)	181.5	160.0
Abnormals ($m)	nil	nil
EPS (c)	72.4	64.3
DPS (c) interim	53	48

Result for the six months to December 31. Net profit is after tax and after abnormals. Dividend is fully franked at 36 per cent.

Lend Lease lost only $3.2 million on currency depreciation and then only because hedging against the baht was unavailable in August.

However, an unwinding of hedging positions would lower exposure to Asia — now at 6.3 per cent of total group assets — to $146.4 million, 80 per cent of which was in Singapore where there was no provisioning for further writedowns.

Asian development exposure would be further reduced to $57 million if the sale of its Nortech project, part of the Admiralty Park industrial complex, in Singapore was completed.

The deferral of Lend Lease's

Asian push came as the group reported a 13 per cent increase in interim net profit to $181.5 million for the six months to December 31 and a further unwinding of its Westpac portfolio, on which the company relies for a $20 million dividend stream.

Lend Lease booked a $60 million net profit after balance date on the sale of 10 million Westpac shares in January, but Mr Higgins said the company would not rely on the sale proceeds for what would be an increase in net profit above last year's $322 million net figure.

He refused to forecast a full-year result, although analysts expect an 11 per cent rise in net profit to $357 million for the June 30 year, which would give the group its 23rd consecutive annual increase.

Lend Lease again relied heavily on its equity division to boost profits. It contributed 30 per cent of the total net profit, including a net profit of $23.5 million from the sale of 25 million Mirvac shares. There was a 22 per cent lift to $92.6 million from funds management and its life insurance net profits.

Mr Higgins said the company was prudent in being almost fully hedged against foreign exchange los²s.

Despite its Asian exposure,

Mr Higgins said the growth was well on track towards its stated goal of a 40 per cent reduction in costs of operating its superannuation and insurance unit, MLC, which would soon be merged with National Mutual.

The proportion of profits from North America and Europe would grow rapidly over the next two years as projects — such as the $15 billion Bluewater shopping centre in Britain — came on stream.

Offshore profits would, from about next year, begin to overtake the contributions from direct investments, which would be wound back to about 13 per cent of total group net profit.

Overall group property sales dipped to $496 million compared with $703 million in the previous corresponding period and the forward construction workload dipped slightly to $2.1 billion from $2.3 billion previously.

Projects in Australia such as the Fox studio site in Sydney and the Pyrmont redevelopment and Olympic village were not expected to contribute to profits before the next financial year.

Figure 0.1 Lend Lease puts the brakes on Asia: The Asian snake pit "feminine, passive, a seductive place where Western masculinity might go limp" (Broinowski 1992: 5), or, in equally stereotypical but more positive terms, as luscious, fertile, and sensuous. The combination of sexually attractive woman and snake has many connotations in the West, and can be interpreted on a number of levels, ranging from Christian interpretations of the Fall, to ritual performances in inner-city red light districts. In this article the image evokes cultural constructs of Asia, as well as being employed to attract the attention of a primarily male readership. However, an intimate connection between culture and economic development is clearly implied, even if the author of the article had not intended or even known about it. Connections such as: Would you want to invest in a snake pit? Are the attractions of Asia worth the danger?

2 Culture and development

This book aims to pull culture out of the shadows in development studies and argue that it is, and has always been, central to our understanding of development processes and their impacts on societies across the globe. The centrality of culture, and its interconnectedness with economic, political, and social change, has been increasingly apparent in contemporary events such as the resurgence of Islam as a political movement, the emergence of indigenous rights movements, and the rise of ethno-nationalism. On the other hand, newly emerging fields of research, such as cultural studies and postcolonial studies, and the impact of postmodernist thought, have provided us with new analytical tools which enable us to take a new look at the relationship between culture and development.

In focusing on culture and development we are not suggesting that cultural factors dominate the process of development, or the ways in which we should conduct the study of development. The interdisciplinary area of development studies will continue to concern itself with the myriad intended and unintended changes which societies are undergoing in the process of modernization, and suggest ways of addressing the crises – poverty, disease, displacement, war, environmental degradation, repression – which this process produces. But we are arguing, along with Tim Allen (1992: 337), that "[t]he study of development . . . necessitates the study of shared values of all kinds, and the examination of their multifaceted transformations. Religion and kinship are just as significant as economic transactions and the political life of nation states, and in fact these things are not really separable or comparable." Development intervention, which is certain to continue at least in the near future, can be more effective and beneficial to those people whose lives are being changed if culture is taken seriously. A painstaking exegesis of a well-meaning but ill-fated Australian development project in Kenya reveals the reasons for its failure as mainly cultural: past lessons were not learnt, historical local circumstances not examined, indigenous knowledge not harnessed, and the superiority of Western knowledge and experience taken for granted (Porter, Allen, and Thompson 1991).

However, the application of new analytical tools and fresh perspectives in development studies has led some scholars to cut to the very core of development. Seen as a cultural construct, the concept of development can be dismissed altogether on the grounds that it is steeped in Western ideologies (capitalist or socialist) of modernization and progress, or irreparably stained by its association with colonialism and imperialism (present and past), or simply outdated and replaced by globalization. While this book attempts to give some space to these arguments, it maintains the terminology with which development studies has operated over the past fifty years or so. We may need to find new terms of reference for processes of development, developing countries, First and Third World, etc., but this will be a project for the future.

3   Points of contact

In the following chapters we focus on some important points of contact between culture and development. One such point is where development, modernization, and westernization occupy the same place, even stand in for each other. As the book explores, a very common portrayal of the Third World and its peoples in development studies is as undeveloped, backward, and non-Western. The solution is invariably seen in terms of a process of modernization implicitly cast as becoming more Western. While often couched in terms of industrialization, urbanization, and the like, in fact what is being advocated is the adoption of Western values and beliefs to underwrite the structural transformation. Hence "culture" is deeply embedded in visions of development.

A second point emerging from our reflections on development and culture is the equation of development with modernization, and of anthropology with culture. A division of labor has become entrenched whereby development studies concerns itself with modernization, conceived primarily in economic and political terms. Culture becomes the preserve of anthropology. This division of labour in part emerged from the earlier anthropological view of culture as bounded, "a self-contained system of traits which distinguishes one community from another" (Bauman 1973: 35). From this perspective, contacts between different cultures were viewed as "cultural clash," and mixing between cultures hence bound to result in undesirable consequences, or even destruction of the cultural "whole." By definition, then, only societies had "culture" which experienced a pace of change slow enough for the "same basic personality type" to be recreated in the next generation (Bauman 1973: 35–6). This implied that rapidly changing modernizing societies lost their cohesive culture, in exchange for something more general and less interesting, described by the term Westernization. At the same time, critics of modernization, using the same concept of bounded culture, can interpret development processes not only as a Western imposition of capitalism on the Third World, but also as cultural imperialism, irrevocably destroying indigenous cultures and identities. In this book we take issue with this notion of culture as bounded, and hence unpack the established division of labor between development studies and anthropology.

There is a third intersection between culture and development, where modernization is equated with development and defined as "the right culture." As Jonathan Rigg reports from Southeast Asia, "the modernization ethic, broadly defined, has been internalized by most people in Southeast Asia. . . . People's desires and aspirations, for themselves and their children, are framed in terms of modernization" (Rigg 1997: 280). In a Third World region where development has rewarded people more than in other regions with higher life expectancy and higher living standards, modernization is apparently readily embraced, and indigenous cultural practices are rejected where they seem to hinder modernization. A global village emerges in the sense of geographically distant people sharing the same values and aspirations, not through cultural or capitalist imperialism, but as a result of the positive effects of development. We suggest that globalization also works to emphasize a community's distinctiveness, and that modernization is not a rolling pin operating on a lump of dough, but meshes with cultural traditions in complex ways.

The fourth, and we argue most crucial, way in which culture and development intersect is that neither can be understood without the other. As Tim Allen (1992) points out, culture is intrinsic to how we look at the world. The same community can be described as backward and uncivilized, or as offering new and more appropriate ways of living to those post-industrial Western societies, depending on the cultural lenses one uses. Moreover, it has been argued, by Escobar (1995) and others, that development is not only an amalgam of processes of change, but also a system of knowledge and power which produces and justifies these processes. As a result, culture no longer makes sense as an entity, but rather becomes intrinsic to all social relations and structures. The question the constructionist view of culture raises, then, is whether or not there is still a need for a notion of culture as something "out there," something coherent which offers its practitioners an identity, a cause, or a home. This is a hotly debated issue, not only in development studies but more generally. On the one hand, there are groups of people who claim "culture" as a coherent and bounded identity; on the other are those who experience and conceive of "culture" as a much more fluid and interactive construct. The book explores a number of instances in which this debate emerges in the context of development.

4 Outline of the book

This book is divided into two sections. Section one includes four chapters surveying the old and new ways of thinking about culture and development. Chapter 1 looks at the concepts of "development" and "culture," tracing the respective histories and debates around each term. Chapter 2 explores how culture has to date been treated in mainstream development studies. It traces the various uses of the term in modernization theory and the ways in which these have influenced the conception of development models pursued by Third World states. Chapter 3 traces the influence of cultural studies, postcolonial studies, and globalization on development studies. Drawing on the new "anthropologies of modernities" (Miller 1995), the chapter argues that the notion of culture as bounded is coming apart at the seams. Chapter 4 provides an overview of feminist approaches to development. We argue that feminist theory has been an important contributor to opening up the debates on culture and development, particularly in terms of the "cultures" embedded in the very concept of development. Initially focused on revealing the male-centered and patriarchal nature of development thinking, feminist scholars and activists were soon embroiled in a much wider set of debates over the cultural politics of difference which, we argue, are having important ramifications for development praxis.

The second section consists of three thematic chapters which work through many of the arguments presented in the first. Chapter 5 unpacks one of the earliest and most pervasive assumptions in development studies and anthropology, namely the dichotomy of tradition and modernity. It does this through a discussion of the different ways this dichotomy is deployed in constructions of national identity. Chapter 6 focuses on human rights and the different ways in which culture is used to define, assert, and contest rights in contexts of development. The chapter discusses two aspects of this, one being the debates over whether human rights are universal. The other aspect concerns the ways in which rights are being redefined and claimed in specific cultural contexts. Chapter 7 concludes the book by revisiting its main themes in terms of the so-called "information revolution" forecast for the new millennium. It considers arguments about the informational society, its relation to new agendas in development, and the arguments being made about its potential to ameliorate or worsen the "development gap."

This book is an introduction into the areas of inquiry which we have sketched out. It does not, and cannot, cover the multitude of ways in which culture and development are interwoven. In pulling together some of the interesting work that scholars all over the world have produced, we are conscious of many omissions. We have relied mainly on English-language sources to ensure that our readers can follow up these sources, but this has restricted the range of material we have been able to include. The authors' location in the Asia Pacific region has influenced our choice of case studies to illustrate our arguments, although we have also drawn on research focused on the African, and to a much lesser extent, Latin American and Caribbean region. And finally, the thematic chapters on tradition (chapter 5), human rights (chapter 6), and the information revolution (chapter 7) by no means exhaust the range of themes where closer attention to culture is relevant in the broad field of development studies. There are several other themes that we wanted to include but had to leave out, for practical reasons. Education, for example, where debates about the need to preserve and foster (traditional) indigenous knowledge, and about the role of (modern) education in development, appear to take place on different planets, imbued as they are with very different notions of "culture." Or health, with its focus on the human body, itself as much cultural as it is physical, so that public health specialists have become increasingly aware of the importance of traditional health practices, human rights, and cultural identity in efforts to deal with the myriad of health problems across the world. Another area we chose to neglect is the environment, despite the fact that it clearly is a key area in development studies today, as a burgeoning literature readily testifies. Cultural constructions of the binaries of culture/nature and humans/environment, the invention of environmental traditions, the ambivalent concept of "wilderness," the patriarchal view of nature as female, contemporary claims of environmental rights are all issues highly relevant to the themes of this book. However, we ask our readers to view this book as a resource in making these connections themselves, and refer to literatures beyond the confines of this book.

References

Allen, T. 1992: Taking culture seriously. In T. Allen and A. Thomas (eds), *Poverty and Development in the 1990s*. Oxford: Oxford University Press, 331–46.

Bauman, Z. 1973: *Culture as Praxis*. London: Routledge and Kegan Paul.

Broinowski, A. 1992: *The Yellow Lady: Australian Impressions of Asia*. Melbourne: Oxford University Press.

Escobar, A. 1995: *Encountering Development: The Making and Unmaking of the Third World*. Princeton: Princeton University Press.

Jomo, K. S. (ed.) 1998: *Tigers in Trouble: Financial Governance, Liberalisation and Crises in East Asia*. New York: Zed Books.

Macleay, J. 1998: Lend Lease puts the brakes on Asia. *The Australian*, February 13, 1998, p. 25.

Miller, D. (ed.) 1995: *Worlds Apart. Modernity through the Prism of the Local*. London: Routledge.

Porter, D., Allen, B., and Thompson, G. 1991: *Development in Practice: Paved with Good Intentions*. London: Routledge.

Rigg, J. 1997: *Southeast Asia. The Human Landscape of Modernization and Development*. London: Routledge.

Acknowledgments

The idea for this book came to us while teaching our new topic on culture and development to first year students in 1997. At the time there was no teaching material that brought together the concerns of development studies with the critical issues raised in cultural studies. Our first year students cheerfully submitted to our teaching experiments and contributed much to the resulting book. As well, our honors and postgraduate students in development studies taught us much from their searching questions, sharp analysis, and new ways of looking at development. We particularly wish to acknowledge our debt to Amy Specht, Catherine Chalk, Shah Nawaz, Somsuan Glagarntai, Tess Escubio, Yuri Banens, Kieleigh Hogan, Monique Mulholland, and Tatsuya Iwama.

The Federal Jobskill Program for new migrants from non-English-speaking backgrounds indirectly supported the book by sponsoring Vicki Pavliv, our first research assistant. She prepared the first bibliographic databases for the book in 1996. Flinders University awarded us a grant of $2500 from its research budget, which allowed us to employ Paul Foley as a tutor and research assistant. He extended the bibliography we worked from, and produced abstracts from texts. Kate Borrett's research assistance made the dreaded task of seeking copyright permissions more manageable and enjoyable. She doubled as photographer for one of the images we were unable to find elsewhere. We also want to acknowledge Sanjugta Vas Dev, whose research with Susanne on NGOs and the new information and communication technologies found its way into chapter 7.

We benefited from conversations with Stephen McNally, whose own PhD research is close to the concerns of this book. He kindly allowed us to use one of his photographs. Jane also thanks Sylvia, Freya, and Stuart for carrying life on around "the book."

The authors and publisher are grateful to the following for permission to reproduce copyright material.

Extract on page 23, from W. Holland, Mis/taken identity, in E. Vasta and S. Castles (eds), *The Teeth are Smiling. The Persistence of Racism in Multicultural Australia*, St Leonards: Allen and Unwin (1996), pp. 97–129; extract on pages 43–5, from E. Cody, Striving to be spiritual, *Washington Post*, January 30, 1997, p. 13, © 1997, The Washington Post. Reprinted with permission; extract on pages 98–9, from Naila Kabeer, *Reversed Realities: Gender Hierarchies in Development Thought*, London/New York: Verso (1994), pp. 223–4; extract on page 167, from S. Alam, Thank you, Mr Harkin, sir! *New Internationalist*, 292 (1997), pp. 12–14; extract on pages 182–3, from M. Ceresa, Stilling the voices of Koori culture. Native tongues refuse to be silenced, *The Australian*, December 21, 1998, p. 11.

Illustrations

Figure 0.1, from John Macleay, Lend Lease puts the brakes on Asia, *The Australian*, February 13, 1998, p. 25; figure 1.4, Steven McNally (1998); figure 1.5, Kate Borrett (1999); figure 3.1, Susanne Schech (1997); figure 3.2, Susanne Schech (1992); figure 3.3, Susanne Schech (1995); figure 4.1, Susanne Schech (1990); figure 5.1, Hulton-Getty Picture Library; figure 5.2, from the Queen Mary Collection of the Royal Commonwealth Society Collections, Cambridge University Library; figure 5.3, from *Sati, the Blessing and the Curse: The Burning of Wives in India*, edited by John Stratton Hawley. Copyright © 1994 by Oxford University Press, Inc. Used by permission of Oxford University Press, Inc.; figure 6.1, International Women's Tribune Center (1998); figure 6.2, Susanne Schech (1990); figure 6.3, Marc French, Panos Pictures; figure 6.4, Bob Muntz (1991), reprinted with permission from Community Aid Abroad; figure 7.1, Susanne Schech (1993); figure 7.2, Adrian Arbib/Still Pictures (1998); figure 7.3, from World Development Report 1998/99 by the World Bank. Copyright © 1998 by the International Bank for Reconstruction and Development/The World Bank. Used by permission of Oxford University Press, Inc.

Every effort has been made to trace all the copyright holders, but if any have been inadvertently overlooked, the publisher will be pleased to make the necessary arrangements at the first opportunity.

1 Thinking about Culture and Development

1 Overview and introduction

The aim of this chapter is to define the two key terms of this book: "culture" and "development." The organization of the chapter, taking each of our two key concepts in turn, itself reflects the surprising lack of connection established between culture and development in the study of development. As we show in section 2 of this chapter, development has most often been thought of as an aspect of economic process: more to do with "getting the prices right" or establishing the conditions for industrialization than with cultural transformation or transfer. However, culture is not absent even from these approaches to "development." In chapter 2, the various strands of modernization theories are explored to show how culture is, explicitly and implicitly, central to the ways in which modernity is conceived of as an outcome of the development process, even when expressed mainly in economistic or technocratic terms. In modernization approaches, culture is seen as something development acts upon.

A different kind of link between culture and development comes into view when we explore development as a *discourse*. The meanings attached to the term development are produced within and by a particular cultural context, that of the so-called West – or, more precisely, the political, economic, and social institutions of Euro-American societies, generating a particular discourse of, or way of talking about, development. Seen in this way, it becomes clear that development is a cultural artefact, rather than a natural process which can be accelerated and guided by development planning. Where do the ideas and measures come from according to which we categorize societies into "developed," "developing" and "underdeveloped"? If development is not an objective status but a cultural construct, what are the implications for development studies as a field of academic inquiry, for development practice as a multi-billion dollar industry, and, more generally, for the way we look at the world in which we live?

But what does "culture" mean? How do we use the term in this book? In section 3, we look at how "culture" has been defined within Western intellectual traditions in ways which relate primarily to development as process: "culture" as something development acts upon. Drawing on the new discipline of cultural studies, we propose a definition of culture which is able to encompass both of the aspects of development we have identified here: as a process, and as a discourse itself implicated within specific cultural contexts of meaning and power.

2   What do we mean by development?

Ask the question what is meant by "development," and you will receive a great variety of answers. Despite, or perhaps because of, the voluminous literature on development that has accumulated over the past 50 years, the concept seems to be impossible to pin down in a neat definition. One reason why confusions arise is that development is variously used to refer to means and goal, process and intention.

2.1   Development as process and development as intention

The question "What is development?" is often confused with "What is intended by development?" Cowen and Shenton (1996: 1) point out that the two questions are different. Outlining a distinction earlier made by Australian economist Heinz Arndt (1987: 165), they explain that the first question relates to development as an immanent process, which creates the new by destroying the old, much like a plant grows. This pre-modern conceptualization of development was already commonly used by the ancient Greeks, who also acknowledged that decay and destruction are an integral part of the development cycle. The second question, about the intention of development, is rather different from the first. It assumes that it is possible to act in the name of development, to give order to the process of development so as to avoid, stop, or at least alleviate its negative dimensions. In this conceptualization, development is no longer immanent and cyclical, but rather it has "come to represent the potential and possibility for a linear movement of human improvement" (Cowen and Shenton 1996: 57). Usually it is the state which expresses the intention of development by imposing order on the often chaotic process of development. It formulates development doctrines and policies of development which spell out the desired outcomes and the strategies by which to achieve them.

Most countries in the Third World provide examples for development as an intent. However, it was not in relation to the Third World that development doctrines first started to emerge. Their history goes back to the early nineteenth century, when Auguste Comte and his followers first sought ways of dealing with urban poverty and unemployment in France, produced, according to their analysis, by capitalist development. Similarly, in Britain the industrial revolution had produced social tension, due to the "combination of working classes despairing because they had not enough to eat and manufacturers despairing because they genuinely believed the prevailing political and fiscal arrangements to be slowly throttling the economy" (Hobsbawm 1968: 59, quoted in Cowen and Shenton 1996: 11).

Around this time Karl Marx and Friedrich Engels provided what was to become a famous description of the rapid rate of change and the intimate relationship between destruction and creation inherent in the capitalist process of development:

> All fixed, fast-frozen relationships, with their train of venerable ideas and opinions, are swept away, all new-formed ones become obsolete before they can ossify. All that is solid melts into air, all that is holy is profaned, and men at last are forced to face with sober senses the real conditions of their lives and their relationships with their fellow men. (Marx and Engels, 1967)

Marx described the capitalist development process as a "constant revolutionizing of production, uninterrupted disturbance of all social relations, everlasting uncertainty and agitation." For many people, the experience was not only deeply unsettling and frightening, but it also did not lead to improvement. On the contrary, they were plunged into unemployment, destitution, and squalor, or what later would be called "underdevelopment." Thus, in the early nineteenth century development doctrines were formulated in the industrializing countries of Europe to "ameliorate the disordered faults of progress" (Cowen and Shenton 1996: 7). Rather than just leaving the movement from the old to the new to an objective, natural process of development, the first developmentalists argued that this movement had to be confronted, compensated, and pre-empted in order to realize universal human improvement. Thus, it was in the European context that development was first conceived of as "one means to construct the positive alternative to the disorder and underdevelopment of capitalism"(Cowen and Shenton 1996: 57).

In the second half of the twentieth century, development has come to refer mainly to the processes of change occurring in the newly independent countries of the Third World. Here, too, the concept is used to describe the "natural" processes of capitalist expansion (industrial development, the development of natural resources), but more frequently it implies the actions of a national government or international organization, such as the World Bank, to purposely enable those types of activities which promise a better life and alleviate suffering. In short, development has increasingly come to mean something we do, rather than something that happens to us.

2.2   Enlightenment, modernity, and progress

As we have seen in the previous section, while development processes have been identified much earlier, development doctrines that prescribe what should be done emerged in nineteenth-century Europe. It was only in the modern era that humans came to believe they were able, entitled, and even compelled (by moral considerations, for example) to have a lasting impact on the processes of nature. Modernity is the broad world view which has become established over the course of the eighteenth century in the West (mainly in Europe and in the USA), and which has subsequently spread, initially through colonization, to other regions of the earth. Echoing Marx's observations, Marshall (1994: 7) explains:

> modernity is associated with the release of the individual from the bonds of tradition, with the progressive differentiation of society, with the emergence of civil society, with social equality, with innovation and change. All of these accomplishments are associated with capitalism, industrialism, secularisation, urbanisation and rationalisation.

Thus, in the writings of the eighteenth-century Enlightenment philosophers and social thinkers, modernity is commonly seen in contrast to traditional social order and beliefs. Traditional forms of knowledge in the old regime were dependent on religious authority, such as the Bible, which kept people ignorant and superstitious. These forms of knowledge legitimized absolutist forms of power, as exemplified by the French kings prior to the Revolution. Modern knowledge, according to the Enlightenment philosophers, was based on experience, scientific experiment, and reason (Hamilton 1992; Porter 1990). Science allowed humans to control nature and make her more productive in ways that improved their lives, through the invention of machinery which would abolish drudgery, and free humans from illness and famine.

Subtle analysis, critical thinking, and a diversity of ideas offered by Enlightenment thinkers also had consequences for the way in which political power was organized. In France, it spelled the end of absolutist rule (at least for a short time) by inspiring the French Revolution, which sought to construct a system of power which was scientific and based on a rational contract between the free individual (who in those days was male and white), and his elected government. The modern state became the representative of the nation of individuals, and a trustee of their interests, hopes, and ambitions for a better future. Nineteenth-century European governments became involved in managing and disciplining people, to regulate and bring order to society which was undergoing massive changes in the industrial and urban revolution.

One of the most powerful ideas of the Enlightenment is that the natural and social condition of humans could improve through application of reason and science. The idea implies ever-increasing well-being and happiness, a movement from badness to goodness. Shanin (1997) maintains that this idea has become so powerful in the modern era that it penetrated all strata of society, and is seen as common sense. In Shanin's (1997: 65) words, the idea of progress "offered a powerful and pervasive supra-theory that ordered and interpreted everything within the life of humanity – past, present and future."

The Enlightenment

The Enlightenment is "a set of interconnected ideas, values, principles, and facts which provide both an image of the natural and social world, and a way of thinking about it" (Hamilton 1992: 21). But the Enlightenment was also a diverse movement, with a plurality of ideas (Porter 1990) which cannot be circumscribed easily within the term "Age of reason." Indeed, many eighteenth-century intellectuals rejected the rationalist philosophies of the seventeenth century, arguing, with Voltaire, that reason can lead to false and absurd conclusions if divorced from experience and sensitivity. Despite numerous internal contradictions, the central ideas of the Enlightenment (Hamilton 1992: 21–2) can be summarized thus:

- **Reason** – the process of rational thought and principal way of organizing knowledge. It produces clear "ideas independent of experience which can be demonstrated to any thinking person," but it must be "tempered by experience and experiment."
- **Empiricism** – all knowledge based on empirical facts and can be apprehended through the senses.
- **Science** – scientific knowledge as the key to expanding all human knowledge.
- **Universalism** – reason and science produce general principles and laws which can be applied to all situations everywhere.
- **Progress** – natural and social condition of humans can be improved through application of reason and science. Propelling progress is the quest of ever-increasing well-being and happiness.
- **Individualism** – the individual cannot be subjected to a higher authority; he/she is the starting point for all knowledge and action. Society is the product of thought and action of individuals.
- **Secularism** – secular knowledge and structures replace traditional religious authority.
- **Toleration** – all humans are essentially the same, and beliefs of other races are not necessarily inferior to European Christianity.
- **Uniformity of human nature** – principal characteristics of humans are always and everywhere the same, i.e., there is a human essence.
- **Freedom** – opposition to feudal and traditional constraints on beliefs, trade, communication, social interaction, sexuality, ownership of property.

In particular, it permitted Europeans to solve two conceptual problems which modernity posed. One was how to deal with the ever-increasing range of different societies and cultures with which European explorers were confronted in their travels to distant lands. The diversity they observed could not be explained with the old dichotomy of civilized and barbaric, and required a more sophisticated way of categorizing and making sense of the range of different societies. The second problem was that in pre-modern times change had been understood in terms of a cycle, similar to the way in which immanent development was understood; the end was the same as the beginning. However, the changes occurring in the modern age, as described by Marx above, were more radical; societies undergoing industrialization, for example, were different at the end of the process. History came to be seen as a linear trajectory, rather than a cycle. The future was uncertain, but this was compensated by a sense of optimism and promise implicit in the notion of progress. After all, those who invented the notion saw themselves as representing the highest achievements of humanity to date. They were able to conceive of themselves as the model for societies which they categorized as less developed. The concept of progress became

> an immensely "energizing" tool of policy and counterpolicy, as well as serving to mobilize the devotion and readiness of its followers, who were often prepared to sacrifice much . . . to help speed up the inevitable approach of the necessary and glorious future. (Shanin 1997: 68–9)

The Enlightenment can thus be seen to have ushered in a new era, that of modernity, which for the first time allowed humans to conceive of development as an intention. Science, rather than God, became central to modern society (Touraine 1995), and the individual, rather than the king, empowered government. Furthermore, the history of human societies came to be understood in terms of linear progress and improvement. These three fundamental changes in how the world was seen and understood had in common the notion that the process of development could be controlled by human agency. Where Shanin (1997) differs from Cowen and Shenton (1996) is that the former sees development as closely linked to progress, and both of these as the *raison d'être* for statehood, while the latter perceive development doctrines emerging from the limitations of the notion of progress.

2.3   Third World development doctrines

Development studies, as an interdisciplinary field mainly devoted to the study of Third World countries, has a recent history. Some writers have located the beginning of development thinking in the immediate aftermath of the Second World War, concurrent with the break-up of the British empire (e.g. Arndt 1987; Escobar 1995). Escobar (1995) begins his book about the making and unmaking of the Third World with a quotation of Harry Truman's inaugural address as president of the United States of America in 1949. Truman defined half of the world's population as poor, hungry, disease-prone, and, in short, underdeveloped, and then went on to argue that the West possessed the knowledge and the skill to redress their suffering:

What we envisage is a program of development based on the concepts of democratic fair dealing. . . . Greater production is the key to prosperity and peace. And
the key to greater production is a wider and more vigorous application of modern scientific and technical knowledge. (Truman [1949] 1964, quoted in Escobar
1995: 3)

Since Truman's speech, a range of different theories have been formulated,
some of which build on his doctrine, others adopting a critical view of it. Each
of these theories shares an intention to develop, but they differ on how this is to
be achieved, what the outcome should be, and what type of principles should
guide it. As Colin Leys points out, these development theories emerged to deal
with a more narrowly defined development issue, namely, how the economies
of (former) colonies of Britain, France, Portugal, and other European countries
might be made more productive. He points out that, surprisingly, few development theorists drew on "the existing body of theory about development that
had been prompted by the original advent of capitalism itself" (Leys 1996: 5).
He mentions three reasons for this: first, the practical orientation of post-war
development theory, which focused on intervention and action, rather than on
reflecting on philosophical questions; second, the tendency to treat development studies as a science, and to ignore political and historical issues; and third,
the dominance in the post-war period of Keynesian economics, which highlighted the role of the state, and of international development agencies, in promoting national economic growth.

What is often forgotten are not only the nineteenth-century writings on development in Europe, but also how at the same time colonialism was perceived
as an exercise in development. In the heydays of colonial expansion, the colonial territories constituted not only a source of wealth, to be exploited by the
colonial administration, but also a convenient workshop in which to invent
and try out the new development doctrines. Generations of nineteenth-century
British social thinkers, including Edmund Burke, James Mill, and John Stuart
Mill, worked as civil servants in India, where they developed their ideas about
development policies in the areas of education, public works, and taxation
(Cowen and Shenton 1996).

The colonial endeavor was often justified in the names of progress and the
civilizing mission. As Ashis Nandy (1997) points out, even some of the finest
minds of nineteenth-century Europe supported colonialism as a vehicle through
which modern structures could be introduced into the barbaric non-Western
world. The European colonial administrations were thus able to perceive themselves not as exploiters, but as benevolent agents of progress who have taken
on the heavy burden of bringing the underdeveloped colonies into the modern
age. Colonies were seen as children for whose mental and physical well-being
the colonial administrations were responsible, but economic progress was not
among the benefits sought for the indigenous populations (Arndt 1987). Thus,
a clear distinction was made in many colonial policies between economic development which was to benefit the colonists, and their obligations to ensure

the social welfare of the "natives." At the same time, in Latin America, European ideas of development and modernization were acted out by the new mestizo elites which had seized power in the early nineteenth century after more than three hundred years of Spanish and Portuguese colonial rule.

Clearly, then, the development theories emerging after 1945 to deal with the postcolonial Third World were not born into a vacuum. They drew on nineteenth-century social theories, on the vast and diverse colonial experience in Asia, Africa, and Australia, and on the postcolonial history of development of Latin America. We should bear this in mind when examining the most influential post-Second World War theories of development in the following sections.

Underdevelopment in the USA

While the president of the United States pledged to fight uneven development on the global stage, one of the most prolific development thinkers, Gunnar Myrdal, had focused his early work on inequality in the USA itself (1944) before going on to write his seminal work on *Asian Drama* (1968). Myrdal's work raises two key issues: first, it puts a question mark over America's claim to an advanced, developed status by suggesting that global inequalities are mirrored in American society; and second, it highlights the role of cultural constructions of racial prejudice, and its associated social and economic inequality, in development.

Myrdal argued that systemic and institutional racial inequality – based in racial theories of the nineteenth century – was one of America's greatest failures, and seriously undermined the ideals of the Enlightenment, which he described as the "first principles" of American democracy (Jackson 1990: 193). With a view to the global process of decolonization, Myrdal warned that unless Western countries abandoned white supremacy and racial segregation, their prestige and influence abroad would suffer, and the "colored nations" could end up taking revenge and inflicting violence on white nations. Conversely, if the United States embraced racial justice, its influence abroad would not only be based on economic and military might, but also on "spiritual power" (Myrdal 1944: 1018, 1022).

While Myrdal was one of the few social scientists at the time to consistently argue that the negro problem was really a problem of white racism, he also believed that black Americans should strive to assimilate into American culture, "to acquire the traits held in esteem by the dominant white Americans" (Myrdal 1944: 928–9). At a time when the dominant social scientist opinion held the view that white Americans and black Americans had fixed and mutually incompatible cultures, Myrdal held out the possibility of assimilation. Foreshadowing much of what would later become Third World development planning, he believed that social engineering, the "supreme task of social science," would help achieve equality and assimilation. Social engineering was to be orchestrated by the state, and involved a range of policies from desegregation of public housing and raising the standard of black education, to full employment, planned migration to areas of high job growth, and the granting of civil rights to all Americans (Jackson 1990: 229–30).

Many of Myrdal's policy recommendations were initially taken up by the President's Committee on Civil Rights, established by President Truman in response to the upsurge of racial violence and liberal protest after the end of the Second World War. The resulting legislative program on civil rights, however, was swept aside as the United States government prioritized its fight against communist tendencies among and embarked on anti-communist wars in the Third World (Jackson 1990).

Modernization theories

Modernization theories are the most widespread and persistent theories of development. These theories dominated development thinking in the 1950s and 1960s, and should be seen as one expression of a long-standing Western concern with progress. They have been so pervasive that it is difficult to separate the idea of modernization from that of development, which in turn is linked to notions of capitalism and economic growth (Roxborough 1988). The distinction between the concepts of modernity and modernization is often blurred, as in Inglehart's recent study (1997), where he defines modernization broadly as

> a process that increases the economic and political capabilities of a society: it increases economic capabilities through industrialization, and political capabilities through bureaucratization. Modernization is widely attractive because it enables a society to move from being poor, to being rich. (Inglehart 1997: 5)

Inglehart goes on to trace modernization back to Marx and Weber, thus identifying the line of descent of the specific set of modernization studies that characterized development studies (and also social sciences in First World countries more generally) in the 1950s and 1960s. Modernization theorists argue that a wholesale change must take place in underdeveloped societies in order to break the vicious cycle of poverty, ignorance, and low productivity. Not only the economy had to be transformed, but also the education system, the ways of thinking, acting, and living. A World Bank "mission" to Colombia in 1949, of the first World Bank visits to a Third World country, called for a "comprehensive and internally consistent" development program. Twenty years later, Gunnar Myrdal wrote about the comprehensive "modernization ideals" he identified in the South Asian region. He argued that although these ideas stem from foreign influences imposed by colonial rule, they have become "the official creed of the South Asian countries." As he points out, they are "composed mainly of the ideals long cherished in the Western world as the heritage of the Enlightenment" (Myrdal 1968: 55). In his listing of modernization ideals we find a number of Enlightenment ideals that have been tailored to the context of the developing world: rationality, development planning, social and economic equalization, improved institutions and attitudes, national consolidation, social discipline, political democracy and grassroots democracy. Myrdal quotes from a speech by the first Indian prime minister, Nehru, to illustrate how modernization requires leaving behind tradition:

> We have got to get out of many of these traditional ways of thinking, traditional ways of acting, traditional ways of production, traditional ways of distribution and traditional ways of consumption. We have got to get out of all that into what might be called more modern ways of doing so. ... The test of a country's advance is how far it is utilizing modern techniques. Modern technique is not a matter of just getting a tool and using it. Modern technique follows modern thinking. You can't get hold of a modern tool and have an ancient mind. It won't work. (Nehru, quoted in Myrdal 1968: 56–7)

Modernization involved development planning as a key strategy to achieve desired change, with the state playing an important role. When the development era began in the 1950s, there was widespread optimism about the capability of Third World governments to guide the development process. Governments made up development plans, often with the assistance from experts of international organizations, such as the World Bank. In these early decades of the development era, development planning was perceived to be the appropriate method by which to apply the economic development theories of Rostow and other development economists (Escobar 1992). More generally, Myrdal defines planning as "the search for a rationally coordinated system of policy measures that can bring about development" (Myrdal 1968: 58).

Economic development – expressed in terms of increasing productivity of labor and rising living standards – was perceived to be crucial to modernization. Rostow (1971) provided an important contribution to the economic component of modernization theory. His book, *The Stages of Economic Growth*, was written in the early 1960s as an anti-communist manifesto. Clearly inspired by a linear concept of history and progress, he described different stages of development which societies all have to go through, from traditional stage, through to a stage of high mass consumption. While he pointed out that industrialization is the most visible sign of a modern society, he traced the antecedents of the industrial revolution far back into Europe's history, with two essential steps toward industrialization being the invention of the mechanical clock and the "discovery of nature" (Arndt 1987: 11). Rostow thus considered industrialization as a part of Western civilization, embedded in the broader changes signaled by the European Enlightenment.

Samuel Huntington (1971: 285), one of the leading proponents of modernization theory, pointed out that the concepts of modernity and tradition were central to post-war modernization theory: "These categories were, of course, the latest manifestations of a Great Dichotomy between more primitive and more advanced societies which has been a common feature of Western social thought for the past one hundred years." In chapter 2 we shall examine this dichotomy in modernization theory in more detail.

To summarize then, in the eyes of the modernization theorists, modernization is

- a revolutionary process, involving radical and total changes in developing societies.
- a complex process, including industrialization, urbanization, social mobilization, differentiation, secularization, media expansion, expansion of political participation, increasing literacy and education.
- a systemic process, in the sense that "economic development, cultural change, and political change go together in coherent and even, to some extent, predictable patterns" (Inglehart 1997: 5).

More controversial are several other characterizations of modernization theory: a process which takes time, going through a number of stages (e.g. Rostow); that it is a global process which in the long term is homogenizing; and that it is an irreversible process from which no turning back is possible.

Modernization theory's assumption, that development was an inevitable process which could, however, be accelerated through an enlightened government and technological assistance from outside, was strangely apolitical. From a critical perspective, Chomsky (1969) pointed out the lack of self-analysis among Western intellectuals in the 1960s, who did not acknowledge how modernization theory was part and parcel of the Cold War competition between the West and the Soviet bloc. He observed that where attempts to solve problems through piecemeal technology failed, methods of coercion would be applied to Third World countries to preserve order and stability, and to keep communism at bay. Chomsky (1991: 58) noted "the striking correlation between US aid and human rights abuses," "elite hostility to democracy," and "the general US opposition to social reform" during the Cold War. He argued that these were all consequences of the United States' determination to maintain a world order that guaranteed the needs of US investors, and to prevent Third World countries from embarking on an independent development path.

Modernization with a human face: the basic-needs approach

The increasingly vociferous critics of top-down modernization approaches (e.g. Myrdal 1968), and the growing realization among mainstream development institutions that their battle against poverty and hunger was failing, led to a crisis of the modernization approach to development. Statistics on poverty were by the mid-1970s indicating that the reliance on the trickle-down effect of high-technology solutions such as the "green revolution" in agriculture or import substitution industrialization to uplift the poor had not worked. Indeed, evidence suggested there might even have been a relative decline in the standard of living for the world's poorest people, particularly women and children. The Food and Agriculture Organization (FAO) estimated that in 1979 eight hundred million of the rural poor were destitute and increasingly reliant on imported food supplies from the West (Blumberg 1981: 34). Dire news of this kind prompted a major policy reorientation within the international development community to the so-called basic-needs approach. This involved moving away from high-technology, top-down development strategies which modernization theorists had advocated. Instead, development should be oriented to providing "the minimum standard of living which a society should set for the poorest of its people" (International Labor Organization 1976). Leading the way on this new development path, the International Labor Organization (ILO) defined the satisfaction of basic needs as:

> the minimum requirements of a family for personal consumption: food, shelter, clothing: it implies access to essential services, such as safe drinking water, sanitation, transport, health and education; it implies that each person available for and willing to work should have an adequately remunerated job. It should further imply the satisfaction of needs of a more qualitative nature: a healthy, human and satisfying environment, and the popular participation in the making of decisions that affect the lives and livelihoods of the people, and individual freedoms. (ILO 1976: 7)

In paying more attention to the experience and objectives of development at the household and even individual level, it was realized that women were central to the provision of basic needs, precisely because of their roles in food production, family consumption, and birth control. Thus the shift to a basic-needs approach went along with a greater attention to women and their part in achieving development. It opened the door to a perhaps more challenging shift in thinking about development which was inspired by feminism – both the social movement for gender equality and the contributions by feminist scholars to social theory (for a more detailed discussion see chapter 4).

In other ways, too, the basic-needs concept was conducive to interpretations that went beyond a technocratic, capital investment approach to development. It raised the issue of investing in humans through greater emphasis on health and education, and identified the equitable distribution of wealth and resources as a development goal and strategy. It also made possible the inclusion of social justice issues, such as gender equality and indigenous rights, in development agendas from the 1970s onwards. Despite the short life of the basic-needs strategy, its main elements have lived on, and have recently been revived under new slogans, as Truong (1992: 8, quoted in Braidotti, Charkiewicz, Häusler, and Wieringa 1994: 19) has pointed out. They inhabit the Human Development

Index of the United Nations Development Program (UNDP) (1990), and the "basic rights" campaigns of non-governmental development organizations (e.g. Simmons 1995; Facio 1995).

Dependency theory and autonomous development

If the basic-needs strategy was a moderate policy-oriented response to the failures of modernization, Marxist theories of development and the so-called dependency school were much more substantial critiques of modernization. Not surprisingly, it was in Latin America where such critiques were first expounded. After all, Latin American countries had enjoyed independence for almost a century and a half, and their level of development remained far below that of the USA and the industrialized nations of Europe. In trying to establish what kept Latin America developmentally retarded, the Economic Commission for Latin America (ECLA), led by the Argentinian Raul Prebisch in the late 1940s, argued that one reason was the unequal exchange between raw material-producing Third World countries and industrialized countries of the First World, who were unwilling to share their technological expertise (Sunkel 1977). The First World was increasingly substituting raw materials and was demanding high prices for its own industrial products (Larrain 1989). This analysis implied an unequal distribution of power between the industrialized centre of the global economy and its underdeveloped periphery.

In the 1960s, André Gunder Frank (1969) expanded on this view of the world with his own theory of underdevelopment. He questioned whether capitalism could bring the benefits of development to the periphery, arguing instead that capitalism was a world system which systematically exploited peripheral countries through monopolistic trade. Indeed, the wealth of Europe and the USA derived from their exploitation of the Third World since the beginning of the colonial era. The developed status of these First World countries was, therefore, structurally linked to the underdevelopment of the Third World, much like "the opposite sides of the same coin" (Frank 1969: 33). Frank perceived the world capitalist system as a hierarchy stretched across the world, so that each stratum was exploited by the next highest stratum, from the rural regions of the Third World, through their regional towns and capital cities, up to the top of the hierarchy where the capital cities of the Western countries resided. Third World nations therefore had to sever the trading and other relations with the First World in order to allow their economies to develop. In a sense, then, Frank turned modernization theory on its head by arguing that the ties with the West were a harmful disruption to the normal course of development in Third World countries (Manzo 1991). He also challenged assumptions that development was a linear process of continuous improvements by interpreting the development process in Latin America as a downward spiral.

In subsequent years, other neo-Marxist development theorists came to exert a strong influence on development thinking. Some of them (e.g. Cardoso and Faletto 1979) associated themselves with the dependency school, which added to Frank's (1969) critique of the capitalist world system an analysis of class structures within developing countries. Cardoso, who has gone on to become the president of Brazil, and his Chilean co-author Faletto did not agree with the view that Third World countries could only "underdevelop," but rather interpreted the socio-economic changes in Mexico, Brazil, and Argentina as "dependent development." The concept of dependence indicated that the empirical events in Third World countries could be understood neither on their own terms nor just by reference to their relations with the First World. Rather, the internal and external structures and processes were linked in complex ways.

Others, such as Emmanuel (1972), Amin (1979), and Wallerstein (1979), developed ECLA's thesis of unequal exchange within a capitalist world system marked by the division of countries into a poor world and a rich world, with limited scope for transition between the two camps. In short, the underdevelopment and dependency theories constituted a structuralist analysis of the obstacles to capitalist development in the Third World (Leys 1996).

Underdevelopment and dependency

While Leys (1996: 45–6) recognizes that there are differences among individual theorists on several issues and concepts, he summarizes the general points that underlie underdevelopment and dependency theories as follows:

1 Today's Third World, its "underdeveloped" social, economic, and political conditions, are the underside of the same world-historical process in which the First World became "developed." This directly contradicts modernization theory's view of the Third World as undeveloped or untouched.
2 "The prime mover in this combined process was capital seeking profits, i.e. seeking opportunities to accumulate capital – specifically, capitalist merchants, capitalist bankers, capitalist insurers, etc., and finally capitalist manufacturers" (46).
3 Capital accumulation is easiest in countries where labor and resources are cheap, and governments weak. This is the case with many newly independent Third World countries, whose economies had already been given an external orientation during the colonial era to fit the economic structures of the imperial center.
4 "Secondary structural consequences of this served to reproduce the process and constantly block local initiatives to pursue an autonomous development path; e.g. the low incomes of the majority due to the creation of surplus labor and marginalization imply a generally small domestic market; highly unequal income distribution implies a narrow import-orientated consumer demand, etc."

> 5   "The corresponding emergence and formation of social classes at
>   the capitalist periphery with interests in common with the
>   bourgeoisie of the metropoles made possible the development of
>   colonial, neo-colonial and semi-colonial states representing
>   successive types of such alliances."

As Leys (1996) points out, the underdevelopment and dependency theorists
revealed the ideological premises of modernization theory. Influenced by Marxist critiques of capitalism, their analyses focused on economic processes and
structures rather than on political, social, and cultural processes. It can be de-
duced from their work that they see the direction and definition of development as an object of political struggle. However, it is not clear what kind of
development Third World countries can strive for that differs from that of capitalist development. In chapter 2 we shall look at some countries that were, at
various times, held up by dependency theorists as examples of positive development, such as China and Tanzania, which in different ways attempted to
forge a socialist path to development.

2.4   The meaning of development

In the literature reviewed thus far, development has a range of different meanings but is generally regarded a desirable objective. Whether capitalist or Marxist, development theorists and policy makers have identified development with
material progress and improved living standards. But how these goals are best
achieved, who should be the primary beneficiaries, and who or what stands in
the way of development, have been matters of ardent debate. Another consensus which emerges from the discussion thus far is that development is closely
related to the broader definition of modernization, as a process of economic
and social change that emerged from Europe and expanded from there to the
rest of the world. Similarly, development policies developed in those parts of
Europe which first underwent rapid industrialization, to respond to the poverty, dislocation, and suffering it produced. Coherent economic development
policies for Third World countries only became common after they had become decolonized, and then they frequently were patterned after First World
policies, or development experiences. It appears, therefore, that development
thinking has its cultural home in the European Enlightenment. A third point
which we have established thus far is that development cannot be conceived of
without a notion of its opposite, whether it be underdevelopment, or non-de-
velopment. The close conceptual link between development and modernization provides a clue for what many development theorists have perceived as
development's opposite – backwardness, stagnation, and, above all, tradition.
Unlike the modernization school, however, dependency and Marxist development theorists, to different degrees, have strongly challenged the idea that de-

velopment is linear and denotes progress. Their work helped to reveal the blinkered vision of modernization advocates by demonstrating that countries and regions can become underdeveloped by colonialist and capitalist expansion, and their people be worse off than before the onset of development.

3   What do we mean by culture?

It is not easy to pin down "culture" with a precise and singular definition. "Popular culture"; "high culture"; "national culture"; "youth culture"; consumer culture; global culture; multicultural; culture clash and so on; in a myriad of phrases, clichés, and references, "culture" is much in vogue as a topic in the media, politics, and in everyday life. Rarely, however, do those who use it say what they mean by it. It is one of those words whose meaning is often taken for granted. Yet, as Raymond Williams, a leading cultural theorist, pointed out, "Culture is one of the two or three most complicated words in the English language" (Williams 1983: 87).

The word has a long and involved history, and this is reflected in the variety of ways the term has been defined and used across various academic disciplines, ranging from literary studies to anthropology and sociology. Many of the everyday ways in which the word is used reflect this history and diversity, often incorporating bits and pieces of several different definitions or historical usages.

Robert Bocock (1992) has identified five ways in which culture has been defined, summarized in table 1.1.

Table 1.1   Definitions of culture

1   Culture = cultivating land, crops, animals
2   Culture = cultivation of mind, arts, civilization
3   Culture = process of social development
4   Culture = meanings, values, ways of life
5   Culture = practices which produce meaning

Source: adapted from Bocock (1992: 234).

3.1   Culture and hierarchy

The first definition of culture listed by Bocock (1992) was the earliest, referring to the cultivation of nature. This had, by the seventeenth and eighteenth centuries, been extended to humans. Culture now referred to the "cultivation" of the human mind as well as the fields and plants. By the late eighteenth century, class was a significant dimension of this meaning of culture. "Culture" became an attribute of birth and rank; "refinement" the exclusive preserve of the aristocracy. Economic and political power underpinned a cultural power, expressed

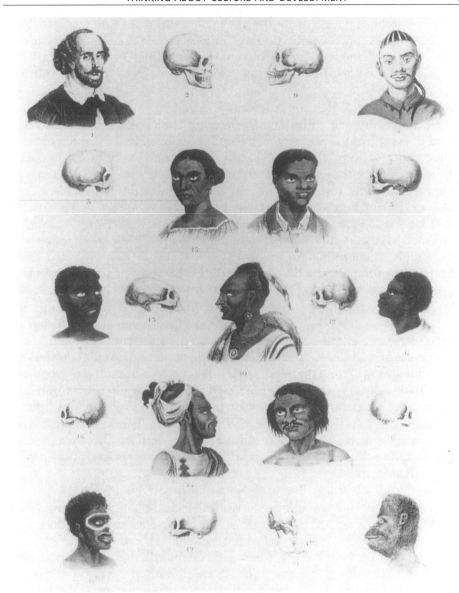

Figure 1.1   A hierarchy of races. Profiles and skulls of various "races" showing facial angles, from a European (top left) through various peoples to "savage" African towards an ape (1850)

in the ability to define what was considered "cultured." Certain human activities were designated as "cultured" – the arts and scholarship – while other activities such as manual labor, trade, and manufacturing were seen as uncultured. Increasingly, "culture" also included particular forms of social conduct, lifestyle, manners, and speech.

This hierarchical notion of culture as the lifestyles of an elite was translated in the nineteenth century into a sense of culture as the pursuit of perfection. In its modern guise, the familiar distinction between "high" and "popular" culture privileges the artistic pursuits of a social elite, while "popular culture," covering those aspects of creative and imaginative life accessible to, and enjoyed by, a mass audience, are considered second-rate.

These distinctions in culture on the basis of class were generalized across groups of people as a distinction between the civilized and the uncivilized, to include entire nations. This extension of the meaning of culture occurred as European societies came into sustained contact with regions, people, and ways of life very different from their own. Exposure to these different societies generated a range of European responses, both negative and positive. A widespread fascination and marvel at the wonders of ancient civilizations such as China and India, particularly in terms of their artistic achievements, often went along with less generous comparisons.

At the same time, the intellectual ferment of the Enlightenment was throwing up new ways of thinking about human societies based on scientific knowledge, displacing religion as the sole basis of knowledge. Human history was no longer seen as one of decline from an original God-given innocence, but as a story of progress, based on the ever-increasing "self-knowledge" of "man." This important shift to a secular understanding of human history was reflected in new scientific models emerging in the nineteenth century, the most famous being Charles Darwin's theory of human evolution. Darwin's linear model of human evolution as a steady progression from ape to man was extrapolated by early social scientists (Robert Young 1995; Nederveen Pieterse 1992: 48) to rank human societies on a scale from "primitive" to "modern." Culture was defined more explicitly as the acquisition of civilization and was conceived of as a process of social development.

By the mid-nineteenth century, as industrialization and imperial expansion established European, and particularly British, technological and economic dominance over large parts of the globe, European societies, and specifically white middle-class men, were cast as the epitome of modernity and progress. Non-Europeans were ranked at lower stages of cultural development, with black people at the bottom of the evolutionary heap, labeled "primitive." Serious debates were conducted amongst social scientists as to the implications of this ranking. Were non-Europeans simply at an earlier stage in a common evolutionary progression to "civilization"? In which case, a "civilizing mission" on the part of Europeans – as missionaries, colonial administrators, and imperial legislators – to bring culture to the less developed, would eventually bring even the primitive into the light of progress and modernity. Or did the different rates of social development indicate biologically different human races, each with specific limits to their respective cultural developments? Such reasoning often legitimated slavery, arguing that Africans were racially suited to physical labor and incapable of self-direction or autonomy. It was even argued that some societies or "cultures" were evolutionary dead ends, best left to "die out."

In the case of Australia's indigenous peoples, such arguments legitimated genocidal and eugenicist policies intended to "breed out" a people caricatured as
"stone-age" and incapable of surviving in a "modern" world.

The Hottentot Venus

This understanding of culture was mapped across class, sexuality, and
gender as well as race. Sander Gilman (1985) shows how all four came
together in the stereotyping of women around race and sexuality.
African women were located in nineteenth-century scientific models of
human development at the opposite end of the evolutionary time line
to European women on the basis of their presumed greater sexual
appetite, itself taken as an indicator of primitiveness. Medical scientists
"proved" this theory of sexuality by documenting its expression in the
"primitive genitalia" and "protruding buttocks" of African women. The
"Hottentot Venus," an African woman named Sara Bartmann (or
Saartjie Baartman), was displayed and exhibited throughout Europe in
the early nineteenth century as living proof of the inherent differences
between the African and European; her body, reduced to its sexual
parts, attesting to the fundamental difference between the "primitive"
and the "civilized," physically and temperamentally.
   By the middle of the century, a connection was made between the
"primitive sexuality" of African women and the "degenerate" sexuality
of prostitutes, that other group of women seen as the antithesis of
virtuous white middle-class womanhood: "The primitive is the black,
and the qualities of blackness, or at least of the black female, are those
of the prostitute" (Gilman 1985). As the two illustrations show (figures
1.2 and 1.3), the same physiology assigned the "Hottentot Venus,"
protruding buttocks, are now assigned the white working-class
prostitute, identified as a pathological form of female sexuality and a
"throwback" to the "primitive" sexuality of the Hottentot.

The example of the Hottentot Venus and the white prostitute illustrates how
the definition of culture as a process of social development, drawing on new
scientific explanations for human history and evolution, was able to rank social groups on a scale of cultural development or "civilization." The two axes
of this scale were, at the lowest point, the primitive or savage, and at the highest, modernity. By the mid-nineteenth century these two notions of the primitive and the modern were firmly tied to ideas about racial difference, and
attached not only to social descriptors such as ways of living but to physical
attributes. Progress and modernity were the pinnacles of cultural development
– civilization – represented by the societies and peoples of Western Europe.

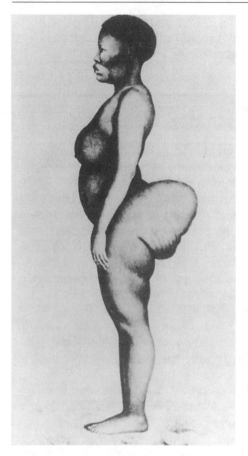

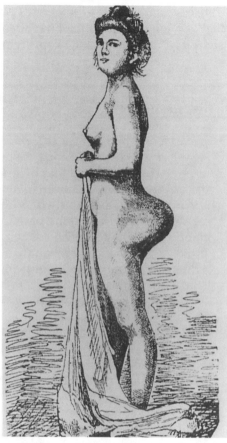

Figure 1.2 "The Hottentot Venus." Georges Cuvier, "Extraits d'observations faites sur le cadavre d'une femme connue à Paris et à Londres sous le nom de Vénus Hottentote" (1817)

Figure 1.3 Italian prostitute. Abele de Blasio, "Staetopigia in prostitute," pl. 1 (1905)

Although, as Gilman's example demonstrates, even within these "modern" societies, certain social groups, such as the working class and women, were distinguished as in some ways lacking the necessary attributes of culture and modernity.

3.2 Anthropology and culture

At the same time as hierarchical notions of culture were becoming established in nineteenth-century social science, another way of defining culture emerged as a core concept of the new discipline of anthropology, whose central concern was the study of culture, specifically non-Western cultures. Western anthropologists were less concerned with culture as a measure of civilization or as a ranking tool for an evolutionary scale than with describing and explaining different cultures. Two main anthropological definitions of culture have been widely influential in the social sciences generally (see 4 and 5 in table 1.1). These two ways of defining culture are not mutually exclusive. They each represent distinct but related ways of approaching the study of culture. The first definition is primarily concerned with what culture is, while the second focuses more on what culture does, or how it does it, rather than on what it is (Bocock 1992: 232).

Culture defined as the meanings, values, and ways of life of a particular group

This is probably the most common definition of culture in contemporary social science. While there is a diversity of ways of interpreting it, these can be broadly included within two main approaches, briefly summarized below.

Functionalist: building on aspects of the work of Emile Durkheim, one of the founders of modern sociology, this approach emphasizes the "shared and normative nature of culture and its functions for integrating the individual into the group." Thus culture is seen as a "design for living," an aspect of the social structure ensuring the cohesion and continuity of society as a whole (Billington, Strawbridge, Greensides, and Fitzsimons 1991: 4).

Interactionist: drawing on the work of another founding father of sociology, Max Weber, this approach puts much less emphasis on the structural dynamic of culture. Instead, it emphasizes how culture, as meanings, values, and ways of life, is formed out of the interaction between individuals and society. A greater emphasis is placed on individual agency. As Clifford Geertz, the foremost exponent of this approach in contemporary anthropology, has elegantly stated,

> Believing, with Max Weber, that man is an animal suspended in webs of significance he himself has spun, I take culture to be those webs, and the analysis of it to be therefore not an experimental science in search of law but an interpretive one in search of meaning. (Geertz 1973: 5)

Culture defined as the social practices which produce meaning

This approach emphasizes the symbolic nature of culture and focuses on the symbols, rituals, and activities involved in the construction of everyday social reality. Structuralism is the main intellectual tradition which has explored this understanding of culture. Structuralists emphasize the centrality of language, by which they mean "any system of communication which uses signs as a way of referencing objects in the real world" (Bocock 1992: 233). Words, drawings, movies, material objects, all function as signs or symbols which enable communication between social actors. "When a group shares a culture, it shares a common set of meanings which are constructed and exchanged through the practice of using language" (Bocock 1992: 233). Lévi-Strauss, the leading exponent of structural anthropology, argued that by analyzing these language or sign systems, it was possible to reveal the underlying rules or structure of a culture. For example, in his study *The Raw and the Cooked*, Lévi-Strauss (1970) argues that the norms of food preparation and consumption, such as when to eat and how to prepare specific foods for particular occasions, are not important in themselves but reveal something about the cultural order as a whole. Take the contemporary concern about "fast food" frequently aired in the press. While this is often expressed in terms of health and nutrition, a structuralist analysis might argue the real significance of the debate lies in the underlying concerns it reflects about changes to family structures and social values as meals become individualized items of consumption rather than home-cooked opportunities for family togetherness (Billington et al. 1991: 33).

3.3   The critique of anthropological conceptions of culture

Anthropology has largely defined itself in terms of the description and explication of "Other" cultures, radically different from those, usually European in origin, within which anthropology and its practitioners have been located. Roger Keesing, a cultural anthropologist himself, has somewhat acerbically written: "If radical alterity did not exist, it would be anthropology's project to invent it. Radical alterity – a culturally constructed Other radically different from Us – fills a need in European social thought: what Trouillot (1991) calls 'the savage slot.'" (Keesing 1994: 301). Keesing goes on to criticize anthropological theories of culture for exaggerating and even inventing "[t]he tribal world . . . of unchanging tradition."

Despite the diversity and vigorous debates conducted between the various anthropological approaches to culture outlined in the previous section, they each share a view of "culture" as a discrete, bounded entity, consisting of particular sets or structures of social relations, practices, and symbolic systems which forge a cohesive unity for the group, whether as society, nation, community, or class. Depicting culture in this way ignores and is unable to grasp the dynamic qualities of cultural flows, trapping anthropological method in a constant search for the "real" or "authentic" Other. These "Other" cultures are caught in a static time warp as unchanging repositories of "tribal," "peasant," or "traditional" ways of living and belief systems, essentially outside of the modernity inhabited by the contemporary West (Fabian 1983). This ignores the broader global context within which contemporary societies, communities, and individuals live, a world in which, to use Keesing's example, dreadlocks, Bob Marley, and Kung Fu movies are as much a part of Solomon Islands' contemporary "culture" as ancestral religion, magic, and ritual are (Keesing 1994: 302; 304).

This anthropological search for and depiction of exotic authenticity has been influential well beyond the narrow confines of the academic discipline. Indigenous Australians are still struggling under the weight of public attitudes and government policy informed by an anthropological construction of "authentic" Aboriginality based on tribal lifestyle, skin color, and remote bush communities which excludes the lived reality of many indigenous people within rural and urban community networks embracing a range of lifestyles as survivors of past and present assimilationist state policies.

White Australian Aborigines: a contradiction in terms?

As a member of an Aboriginal family in the southwest of Queensland, Wendy Holland writes about not fitting into the images that white Australians have of Aborigines. She writes: "growing up blonde, blue-eyed, and fair-skinned, I certainly cannot deny my english and irish heritages. Nor can I deny the opportunities I have been afforded as a result of my whiteness and being mis/taken as white in this racist society" (Holland 1996: 97). She grew up in an ethnically mixed neighborhood, where it was not necessary for her family to name themselves Aboriginal – the family was accepted for who they were.

It was in school that Holland first remembers learning about her "own family difference via racism":

> "Aborigines" and their society (note singular usage, as if "aborigines" were monocultural, which was clearly not the case) were depicted as simplistic, childlike and heathen. . . . "Aborigines" were presented as if they were transfixed in time. There was no reference, let alone any discussion, in relation to the british invasion and colonization of this land and its impact on indigenous people. The one and only illustration on the page of the text was of a naked black man standing on top of a rock with one leg up on the other, poised holding a spear as he gazed into the distance . . . ah, the timeless "noble savage"! When I explained in class that some of my mother's family were aboriginal and that we did not live like the murris depicted in the textbook, I [remember] feeling really embarrassed and confused when the teacher dismissed my family as not *real* "aborigines." (Holland 1996: 101)

Holland goes on to explain that since British colonial administration there had been a fixation on classifying Aboriginal people according to racial criteria which some Aboriginal people themselves have adopted in coming to terms with their identity. Claiming that one is either Aboriginal or not, some Aborigines romanticize the "traditional" Aboriginal society while denying "difference that has always existed and continues to exist within our communities" (Holland 1996: 106).

More generally, the essentializing of culture as a discrete set of forms and behaviors marking identity has lent itself to a diverse range of effects, including:

- a global tourism industry geared to locating the authentic and exotic "Other" for commercial consumption. For example, the hill tribes in parts of Southeast Asia are "integrated" into the postcolonial nation-state and coerced out of opium growing (under the pressure of powerful foreign interests) by relocation into "traditional" villages as tourist exhibits for a tourism industry that is a cornerstone of national development plans.
- Third World nationalist discourses that reify "tradition" as a counter to the perceived threat of "westernization" or "neo-colonialism." As chapter 5 discusses in more detail, this is often a process of invention, frequently reducing a complex and varied history into a singular version which is then liable to imposition on subaltern groups or used to exclude those not seen to follow the "tradition," of belief, language, dress, lifestyle, from the new national collectivity.
- romanticized notions of "traditional," particularly tribal societies, usually by outsiders, often expressed as an anti-development rhetoric to preserve a "vanishing world" against the influx of modernity. This frequently pits Western activists against Third World communities or states who see themselves not as remnants of a past world but as agents in a dynamic present.

Emphasizing culture as an integrative mechanism shared by all fails to acknowledge the power dimensions of cultural cohesion and uniformity. It

Figure 1.4 A tourist exchange in Sapa, Lao Cai Province in northwest Vietnam

Figure 1.5   Doors from a ceremonial house in Tutulala, East Timor, adorning an Australian living room

ignores the ways in which apparent homogeneity and conformity are manufactured through subtle mechanisms of hegemony which define non-dominant cultural practices as deviant and marginal. It gives no sense of the ways in which "culture" is resisted and contested in any social unit. This is reinforced by the definition of "culture" as a discrete component of the social, separate from the economic and political dimensions of social life, as if ways of living, belief systems, rituals, and symbols are quarantined from the arenas of production and power. The Islamic revolution in Iran in 1979 is only one example showing the interconnectedness of culture, economics, and politics to which many Western observers had been blind (Allen 1992). As Tim Allen (1992: 333, 337) points out, Middle East expert Fred Halliday, in a book written on the eve of the revolution, "ends up deflecting attention away from religion as a key factor," glossing the apparent revival of Islam as "the consequence of supersti-tion, ignorance and poverty" and much less significant than the real issue of class inequalities.

These anthropological theories of culture have had particular consequences in terms of the study of development and the Third World, often unintention-ally reinforcing and extending the hierarchical notions of culture developed in the nineteenth century, outlined in 2.1 above. Cultural difference between the West and the non-West or Third World is depicted as a gulf not only of lifestyle and belief systems but of time. Effectively, the non-West is removed from mo-dernity and described as inhabiting a qualitatively different temporal space, a contemporary location which bears all the hallmarks of the West's past rather than its present. A location, moreover, implicitly devoid of any dynamic of internal change, given the static, unchanging quality ascribed to these socie-ties. As a consequence, any impetus for change is reserved for external influ-ences, particularly those from the dynamic and modern West. Hence "development" in this context inevitably meant processes of westernization. "Traditional cultures" are variously seen as either barriers to the – desirable and/or inevitable – march of progress, or as helpless victims of a relentless modernity, doomed to disappear. The idea of modernity as a temporal space inhabited only by the West or westernized has had a pervasive influence throughout the "development industry" and within the Third World, with per-haps its most tragic manifestation in the apparent intentions of the Pol Pot re-gime in Cambodia to remove their war-devastated country and its people from any contact with modern time and return them to a cleansed "culture" of the past – Year Zero (see chapter 2).

3.4 Culture and power

An alternative approach to defining and studying culture has emerged recently out of a synthesis of literary studies and social science, institutionalized as the new discipline of cultural studies. Originally motivated to both dismantle the elitism of the distinction between high and popular culture within literary stud-ies and to challenge the economic determinism of orthodox Marxism, cultural studies has synthesized and extended the anthropological definitions of cul-ture in ways which overcome some of the criticisms made of them. Culture is, from this perspective, no longer conceived as a discrete, bounded entity dis-tinct from the economic and political. Rather, as Frow and Morris (1993: viii) put it, "[i]t is a network of representations – texts, images, talk, codes of behav-iour, and the narrative structures organising these – *which shapes every aspect of social life*" [emphasis added].

Culture, from this perspective, is not apart from, or derivative of, other are-nas of social life. It is, as the highlighted phrase emphasizes, productive, in the sense of being an active component in the production and reproduction of so-cial life. In Raymond Williams's (1961) phrase, it is the "whole way of life" of a social group as it is structured by representation and by power. Social groups

coalesce around a variety of circumstances that form the basis of a se
shared identity, the most important being the categories of class, gende
"race," nation, but including a range of other axes such as rural/urban
region, and so on. These categories of identity formation are not discrete but
intersect, even within the life of an individual, in ways which often conflict or
contradict one another. Take for example the ways in which race and class can
intersect in conflicting ways, as when a minority ethnic group may share an
economic location with another dominant ethnic group, the divide of race and
ethnicity may lessen the sense of shared class interest, in Malaysia or the USA.
The shared or cohesive quality of "culture" is thus limited to a social segment
rather than the social whole, consequently building in to this model of culture
the dynamic of difference. "Culture" is, from this perspective, a site of contestation rather than a force for social cohesion.

Frow and Morris's definition also collapses the distinction drawn in anthropological approaches between culture as a way of life and culture as the production of meaning. The two are linked by the concepts of reproduction and
power, such that ways of life are here conceived as being constituted by, or
made up of, meaning-producing practices: "texts, images, talk, codes of behav-
iour, and the narrative structures organising these" (Frow and Morris 1993:
viii). Reproduction and power are two key tools used by cultural studies to rework anthropological approaches to culture in ways which have particular relevance for the study of development as concept and as process. What does
representation mean and how does it relate to power?

Representation

Stuart Hall (1997) provides a clear introduction to representation and its role in
the study of culture generally. Language lies at the heart of culture understood
as shared meanings, and language constructs meanings through representation. By language, Hall does not mean only spoken languages such as English
or Vietnamese, but a range of ways of communicating and comprehending
between people, including body language, visual images, dress, and so on.
"They are 'systems of representation'" in the sense that they "all use some element to stand for or represent what we want to say, to express or communicate
a thought, concept, idea or feeling" (Hall 1997: 4).

The emphasis placed on the construction of meaning through and within
representational systems is why this approach is often labeled the constructionist
perspective. It turns on its head the materialist approach to culture, which assumes a "true" meaning exists external to representation, in the material world,
a meaning language seeks to represent accurately. Representation, from a materialist perspective, is less important in the study of culture than identifying
this underlying structure. Another important distinction between the two approaches is, therefore, that for materialists, meaning is fixed – there is one "real"
or "true" meaning more or less accurately rendered in the symbolic realm of
representation. Taking a constructionist approach, however, necessarily assumes

meanings are multiple and variable, specific only to particular systems of representation.

Discourse, knowledge, and power

The constructionist understanding of representation and its role in the production of meaning was extended by the French philosopher-historian Michel Foucault (1985; 1991) through his notions of discourse and power/knowledge. Foucault was concerned to address not simply how meanings were produced through representation, but also the relations of power underpinning the production of meanings and the processes by which certain meanings were rendered "true." In a series of historically based studies of the European systems of crime and punishment, sexuality, and madness, Foucault developed the concept of discourse to refer to the systems of representation which produced a particular kind of knowledge about a topic. In any given time and place, certain discourses acquire paradigmatic status as "truth," providing the boundaries within which shared meanings are construed through a particular system of representation. Hence knowledge is inextricably caught up with power – the power to "make itself true" (Hall 1997: 49). It is important to note, however, that the notion of power developed by Foucault is not linear, in which power is deployed from above to exploit and oppress those below. His conception of power/knowledge conceives of power as circulatory, pervasive, and multicentered, operating in diffuse and productive ways through discourse in ways which imbue all social actors with degrees of agency – and complicity – within the effects of power/knowledge (Foucault 1980).

Sander Gilman's case study of the "Hottentot Venus," which utilizes a Foucaultian analysis, summarized in 1.3 above, illustrates how a "discursive regime" of representation can operate to construct power/knowledge – in this case, about race, sexuality, class, and female bodies – across a range of topic areas, including visual art, medicine, science, and criminology, as "truth." The body of Sara Bartmann is pathologized and generalized into a model of deviant female sexuality powerfully deployed to police, coerce, and stereotype certain subjects, in this case, black people and (black and white) women. Yet this same "regime of truth" was also productive of vibrant bordello cultures (e.g. late-nineteenth-century London and Paris) in which an active female (and male non-hetero) sexuality was aligned to free-thinking intellectuality in counterpoise to a constrained and repressive respectable society (Showalter 1990).

Culture, power, and development

Foucault's concepts of discourse and power/knowledge, along with representation, constitute the analytical toolbox of cultural studies. "Culture" is no longer defined as an entity in the common-sense way we talk about "a culture," whether we are referring to a national culture or particular subcultures. As Keesing (1994) observes, from this perspective it makes much more sense to talk about "the cultural," implying practices and processes intrinsic to all social relations and structures. Power and difference now lie at the heart of the definition of culture, placing an emphasis on how shared meanings are constructed through discourse in ways which are productive of contestation and resistance as much or more than social cohesion and unity.

This framework for the study of culture has had a profound effect on development studies, opening up in new ways the question of what is meant by development and in whose interests it operates. Focusing on representation, power, and discourse, a number of scholars have now convincingly demonstrated how "development" operates as a discourse of power/knowledge within which the global relationships between the so-called First and Third Worlds are constructed, imagined, and operationalized. Development, they have argued, is not a means of addressing global inequalities and power differentials. On the contrary, it is itself constitutive of those very inequalities it purports to address. As Arturo Escobar passionately writes,

> instead of the kingdom of abundance promised by theorists and politicians in the 1950s, the discourse and strategy of development produced its opposite: massive underdevelopment and impoverishment, untold exploitation and oppression … it is about how the "Third World" has been produced by the discourses and practices of development since their inception in the early post-World War ll period. (Escobar 1995: 4)

Chapter 3 will look at how Escobar and others have deconstructed development as both discourse and process in ways which reveal the multifaceted ways in which it relates to and is part of the cultural.

4 Summary

The initial meaning of culture to refer to the cultivation of nature was extended to apply to the cultivation of the human mind. During the seventeenth and eighteenth centuries, this meaning became enmeshed with the development of class distinctions within Western European societies, establishing a hierarchical quality to the term between those social groups, activities, and lifestyles recognized as cultured and those which were not. By the mid-nineteenth century, the Enlightenment shift from a religious to a secular view of human history had become entrenched in scientific models of human evolution which fostered a definition of culture as the process of social development. Against a background of European technological and industrial advancement and imperial expansion and aggrandizement, the idea of culture as social development drew on scientific models of human evolution to describe a hierarchy of cultural development across societies and social groups. Mapped across race, sex, class,

> and gender divisions, this definition of culture placed Western European societies at the pinnacle of cultural achievement and social development as modern progressive nations, ranking other societies at various "stages" of development down to the lowest level of primitive.

Having traced the two key concepts of "development" and "culture" through time, and viewed them from a number of perspectives, we now turn to the question where development and culture connect. One way of responding to this question is by excavating and analyzing the assumptions about culture, both Western culture and Other cultures, in the various approaches to development that have dominated development studies in the past few decades. Such an analysis reveals, as chapter 2 will do, that many studies which ostensibly concern themselves with economic development are actually laden with assumptions about culture and its interaction with development. What is puzzling here is that on the one hand, many of these studies tend to relate culture to tradition, and to argue that the cultural traditions of non-Western societies must change under the impact of development, which is conceived in terms of a universal modernity. On the other hand, however, this universal modernity clearly has its cultural roots in the European Enlightenment, and therefore it easily slips into the concept of the West, or westernization, even when it is not expressly identified in these terms. The shorthand of this connection is development = modernization = westernization.

References

Allen, T. 1992: Taking culture seriously. In T. Allen and A. Thomas (eds), *Poverty and Development in the 1990s*. Oxford: Oxford University Press, 331–46.

Amin, S. 1979: *Unequal Development*. Delhi: Oxford University Press. First published in French in 1973.

Arndt, H. W. 1987: *Economic Development. The History of an Idea*. Chicago and London: University of Chicago Press.

Billington, R., Strawbridge, S., Greensides, L., and Fitzsimons, A. 1991: *Culture and Society: A Sociology of Culture*. Basingstoke: Macmillan Education.

Blumberg, R. L. 1981: Rural women in development. In N. Black and A. Baker Cottrell (eds), *Women and World Change: Equity Issues in Development*. London: Sage, 32–56.

Bocock, R. 1992: The cultural formations of modern society. In S. Hall and B. Gieben (eds), *Formations of Modernity*. Cambridge: Polity with Open University Press, 229–74.

Braidotti, R., Charkiewicz, E., Häusler S., and Wieringa, S. 1994: *Women, the Environment and Sustainable Development: Towards a Theoretical Synthesis*. London: Zed Books in association with INSTRAW.

Cardoso, E. H. and Faletto, E. 1979: *Dependency and Development in Latin America*. Berkeley: University of California Press. First published in Spanish in 1971.

Chomsky, N. 1969: *American Power and the New Mandarins*. London: Chatto and Windus.

Chomsky, N. 1991: *Deterring Democracy*. London: Verso.

Cowen, M. P. and Shenton, R. W. 1996: *Doctrines of Development*. London: Routledge.

Emmanuel, A. 1972: *Unequal Exchange: A Study of the Imperialism of Trade*. New York: Monthly Review Press.

Escobar, A. 1992: Planning. In W. Sachs (ed.), *The Development Dictionary*. London: Zed Books, 132–45.

Escobar, A. 1995: *Encountering Development: The Making and Unmaking of the Third World*. Princeton: Princeton University Press.

Fabian, J. 1983: *Time and the Other: How Anthropology Makes its Object*. New York: Columbia University Press.

Facio, A. 1995: From basic needs to human rights. *Gender and Development*, 3 (2), 16–22.

Foucault, M. 1980: *Power/Knowledge: Selected Interviews and Other Writings, 1972–1977*. Ed. Colin Gordon. Brighton: Harvester Press.

Foucault, M. 1985: *The Order of Things. An Archaeology of the Human Sciences*. London: Tavistock Press.

Foucault, M. 1991: *The Archaeology of Knowledge*. London and New York: Routledge.

Frank, A. G. 1969: *Capitalism and Underdevelopment in Latin America*. New York: Monthly Review Press.

Frow, J. and Morris, M. (eds) 1993: *Australian Cultural Studies: A Reader*. St Leonards: Allen and Unwin.

Geertz, C. 1973: *The Interpretation of Cultures: Selected Essays by Clifford Geertz*. New York: Basic Books.

Gilman, S. L. 1985: Black bodies, white bodies: toward an iconography of female sexuality in late nineteenth-century art, medicine and literature. *Critical Inquiry*, 12, 259–74.

Hall, S. (ed.) 1997: *Representation: Cultural Representations and Signifying Practices*. London: Sage/The Open University.

Hamilton, P. 1992: The Enlightenment and the birth of social science. In S. Hall and B. Gieben (eds), *Formations of Modernity*. Cambridge: Polity with Open University Press, 17–58.

Hobsbawm, E. 1968: *Industry and Empire*. London: Weidenfeld and Nicolson.

Holland, W. 1996: Mis/taken identity. In E. Vasta and S. Castles (eds), *The Teeth are Smiling. The Persistence of Racism in Multicultural Australia*. St Leonards: Allen and Unwin, 97–129.

Huntington, S. P. 1971: The change to change. Modernization, development, and politics. *Comparative Politics*, 3 (3), 283–322.

Inglehart, R. 1997: *Modernization and Postmodernization: Cultural, Economic and Political Change in 43 Societies*. Princeton: Princeton University Press.

International Labor Organization (ILO) 1976: *Employment, Growth and Basic Needs: A One-world Problem*. Tripartite World Conference on Employment, Income Distribution and Social Progress, and the International Division of Labor. Report of the Director-General of the International Labor Office. Geneva: ILO.

Jackson, W. A. 1990: *Gunnar Myrdal and America's Conscience. Social Engineering and Radical Liberalism, 1938–1987*. Chapel Hill and London: The University of North Carolina Press.

Keesing, R. M. 1994: Theories of culture revisited. In R. Borofsky (ed.), *Assessing Cultural Anthropology*. New York: McGraw-Hill, 301–12.

King, A. 1990: *Urbanism, Colonialism and the World-Economy*. London and New York: Routledge.

Larrain, J. 1989: *Theories of Development*. Cambridge: Polity.

Lévi-Strauss, C. 1970: *The Raw and the Cooked*. Translated from the French by John and Doreen Weightman. London: Jonathan Cape.

Leys, C. 1996: *The Rise and Fall of Development Theory*. Bloomington: Indiana University Press.

Manzo, K. 1991: Modernist discourse and the crisis of development theory. *Studies in Comparative International Development*, 26 (2), 3–36.

Marshall, B. 1994: *Engendering Modernity*. Cambridge: Polity.

Marx, K. and Engels, F. 1967: *The Communist Manifesto*. Harmondsworth: Penguin.

Myrdal, G. 1944: *An American Dilemma: The Negro Problem and Modern Democracy*. New York: Harper and Brothers.

Myrdal, G. 1968: *Asian Drama: An Enquiry into the Poverty of Nations* (3 vols). Vol. 1. New York: The Twentieth Century Fund.

Nandy, A. 1997: Colonization of the mind. In M. Rahnema with V. Bawtree (eds), *The Post-development Reader*. London: Zed Books, 168–177.

Nederveen Pieterse, J. 1992: *White on Black: Images of Africa and Blacks in Western Popular Culture*. New Haven and London: Yale University Press.

Porter, R. 1990: *The Enlightenment*. Harmondsworth: Penguin.

Rostow, W. W. 1971: *The Stages of Economic Growth: A Non-communist Manifesto*. Cambridge: Cambridge University Press.

Roxborough, 1988: Modernization theory revisited – a review article. *Comparative Studies of Society and History*, 30 (4), 752–61.

Shanin, T. 1997: The idea of progress. In M. Rahnema with V. Bawtree (eds), *The Post-development Reader*. London: Zed Books, 65–72.

Showalter, E. 1990: *Sexual Anarchy: Gender and Culture at the Fin de Siècle*. New York: Viking.

Simmons, P. 1995: *From Words to Action*. Oxford: Oxfam.

Sunkel, O. 1977: Development of development thinking. *Institute of Development Studies Bulletin*, 8 (3), 6–11.

Touraine, A. 1995: *Critique of Modernity*. Translated by David Macey. Cambridge: Cambridge University Press.

Truman, H. [1949] 1964: *Public Papers of the Presidents of the United States: Harry S. Truman*. Washington: US Government Printing Office.

Truong, Thanh-Dam 1992: Human development: conceptual and practical issues. Paper prepared for the International Forum on Intercultural Exchange, Saitama, Japan, National Women's Education Center, September 30–October 2.

United Nations Development Program 1992: *Human Development Report 1992*. New York: Oxford University Press.

Wallerstein, I. 1979: *The Capitalist World-Economy: Essays*. Cambridge: Cambridge University Press.

Williams, R. 1961: *The Long Revolution*. London: Chatto and Windus.

Williams, R. 1983: *Keywords: A Vocabulary of Culture and Society* (Flamingo edn, rev. and expanded). London: Fontana Paperbacks.

Young, R. 1995: *Colonial Desire: Hybridity in Theory, Culture and Race*. London: Routledge.

2 Bringing Culture and Development Together

> **Contents**
> 1 Introduction   33
> 2 Third World models of development   40
> 3 The crisis of development and the new
>   neo-liberal hegemony   50
> 4 Summary   53

1 Introduction

In chapter 1 we have surveyed the main theoretical perspectives which have dominated development thinking in the postcolonial era. This chapter brings culture and development together and looks at the ways in which the links between the two have been conceived. What kind of culture is required for development? How does development change cultural practices?

1.1 Having the right culture

As discussed in chapter 1, modernization studies dominated development thinking in the 1950s and the 1960s. As Alvin So (1990) points out, they were the historical product of the disintegration of the European colonial empires, the rise of the United States of America as a superpower, and the growing influence of a communist movement on world politics. Culture played an important role in distinguishing modern from traditional societies. One influential study was Talcott Parsons's formulation of five sets of pattern variables which provided a simple binary model. Alvin So (1990: 21) observed that "[p]attern variables are the key social relations that are enduring, recurring, and embedded in the cultural system – the highest and the most important system in Parsons's theoretical framework."

Some modernization theorists developed Parsons's schema further by arguing that policy makers should promote modern cultural traits in Third World countries which would enable modernization to occur. A study by McClelland (1964) suggested that stronger achievement motivation could be instilled in individuals both through non-authoritarian socialization within the family and through Western-style education. But Smelser (1964) pointed out that mod-

Table 2.1 Parsons's pattern variables of traditional and modern societies

Criteria	Traditional society	Modern society
Type of relationships	affective (personal, emotional, face-to-face relationships)	affective-neutral (impersonal, detached, and indirect relationships)
Type of interaction	particularist (people are bound to each other by obligation, duty, and trust, and each member has a particular role which is known to all other members)	universalist (people frequently interact with strangers, and apply universalist rules and norms to these interactions)
Identification	collective (loyalty to the family, community, or tribe)	individualistic (people are encouraged to develop their own interests, talents, and identity)
Status	ascriptive (a person's position and life path are determined by who they are)	based on achievement (a person is evaluated according to what they have achieved)
Division of labor	functionally diffused (a person usually has multiple functions, e.g. farmer, healer, and local chief)	functionally specific (a person has a more narrowly defined role, and can be more efficient in what they do)

Source: adapted from So (1990).

ernization may bring problems of integration and social and political upheaval. He understood this to be caused by the process of structural differentiation, whereby the multifunctional institutions, such as the extended kinship network of traditional societies, are divided into a multitude of specialized structures. This creates the danger of institutions disintegrating before new ways of coordinating these institutions have been developed, and may cause hardship and resistance. For example, as "traditional" extended families are separated into modern nuclear family units, new institutions are needed to look after their small children, or to support the older generation.

Lerner's parable of the grocer and the chief

American sociologist Daniel Lerner's study of a small village at the outskirts of Ankara in Turkey shows how Parsons's pattern variables were used to make sense of the rapid pace of change in the 1950s. The village of Balgat becomes a microcosm of the Middle East, and two villagers, the chief and the grocer, come to represent tradition and modernity, respectively. The chief represents the values of tradition: obedience, loyalty, and courage, the principal values of the Ataturk Republic. He is described as austere but content with his life, confident in the appropriateness of his world view, and a devout Muslim. The grocer "is a very different man." Though born and bred in Balgat, he "lives in a different world, an expansive world, populated more actively with imaginings and fantasies – hungering for whatever is different and unfamiliar" (Lerner 1958: 23). His dream is to travel to the city, move to America, be rich, all ambitions which traditional society considers improper, according to Lerner, since "[t]o reveal excessive desire for money is – Allah defend us! an impiety" (Lerner 1958: 25).

Four years later, Balgat had become integrated into the rapidly expanding city of Ankara. Lerner found that the grocer had died, but the chief's sons had both become shopkeepers. After asking several villagers about their opinions of the grocer, "[t]he light finally shone in one of the wiser heads and he spoke the words I was seeking: 'Ah, he was the cleverest of us all. We did not know it then, but he saw better than all what lay in the path ahead. We have none like this among us now. He was a prophet'" (Lerner 1958: 41). Once Lerner had satisfied himself that the villagers had recognized modernization as their new religion, his visit to Balgat had ended – there was nothing left to find out.

This study raises some interesting questions. For example, how does Lerner establish the difference between tradition and modernity in Balgat? What is the impact on his study of focusing his analysis on two men (Scott 1995)? On what assumptions does he ground his interpretation? What does development do to the village of Balgat and its people, their culture, livelihoods, ways of life, attitudes, etc.?

1.2   Culture and westernization

Once the differences between modern and traditional societies were explained in terms of these deeply embedded cultural traits, the next question was how modernization could occur. One way of explaining this was by seeing modern patterns of social relations as a "universal social solvent" (So 1990: 34), which dissolves the traditional traits of Third World societies through contact. As Levy

(1967: 190) explained, "once the penetration has begun, the previous indigenous patterns always change; and they always change in the direction of some of the patterns of the relatively modernized society." The implication of Levy's argument is that modernization is a process of westernization, which will result in Third World societies resembling Western Europe and the United States.

The close link between modernization, development, and westernization has also been noted by critics of modernization. Serge Latouche (1996: 50) has argued that "Westernisation is a two-pronged economic and cultural process: universal in its expansion and its history, reproducible through the West's capacity to act as a model and through its identity as a 'machine.'" He describes westernization as a machine because it can no longer be identified with a geographical region (Western Europe), nor with a collection of shared beliefs. Echoing Karl Marx, he sees it as a soulless, mad machine which

> has shaken off all human attempts to stop it and now roves the planet, uprooting what and where it will: tearing men [sic] from their native ground, even in the furthest reaches of the world, and hurling them into urban deserts without any attempt to adjust them to the limitless industrialisation, bureaucracy and technical 'progress' which the machine is pursuing. (Latouche 1996: 3–4)

In Latouche's view, Western Europe destroyed the traditional organization of production and consumption in the course of colonization, leaving the Third World no choice but to aspire to the Western model of consumption. Even societies which were not actually colonized became obsessed with "backwardness." Kemal Ataturk's project to modernize Turkey in the early twentieth century involved transforming the country's culture according to Western ways, from the script to hairstyles and clothing. Despite these efforts at westernization, Lerner (see p. 35) still was able to contrast Ataturk's "traditional" Turkey with modernity, because, says Latouche, modernization is a race which has no goal.

While Levy's (1967) image of the "universal solvent" implies a superiority of Western culture vis-à-vis Third World cultures, Latouche (1996: 20) describes the Third World as subject to a "cultural" invasion of "images, words, moral values, legal notions, political codes, criteria of competence" through the media of the North. As an example of the globalization of Western culture, Latouche points to the empty streets of Algiers one late afternoon in 1985 – everyone was watching the American soap opera *Dallas*. But unlike previous cultural invasions, westernization does not offer a new culture as compensation for lost traditions. Rather, "[i]ts prodigious success depends on the uncontrollable mimetic spread of deculturating fashions and practices. It universalizes loss of meaning and the society of the void" (Latouche 1996: 73). In other words, the culture of Coca Cola and McDonald hamburgers is a universal anti-culture.

1.3 Critical comments

Culture has an important place in modernization studies. However, it is difficult to analyse because it is the modernization studies themselves which produce the differences between traditional and modern culture. As Pigg (1996: 163) points out, the "dichotomy between tradition and modernity makes sense only within the narrative of modernization," which imagines "space and people through temporal idioms of progress and backwardness." In modernization studies traditional culture is something modernization acts upon, usually by rupturing, breaking, and even destroying cultural traditions of Third World societies: their ways of speaking, celebrating, their beliefs, techniques, art forms, and values. The processes of modernization are thus placed in opposition to culture. Civilization, on the other hand, is heralded as the culture of modernity (Latouche 1996: 43), expressed in a world view which is irreconcilable with traditional (Third World) culture, and which can be universally shared. And because both the impulse to civilize and scientific and technological know-how emerged from the West, modernization, development, and westernization are perceived to be interconnected processes.

However, the way in which Third World culture was conceptualized soon came under attack. Critics questioned the modernization school's representation of Third World cultures as homogeneous, stable, and ahistorical. Similarly, they doubted whether Western culture could be portrayed as a unified world view shared by all Western or westernized people. Instead, they pointed out that Third World cultural systems were diverse, conflicting, and had experienced change even before the onset of modernization. In contrast to followers of the modernization school who regarded culture, whether traditional or modern, as determining people's world view and behavior, their critics argued that culture is not the only thing that influences a person's interests and attitudes. Furthermore, "culture is not a finished social fact 'internalised' by passive cultural subjects," but rather, "cultural knowledge is accommodated to an already complex world of emotion, recognition, and previously assimilated social knowledge" (Hefner 1998: 4).

More generally, critics contend that the binary distinction between traditional and modern could not accommodate empirical evidence of the coexistence of "modern" and "traditional" traits in many Third World countries, and indeed in Western societies. This is to some extent due to the tendency to label traditional everything which is not modern. As Huntington (1971: 294) notes, "Pygmy tribes, Tokugawa Japan, medieval Europe, the Hindu village are all traditional. Aside from that label, however, it is difficult to see what else they have in common." He argues that in modern societies modern and traditional attitudes and behavior patterns often existed side by side, or were integrated with one another. In fact, there was plenty of reason to doubt whether modernization could ever completely dissolve traditional cultural traits. To the contrary, traditions are frequently revitalized in order to unite people for the difficult and arduous task of development and modernization, or to promote certain aspects of modernization (Bernstein 1971; So 1990: 55–6).

Finally, the cozy post-war consensus on which the modernization school was based, with its emphasis on market development and liberal democracy, began to shatter under the impact of the Vietnam war and other conflicts. Its close association with US foreign policy interests (So 1990; Hefner 1998: 6) cast the modernization approach into disrepute, and people looked for other frameworks to understand what was happening in developing countries. However, as Hefner (1998: 7) points out, one "lamentable consequence" was that economic and cultural analyses of development increasingly went separate ways. While some economists went so far as to dissolve cultural, social, and political factors into their discipline as externalities, on the cultural wing of human sciences some argued that the culture concept could virtually on its own "unlock the mysteries of human experience."

1.4 End of history and culture clash

The arguments presented in modernization studies experienced a revival in recent years. Two American political scientists, Francis Fukuyama and Samuel Huntington, have been pivotal in this revival, taking positions on opposite sides in a debate over the universality of Western culture. In an article in 1989, Francis Fukuyama argued that as the Soviet empire crumbles, we are witnessing not the end of a historical period – that of the Cold War – but the end of history:

> At the core of my argument is the observation that a remarkable consensus has developed in the world concerning the legitimacy and viability of liberal democracy. In order to refute my hypothesis it is not sufficient to suggest that the future holds in store large and momentous events. One would have to show that these events were driven by a systematic idea of political and social justice that claimed to supersede liberalism. (Fukuyama 1990: 10)

For Fukuyama, liberalism is the ideological core of Western culture, and it – like other major ideologies of global significance – was created in the West and flowed to the Third World. Over time, most societies have come to the consensus that liberal democracy and free markets are "the best of the available alternative ways of organizing human societies" (Fukuyama 1995: 29). This consensus has been produced by the development of the scientific method which makes possible the satisfaction of deep-seated human desires for utility maximization (or happiness), as well as social recognition. Echoing the modernization studies of the 1950s and 1960s, Fukuyama contends that the process of economic modernization is universal because aspiration to modernization is universal. "The only parts of humanity not aspiring to economic modernization are a few isolated tribes in the jungles of Brazil and Papua New Guinea, and they don't aspire to it because they don't know about it" (Fukuyama 1995: 32). Thus, as in Levy's (1967) and Lerner's (1958) studies, those who have been touched by modernization's breath inevitably become its advocates. Ultimately, it is simply reasonable to be persuaded by modernization and liberalism because human nature, though self-created, "follows a clear directionality dictated by the unfolding of reason" (Fukuyama 1990: 13).

Fukuyama's claim, that we have reached a global consensus based on the linked ideologies of modernization and liberalism, is another way of saying that we are now all sharing the same culture, a culture which emanated from the West. However, Samuel Huntington, whom we have already encountered in chapter 1 as a proponent of modernization theory, does not agree with this view. In his book, entitled *The Clash of Civilizations* (1996), he argues that the non-Western countries have not lost sight of their indigenous cultures. On the contrary, some have even reinforced and mobilized their traditions in ways which can be seen to threaten Western hegemony. Against Fukuyama's thesis of the universal victory of Western liberalism, Huntington posits his own very different view of the relationship between modernization and westernization, and the prospect of a universal civilization. In the early 1970s he had pointed out that modernization studies, such as Lerner's (1958), often failed to distinguish modern from Western, and had argued that "to a non-modern, non-Western society, the processes of modernization and Westernization may appear to be very different indeed" (Huntington 1971: 295).

In contrast to Fukuyama's universal civilization, Huntington (1996) sees several distinctive civilizations coexisting on the planet, of which Western civilization is only one. While Fukuyama may be correct in his assumption that communism has collapsed, he has overlooked the fact that there are still many forms of rule that are different from liberal democracy, as well as several religious alternatives. Thus, Huntington (1996: 66–7) argues that after the collapse of communism, "[t]he more fundamental divisions of humanity in terms of ethnicity, religions, and civilizations remain and spawn new conflicts." He explains the persistence of these divisions with the argument, borrowed from social psychology, that people define themselves by what makes them different from others. This fundamental human trait is not diminished by processes of globalization and homogenization, but rather it is heightened by them: "As increased communications, trade, and travel multiply the interactions among civilizations, people increasingly accord greater relevance to their civilizational identity" (Huntington 1996: 67).

Huntington's key argument deals with the assumption that modern civilization is also Western civilization. He argues that the "West was the West long before it was modern," having built its distinctive characteristics on the legacy of Greek and Roman civilizations, on Christianity, and a multitude of different languages. Pre-modern are also traditions of governance, such as the separation of spiritual from worldly authority, a legislative, social pluralism, and representative bodies. Central to Western civilization is individualism, which developed in the fourteenth and fifteenth centuries, and which "contrasts with the prevalence of collectivism elsewhere" (Huntington 1996: 71). None of the characteristics is unique to the West, but the combination of these characteristics gave the West its distinctive quality.

> These concepts, practices, and institutions simply have been more prevalent in the West than in other civilizations. They form at least part of the essential continuing core of Western civilization. (Huntington 1996: 72)

Therefore, while modernization theories have made a come-back in the work of Fukuyama and Huntington, these two American political scientists differ in their views on the links between modernization and westernization. While Fukuyama argues that modernization is seen as universally desirable, and that the majority of the world's societies are now embracing the twin objectives of capitalism and liberalism, Huntington distinguishes between modernization and westernization, and predicts continuing conflicts and wars between the world's major civilizations. However, both Huntington and Fukuyama follow in the old modernization theorists' footsteps in perceiving culture as a bounded and coherent entity, which is acted upon by the forces of modernization.

2   Third World models of development

In this section we look at two distinctive models of development which diverge in different ways from the Western development canon, and contest various of its assumptions about traditional and modern cultures. Here we are not aiming to provide an exhaustive survey of all the development visions and alternative understandings of development which Third World societies have entertained. We only want to briefly examine some of the better-known variants of development strategies that have emanated from Third World countries as versions of modernization different from modernization theory.

We begin by looking at how the developmental success of East Asian countries over the past decades has challenged modernization theory's claims about culture and development. Rather than abandoning traditions, East Asian leaders and scholars have argued that their traditional cultural values have played a crucial role in their countries' rapid capitalist development. However, explanations based on "Asian values" simply turn the modernization school's hierarchy of traditional and modern values on its head, and thus become vulnerable to the same criticisms of inappropriate generalization, simplification, and lack of historical perspective. Nevertheless, the East Asian examples show that modernization does not require countries to change their culture in line with Western values and practices.

A different challenge to modernization theory is evident in socialist models of development, which in one way or another were inspired by Marxism. In the late 1950s, Marxist development paths separated into two fiercely opposed directions. One is the Soviet model, which shares with the Western modernization model the idea that modern consumption, technology, and labor organization modes are "neutral" in relation to the social system (Amin 1977). The other was the Chinese Maoist model, which sought to combine tradition with development to achieve an egalitarian society, using the country's indigenous technologies. The Maoist model, which was practiced in China between 1958 and 1976, considered Western aid and technologies to be tools of imperialism, and regarded westernization as a cultural threat to China's national identity and independence. While harnessing indigenous resources was successful to a

degree in China, another version of the Maoist model was applied
dia under Pol Pot in the mid-1970s, with disastrous results. In Cam.
vision of a communist Khmer peasant society was based on an idealize.
of Khmer culture that was contrasted to Western (US and French) imperia.
Here, too, the hierarchy of traditional and modern had been turned on its hea.

Tanzania's socialist development path was more open to Western assistance
and trade, and was observed with great hopes and interest by Western aca-
demics and development activists. Julius Nyerere, the country's first president
after independence in 1961, argued that Tanzania did not have to follow the
European path through capitalism to socialism, but would be able to draw on
traditional African socialist principles which were practiced in rural communities. In his vision of Tanzania's *ujamaa* future, the country would be organized
into self-reliant rural villages. What the Maoist, the Khmer Rouge, and the Tanzanian models have in common is an emphasis on rural development and a
critical view of cities and towns as exploitative of the peasantry. They drew in
different ways on what they perceived the cultural essence of the country to be,
and these cultural traditions gave direction to their development strategies,
and at the same time shaped a specific cultural and national identity. These
development models thus stood in contradiction to modernization theory, which
gave prominence to industrialization and urbanization and sought to transform the national culture toward a westernized set of values.

2.1 Modernization the Asian way

In many ways, East Asia presents a challenge to Western theories of modernization, westernization, and development. By the 1980s, the academic world had
identified East Asia's high and enduring economic growth rates as a "miracle."
The miracle was at least in part the fact that industrial growth rates and living
standards similar to those enjoyed in Western Europe and the United States had
been achieved in some Asian countries (notably Japan, the Republic of Korea,
Singapore, and Hong Kong), challenging beliefs that these could be "realizable
only within the framework of Occidental civilisation" (Hefner 1998: 1). In the
search for explanations, some analysts turned to culture, in particular to those
cultural features of Chinese societies that are shaped by Confucian ideas.

The Confucian cultural features (which have applied to the whole of Asia in
the concept of "Asian values") most prominent in cultural explanations of East
Asian economic development usually include:

- human relations and social harmony based on the idea of filial piety;
- respect for authority and a strong identity with the organization;
- subjugation of individual rights in favor of community obligations; and
- diligence.

These features are clearly in contrast to the individualism which runs through
the cultural attributes of the "modern man" identified in modernization ap-

proaches, and have, in fact, been considered unfavorable to capitalism in the past by Western scholars. This was in part due to the fact that these earlier analyses

> specified social and economic consequences based on differences between [Chinese elite descriptions of cultural] ideals and an equally idealized version of Western market culture. Instead of placing actual behavior in real contexts, they assumed an automatic translation of a unitary culture into action. The new version, in part because Chinese scholars have taken the lead in its development, grounds its claims in a far better understanding of Chinese culture and history. (Weller 1998: 81)

These Chinese cultural tenets clearly influence the manner in which Chinese businesses operate. For example, while Lerner's modernization approach to promoting entrepreneurship, this crucial ingredient of economic development, focused on individualism, in Chinese businesses the family is the basic building block, and reciprocal relationships (*guanxi*) are the glue. While family relationships are patriarchal, allowing the male head of household to "lay claim to the labor power and wages of working children" (Hefner 1998: 13), *guanxi* are more egalitarian relationships between kin, neighbors, former schoolmates, or Chinese migrants who come from the same local area. Numerous studies (e.g. Hefner 1998; Lever-Tracy, Tracy, and Ip 1997; Hamilton 1991) have shown that these ties play a central role in Chinese business. While such evidence may lead to the conclusion that Chinese societies have found an alternative to Western market culture, which highlights rational and individualistic behavior, Weller (1998) warns us against premature conclusions. After all, early Western capitalism also relied on family networks, and then gradually moved away from them as businesses became bigger, and competition put such personal ties under increasing strain.

If Chinese cultural values have been cited in explanations of economic success stories, there is also evidence that East Asian governments are concerned about capitalism gradually eroding these values. In Singapore, a heated debate in the city-state's newspapers suggests that retired citizens are no longer just seen as revered elders, but are regarded by some as "an 'impediment to growth' in youthful, raring-to-go, and bottomline-conscious Singapore" (Long 1997: 9). A trend toward nuclear family units, encouraged by government housing policies, leads to looser family ties. Daughters and daughters-in-law, who traditionally bear the brunt of caring for older family members, are now more likely to be in full-time paid employment to maintain rising standards of living that Singaporeans and their government have come to expect. The Singaporean government does not consider caring for elderly citizens as its responsibility, and responded to the debate with a policy to raise the retirement age to 67 years by 2003 (Ahmad 1996) and by undertaking campaigns to promote caring attitudes among family members of different generations (Teo 1994). Thus, Chinese cultural values, such as filial piety and family solidarity, appear to clash with other values that are promoted by the capitalist system (e.g. nuclear

family, productivity orientation, increasing standard of living), which are identified with Western cultures. Governments respond by reworking traditional
concepts in the contemporary context in an attempt to maintain Chinese cultural traits in a modern post-industrial society.

Besides evidence that Chinese cultural traits are not indelibly stamped on
East Asian societies, there is also concern with portrayals of Chinese culture as
a unitary construct (Weller 1998). Such a portrayal, whether by Asian or Western scholars, fails to take into account the multitude of sometimes conflicting
cultural currents in traditional Chinese culture, or the various ways in which
present-day Chinese adapt their cultural heritage at the local level of everyday
life.

Chinese spirituality versus Western values

In his article for the *Washington Post*, Cody (1997) presents a view from
the West on the efforts of a local government in China to maintain
Chinese cultural values in the face of rapid capitalist modernization. It
portrays Chinese values as different from Western values, but
compatible with modernization, and indicates that there are debates
about the nature and permanence of Chinese values.

(. . .) China's "spiritual civilization" campaign has really taken root in
Dalian, a Manchurian port that used to be notorious for rough language
and now is heralded for civic pride. Mayor Bo Xilai, a rising political star
and the son of a Communist Party elder, has pushed his city into the
forefront of a national effort to revive traditional Asian values and civic
spirit among a people who for the last 12 years mostly have been caught
up in a race to get rich.

The campaign arose partly from a desire among Beijing's top leadership
to prevent Western values from invading China along with Western
capital and flooding the country with hamburger joints and all-night
discos. This concern, voiced especially by President Jiang Zemin, echoes
similar sentiments elsewhere in Asia, particularly Singapore and Malaysia,
where leaders seek to benefit from Western-style economics, but without
seeing their own culture eclipsed in the process. (. . .) The Chinese
campaign also reaches back into the country's revolutionary past, when
the egalitarian Communist society formed by Mao Zedong fostered a
spirit of self-sacrifice and concern for others. That society, largely
abandoned under the economic and social liberalization started by Deng
Xiaoping, also included heavy-handed repression, which kept people in
line even if the Little Red Book's civic-mindedness did not.

For that reason, many Chinese have interpreted the spiritual civilization
campaign – and particularly Jiang's recent emphasis on it – as an attempt
by the Beijing leadership to solidify controls at a time when exploding
capitalism has turned much of the population away from the authoritarian
government and its proclaimed ideology of "socialism with Chinese

characteristics." "What it really means is to obey the government," remarked a successful Chinese businessman here who wanted to be known as "Steve" and says he pays little attention to declarations from Beijing.

Chinese officials frequently have cited fear of chaos as a reason for continuing their authoritarian style of government even though its Communist underpinnings have gone by the wayside since Deng became paramount leader. And judging by largely feckless attempts to control culture or rein in the pirate recording industry, they seem to have a point.

At another level, China's rapid economic growth – and the potential to grow even more – have given rise to a newly assertive nationalism in which traditional values and Chinese history also have a place. A recent hit in Beijing was a book titled "China Can Say No," in which the authors argued that China, with its new place in the world, is entitled to pay less attention to what Western nations have to say about human rights, trade practices or regional diplomacy.

The idea of a spiritual civilization for China has been around since the mid-1980s, shortly after Deng's liberalization moved beyond Mao's vision and began to produce the corollaries of official corruption, ruthless business practices and materialism. It was to include the Five Talks – politeness, civility, morality, social relations, hygiene – and the Four Beauties: language, behavior, heart and environment. (. . .)

Lying 450 miles east of Beijing and only 350 miles west of Pyongyang, North Korea, Dalian is a close neighbor of the port of Lushun, known as Port Arthur at one time. Dalian was Dalny to the Russians when they occupied it until the Russo-Japanese war in 1904–05 and Darien to the Japanese, who ran things here from 1905 until the end of World War II. In more recent times, it has been known as the home of China's championship soccer team – and the city that, through the spiritual civilization campaign, overcame a reputation for foul language and over-ardent fans who threw insults at visiting teams.

"As Asian citizens of China, we pay attention to our ethics," said Zhan Jia Shu, secretary and deputy chairman of the Dalian City Soccer Fans Association, a city hall-sponsored group. "So as President Jiang Zemin said, the campaign has new meanings and old meanings. We don't want our soccer fans to be hooligans like in England. We want them to be warm, but civilized."

To make sure of this, Zhan said, the association broadcasts warnings against rude behavior over stadium loudspeakers during matches and seeks to channel enthusiasm with a People's Liberation Army band and blue-suited cheerleaders who kick their bare legs and sway their bodies like their National Football League counterparts.

Zhu Fenxiang, deputy director of the Dalian City Spiritual Campaign Office, said city officials in pursuit of ways to improve Dalian also have traveled to Singapore. Under former prime minister Lee Kwang Yew, the city-state acquired a reputation for no-nonsense civic behavior enforced by fines and even jail. (. . .)

Zhu said Bo's administration has doubled the amount of green space in the city to 7.8 million square yards planted with grass or trees and has started a slum eradication program to get rid of substandard housing. Because of the parks – along with a street layout and architecture inherited from its Russian and Japanese occupiers – Dalian seems remarkably ordered, clean and spacious compared to other, more crowded and run-down Chinese cities.

2.2 Third World socialist development models

If some East Asian countries can be seen to have challenged Western modernization views of development and culture within a capitalist paradigm, other developing countries have opted for socialist paths of modernization. Socialist development models took different forms in different countries, and were influenced by Marxist theories of imperialism and the Marxist-influenced dependency school (see chapter 1). From the mid-1950s until the mid-1970s, the most influential socialist model was Maoist China, but the Democratic Republic of Vietnam, Cuba, Angola, and Nicaragua have been, at various times and to varying degrees, influenced by Soviet development policies, and many other countries in Asia, Africa, and Latin America had strong popular movements which took their inspiration from Marxism. Samir Amin (1977), a well-known Egyptian Marxist scholar, believed that African and Asian countries were more likely to embrace the Maoist model than Latin American countries, because pre-capitalist traditions were still stronger in the former, allowing a bridge to be built between the past and a communist future. Without doubt, the multifarious shape of socialist development experiences is to a large extent due to the different ways in which popular movements and governments have harnessed local cultural traditions.

The Maoist path to socialism in China

The Maoist development model trod a precarious path between tradition and modernity which distinguished itself from that of other East Asian countries by its emphasis on socialism. Rather than following the Soviet policies of capital-intensive industrialization and centralized economic planning, Mao Zedong favored a decentralized development model in which each county and prefecture would become self-sufficient economic units, and emphasized the importance of political consciousness and of spiritual rather than material rewards. According to Ogden (1988), the Maoist development model did not aim at modernization, but sought to move China toward socialism. The developmental successes of this model, particularly in achieving self-sufficiency in grain and improving access to primary health care and education despite continuing low per capita incomes, were widely recognized in the 1970s (Ogden 1988; Selden and Lippit 1982). The Maoist regime's attitude toward Chinese cultural traditions was ambivalent, as seen during the heydays of the Cultural Revolution (1966–9). As Ogden (1988: 64) observes, "[t]here can be little question that the leftists were committed to eradicating the entrenched elitism of traditional

Chinese culture. Their efforts to present the peasant as the model of Chineseness, to glorify the simple, hardworking, self-sacrificing values of peasant life" are evident in the kind of proletarian culture which was endorsed.

In the 1980s, the reformist leaders reworked the connections between Chineseness, socialism, and modernization. Socialism is now more closely linked to development, with the argument that socialism will only succeed if it produces a better lifestyle than capitalism. As the strength of socialist ideology is waning in the drive toward development, Chineseness becomes the most important of the three clusters of values:

> the Chinese leadership has seemingly developed a far greater tolerance for market forces of supply and demand, which challenge socialism, than for Western values which might pollute Chinese culture. (Ogden 1988: 7)

However, according to Ogden (1988), the process of development, or modernization, levels the extremes of ideological and cultural differences in any society – Chinese culture and socialism will become less important in determining how China resolves its problems.

Pol Pot's Cambodia

Similar tensions between modernization and cultural tradition as in China emerged in Cambodia when the country attempted to embark on an autonomous development path under Pol Pot. At the beginning, Western left-wing intellectuals welcomed Pol Pot's victory in 1975 as a successful revolution against American imperialism, and a promising beginning of an egalitarian society based on rural development. However, Ponchaud's (1978: xiv) observations of the first two years under Pol Pot paint a picture of a regime which had turned the hierarchy of Western modernity and non-Western traditionalism on its head.

The Khmer Rouge categorically rejected, and indeed destroyed, any Western paraphernalia and structures in the country, including the city of Phnom Penh, which was evacuated immediately after the Khmer Rouge soldiers had captured it. According to the regime, in an egalitarian rural society even the idea of a city had no place. Phnom Penh, in their view, owed its existence to French colonialism, Chinese commerce, and the bureaucracy of the monarchy, all of which had been exploiting the Khmer peasantry for centuries. Many Phnom Penh residents and refugees from the war-torn countryside were forced to leave their houses in the city on foot because it was forbidden to start up motor vehicles. Meanwhile, the Khmer Rouge cadres stripped the city of any reminders of Western culture, by burning libraries, TV sets, furniture, whitegoods, and so forth. Coupled with this drive to purify a culture which the Khmer Rouge leadership saw as corrupted by imperialists was an equally determined effort to make agriculture (especially rice production) the main focus of the economy and of culture, under the motto "The fountain pen of today is the hoe!" (Ponchaud 1978: 122).

The tensions between town and countryside have been evident in the Marxist and Maoist theories which influenced the Khmer Rouge leaders (McIntyre 1996). As McIntyre (1996: 736) points out, "[f]or Marx, capitalism necessarily represented the triumph of the town over the countryside." The village was the seat of feudalism and despotism. Lenin and Stalin went further in that they "shared a strong belief that Russia's countryside was backward and that the town was crucial to achieving socialism." However, the Maoist perspective differed in that it saw capitalist industry as a product of colonial influence, and the cities in which industry was located came to be seen as sites of foreign domination.

The Khmer Rouge took a perspective similar to the Chinese Communist Party under Mao, in that they considered cities to be imperialist products. The predominantly rural population tended to regard cities as symbols of oppression, where the Cambodian ruling class, the French, and the Americans reigned supreme (Tan 1979). Furthermore, far from being modern, cities were perceived to be unproductive, with the vast majority of city inhabitants engaged in activities such as administration, services, and commerce (McIntyre 1996). Agriculture and small industry and crafts, in contrast, were classified as productive activities, and therefore a rational restructuring of society would involve moving people out of unproductive and into productive activities. According to McIntyre, the Khmer Rouge vision of a rural communist society was a reversal of the Western (Marxist) hierarchy of city and country. Instead of seeing progress as emanating from the city, they believed that the city was polluted and the rural peasantry was the true Khmer society. The Pol Pot regime identified agriculture as the key to all other self-reliant development, industrial or cultural. In a statement published in 1976, it justified its policy of forcing everyone into agricultural activities: "The important point is to solve the food problem first. When we have the food, we will expand simultaneously into the learning of reading, writing and arithmetic" (*Tung Padevat* 1976, quoted in Kiernan 1982: 242).

The new communist society could, however, by no means be created simply by returning to the country's traditions. To the contrary, the notion of "Year Zero" implies a new beginning, virtually out of the ashes of the past. It involved abandoning Khmer cultural practices just as much as eradicating the symbols and artefacts of Western culture. Hence, Ponchaud (1978: 120) reported that by army command

> the gracious Khmer greeting has been replaced by the ordinary European hand-shake, as a symbol of liberation. In the past no woman of modest status, whatever her age, would have dared to shake a man's hand; it would have shown a want of feminine modesty.

Human relations were completely transformed when the term "comrade" was introduced to replace the highly complex linguistic code through which ties of blood, age, social rank, and quality of the persons communicating were expressed in the Khmer language. With few exceptions, Buddhist temples were destroyed by the army as Buddhism was seen as a reactionary religion which lead to passivity, and hence, to an unproductive disposition.

However, these policies, seen from a position more sympathetic to the Khmer Rouge, may have aimed at ridding the country of oppressive traditions. Tan (1979: 6) pointed out that Cambodia before the Khmer Rouge was a rigidly hierarchical society, in which language "was imbued with rank, class, place in the society, and it reinforced respect for these values." These language structures were not deemed appropriate by a regime which was a "fierce advocate of egalitarianism" (Kiernan 1982: 239). The Khmer Rouge thus distinguished between what they considered true Khmer culture, and oppressive traditions which stood in the way of communism. Tan (1979: 9) argues that the violence with which the Pol Pot regime pursued its vision can at least in part be attributed to "the primitive hatred of rural people for their oppressors," and "the traditional Cambodian penal system that political criminals or traitors *and their whole families* are executed together."

Nyerere's vision for Tanzania: self-reliance

A self-reliant economy based on a strong agricultural sector was also the objective of the newly independent government of Tanzania in the 1960s, where similar contradictions were played out in ways different from both China and Cambodia. Julius Nyerere, the country's first president, identified a traditional form of socialism in *ujamaa*, the extended family, which, he claimed, was opposed to capitalism and class exploitation, as well as to doctrinaire socialism, which was based on class conflict (Kitching 1982: 64). The basic principles of *ujamaa* were mutual respect and recognition of the rights and needs of family members; sharing of property and income among all members of the family unit; and a universal acceptance of the obligation to work. Nyerere argued that

> These principles were, and are, the foundation of human security, of real practical equality, and of peace between members of a society. They can also be a basis of economic development if modern knowledge and modern techniques are used. (Nyerere 1967, quoted in Kitching 1982: 66)

Kitching (1982) points out that Nyerere's stress on the central importance of agriculture in Tanzania's development had two justifications. One was that Tanzania's economy and population were predominantly rural, and the country did not have the capital resources to throw into industrialization. The other was a moral and social reason: the traditional extended family was engaged in farming, and urbanization and industrialization would lead to the break-up of the country's closely knit communities. However, Nyerere's concern with economic growth and the need to lift the country out of poverty led him to a more cooperative relationship with the West, and to accept foreign capital as a way to complement domestic savings and thus allow for higher investment, more imports, and faster growth rates (Wuyts 1994).

The *ujamaa* movement was formally initiated in the Arusha Declaration of 1967, which identified agriculture as the main foundation for Tanzania's future development (Kjekshus 1977: 269). In this strategy, the purpose was to gather the scattered rural population in villages in order to achieve peasant self-reliance and collective land exploitation. It was argued that in this way peasants would increase productivity through division of labor and shared services and technological innovations. "Socially, the village would offer a life without exploitation, politically, village life was equated with grass-roots democracy and popular participation" (Kjekshus 1977: 275). At first a voluntary program, the *ujamaa* strategy was made compulsory in 1973 when the ruling party, the Tanzanian African National Union (TANU), decided that the entire peasantry was to live in *ujamaa* villages within three years.

Most scholars agree that the strategy failed for a number of reasons, ranging from inadequately planned villages and lack of knowledge of collective production methods, to peasant resistance to leaving their homesteads and lands. According to Kitching (1982: 120), Nyerere's vision of African socialist traditions was also overly romantic and did not sufficiently recognize the degree to which pre-colonial and colonial farming systems relied on de facto individual land tenure:

> In creating nucleated villages which were to depend for the bulk of their income on communal production on a collective farm, Tanzania was *not* simply extending "traditional" practices in new directions. It was creating completely novel forms of social and economic organization that were totally strange and alien to the vast majority of the people. (Kitching 1982: 120)

However, it seems that the *ujamaa* strategy was not so new. Kjekshus (1977) observes that rural Tanzanians had experienced villagization strategies already under the British colonial government, which argued in the late 1940s closer settlement patterns were a precondition to real progress. The colonial administration held the view that the Tanzanian peasant was a

> lazy, good-for-nothing agriculturist whose practices depleted, eroded and eventually destroyed the land. It was held that no development hopes could be pinned on the "traditional" peasant and herdsman. Initiative for change had to come from elsewhere, from the colonial government which thus cast itself in the role of a "modernizing agent." (Kjekshus 1977: 271)

The Tanzanian peasants did not support the colonial villagization process, which threatened to disrupt their way of life. They were more willing to follow Nyerere's *ujamaa* vision, but many also resisted the government's efforts to uproot them. Ten years after the Arusha Declaration, Nyerere admitted that the goals of self-sufficiency and socialism had not been achieved. Villagization had facilitated considerable progress in the provision of basic social services to rural Tanzanians, such as primary schooling, a system of basic preventive and curative health care, and much increased provision of clean water supply in

rural areas (Kitching 1982: 123). But maintaining these basic services relied heavily on foreign aid (Rist 1997). According to Rist (1997: 132), Nyerere's approach
was contradictory: "How could he have thought that the people most attached
to the land where their ancestors lay buried would spontaneously choose to
leave it for co-operatives directed by the state personnel, and to modernize
their agricultural practices?" He concludes that "it was difficult at one and the
same time to base actions upon tradition and to modernize production by changing technology and adopting new crop strains linked to chemical fertilizers
and pesticides" (Rist 1997: 133). Perhaps Nyerere's own assessment should also
be taken into account. Asked why his attempt to find a new way foundered on
the rocks, he said when he stepped down as president:

> there was 91-per-cent literacy and nearly every child was in school. We trained
> thousands of engineers and doctors and teachers. In 1988 Tanzania's per-capita
> income was $280. Now, in 1998, it is $140. So I asked the World Bank people what
> went wrong. Because for the last ten years Tanzania has been signing on the dot-
> ted line and doing everything the IMF and the World Bank wanted. Enrolment in
> school has plummeted to 63 per cent and conditions in health and other social
> services have deteriorated. I asked them again: "what went wrong?" These peo-
> ple just sat there looking at me. (Nyerere, quoted in Bunting 1999: 15)

To summarize, in the first section we argued that modernization approaches
to development assumed Third World cultures to be a hindrance to modernization. In order to experience progress, people in developing countries were
urged to embrace modern culture, which was by definition Western. However,
many societies resisted the identification of modernity with the West. Their
various alternatives, whether capitalist (Singapore) or socialist (China, Cambodia, Tanzania), sought to graft development onto native root stock. As Rist
(1997: 138) points out, "[t]he theoretical sequence of modernization is replaced
with a multiplicity of new practices that spring forth at the crossroads of history and cultures." Development itself is not challenged – Tanzania's Nyerere
hoped to chart a non-capitalist, African socialist modernity, and even Cambodia under Pol Pot held on to a notion of progress.

3   The crisis of development and the new neo-liberal hegemony

It is this very notion of development which came under attack in the 1980s.
This section distinguishes three aspects of the crisis of development: the crisis
of development theory, the gap between development theory and praxis, and
the declining credibility of development as a path to a good life for all. Stripped
of its normative definition, development is redefined in terms of a society's
integration into the world economy, which is to be achieved through the free
forces of the market. This neo-liberal view of development became the dominant discourse in the 1990s.

3.1   The crisis of development theory

The crisis in development thinking was first identified by Marxist-inspired theorists who had dominated the theoretical debates in the 1970s. One such voice was David Booth's (1985), who criticized Marxist development theorists for focusing their efforts on demonstrating how social, economic, and political structures maintained developing countries in poverty, rather than exploring how these structures might be changed. Booth argued that these critics of development were dogmatic, and too obsessed with political economy. Radical development perspectives thus had failed in charting alternative development paths that were sustainable, and by the end of the 1970s socialist strategies (such as those sketched out above) had been discredited or abandoned. This failure was compounded by the demise of centrally planned socialist economies in the 1980s.

3.2   The theory–praxis gap

There was a second strand to this crisis talk which concerned the gap between theory and praxis. On the one hand, it was argued that theorists of dependency and underdevelopment had been too pessimistic about capitalist development. As a result, they were unable to make sense of the East Asian countries that had been experiencing high rates of economic growth and improving standards of living (Warren 1980; Corbridge 1993a). They had become the success stories to which other developing countries looked for inspiration. On the other hand, critical voices among those who were in the thick of development action pointed out that current development thinking was not relevant to the problems they encountered. Instead of seeking solutions in theory, Edwards (1989: 127) proposed an empirical approach – arguing that "we find solutions to the problems we encounter through direct participation in a long process of trial and error."

Edwards's critique of "conventional development studies" raised some concerns with power and knowledge which we will look at in more detail in the next chapter. For example, he claimed that development studies treated people in the Third World as objects to be studied rather than as subjects of their own development, and devalued their knowledge. In addition, he claimed that "[t]he barriers created by jargon, language, literacy, price, availability and method create a situation where people are denied access to the information which is supposed to concern them" (Edwards 1989: 123).

While Edwards turned his back on development theory, Booth (1993) sought to develop new theoretical approaches from the bottom up. This new theory was to build on a wealth of empirical studies that had accumulated in the 1980s, and therefore be much more useful to development practitioners. Furthermore, the new theory

> would be sensitive to the great diversity of situations in the Third World ... and would allow for the possibility of "room for manoeuvre" at the "micro" and

"meso" levels of action, as well as the "macro" level, which had been the focus of previous development theory. (Leys 1996: 27)

However, the retreat from the macro level of theorizing to the local level may not give us new answers to the question of what development means today. As Leys (1996) points out, a new theory of development would involve choices about whom the theory is for, and what should be the goals of development – that is, political choices. It appears, therefore, that a vacuum remains where development theory once was, and this vacuum has been filled by the neo-liberalist view of market forces.

3.3   The crisis of the concept of development

In the eyes of another group of critics, there is a more fundamental crisis underpinning the problems of development theory and its inadequate links with praxis. It is a credibility crisis, in that few still believe in development being able to deliver the goods, according to Rist (1997: 218):

> it is a simple fact that the enthusiasm of the early sixties has gradually crumbled away. Nor can it be denied that projects intended to "enable communities to take their fate in their hands," or to assist "the development of each and all," have most often ended in failure.

Despite temporary successes in some East and Southeast Asian countries, the gap between North and South, and between the rich and the poor in each, is widening. Many countries in Africa are worse off now than they were thirty years ago (e.g. Stewart with Basu 1995). Thus, the great development project, which is based on faith in technology, growth, and progress, has brought to many Third World countries the opposite of what it promised (Schrijvers 1994: 20). In industrialized countries, the technological revolution has produced an underclass which is excluded from the formal labor process. If this underclass is marked as racially or ethnically different from the mainstream, then it is sometimes described as Third World within the First World. Such observations in the Third and the First Worlds have led some to the conclusion that development itself is fundamentally flawed (Rist 1997).

3.4   Enter neo-liberalism

The real crunch came in the 1980s, when the economic crisis hit the Northern countries. It became difficult to maintain the welfare system which many Western countries had built up in the post-war era, and tight control of government spending was prescribed as the only remedy. Banks began to retrieve their outstanding debts from developing countries and to charge higher interest rates. In order to service their loans, developing countries now have to borrow more capital from the International Monetary Fund, which agrees to further loans only subject to a structural adjustment program to bring the economy in line with the global capitalist system. This usually entails heavy reductions on governments' social spending (such as on food, education, health, and other basic services), which tend to hit the poorest most heavily (Schrijvers 1994: 14–15). The effects of this strategy are that most African and Latin American countries began to experience a process of development reversal by the early 1980s (Corbridge 1993b).

In terms of theory, the impact of the 1980s has been to undermine the idea that development could be organized by the state. Neo-liberals, who had long argued that the main obstacle to development was state intervention, now came to dominate financial institutions, governments, and even the development industry. Privatization, free markets, and globalization of the economy are now seen to be the solution to problems of poverty and underdevelopment. These solutions are seen to be universal, and applicable to all societies, whatever their social, cultural, and political make-up.

4   Summary

In this chapter we explored the contradictory ways in which culture has been deployed in Western studies of modernization and in various non-Western development strategies. All of these visions of development rely on a bounded view of culture, whether seen as hindrance or resource in the quest for development. This view of culture assumes that the world consists of separate societies each with its own distinctive culture, which is an integrated totality radically different from others (Gupta and Ferguson 1997). The implication is that modernization must either lead to the destruction of a developing society's traditions, or else build on these traditions which constitute the essence of that society. While early critics of modernization theories of development focused on the underlying assumption that developing societies had to shed their own traditions and become westernized, more recent critics argue that development is itself a cultural construct of the West. In examining the claim that development is in crisis, we have surveyed a number of possible causes for such a crisis, both at the level of ideas and at the material level. Rist argues that development has become a concept of the past – it has become absorbed by the globalization process. But development is still needed to legitimize globalization because while the former has a meaning, the latter has none (Rist 1997: 227). We need something we can believe in, only now we no longer need to distinguish between the virtual and the real.

"Development" (as a programme for collective happiness) no longer exists except as virtual reality, as a synthetic image in the full-length film of globalization. *It is like a dead star whose light can still be seen, even though it went out for ever long ago.* (Rist 1997: 230)

Another perspective, however, is put forward by Gardner and Lewis (1996), who argue that despite the undeniable crisis of development there is still a need to redress poverty. Like Rist, they argue that development as an idea and as a set of institutions and practices will remain with us for some time, and the challenge is therefore to make it more effective. They believe that anthropological approaches to development can contribute to this end – by turning the anthropological gaze on development institutions and professionals. This would involve, among other things, examining the cultural locations from which development professionals, scholars, and other key agents speak. Chapter 3 explores the new ways in which "the cultural" is conceived in the context of the crisis in development.

References

Ahmad, Y. 1996: The time to retire. *New Straits Times Press (Malaysia)*, January 1, 1996, p. 36.

Amin, S. 1977: Universality and cultural spheres, *Monthly Review*, 28 (9), 25–38.

Bernstein, H. 1971: Modernization theory and the sociological study of development. *Journal of Development Studies*, 7, 141–60.

Booth, D. 1985: Marxism and development sociology: interpreting the impasse. *World Development*, 13 (7), 761–87.

Booth, D. 1993: Development research: from impasse to a new agenda. In F. J. Schuurman (ed.), *Beyond the Development Impasse: New Directions in Development Theory*. London: Zed Books, 49–76.

Bunting, I. 1999: The heart of Africa. *New Internationalist*, 309, 12–15.

Cody, E. 1997: Striving to be spiritual. *Washington Post*, January 30, 1997, p. 13.

Corbridge, S. 1993a: Marxisms, modernities, and moralities: development praxis and the claims of distant strangers. *Society and Space*, 11, 449–72.

Corbridge, S. 1993b: *Debt and Development*. Oxford: Blackwell.

Edwards, M. 1989: The irrelevance of development studies. *Third World Quarterly*, 11 (1), 116–35.

Fukuyama, F. 1990: The end of history debate, *Dialogue*, 89, 8–13.

Fukuyama, F. 1995: Reflections on *The End of History*, five years later. *History and Theory*, 34 (2), 27–43.

Gardner, K. and Lewis, D. 1996: *Anthropology, Development and the Post-modern Challenge*. London and Chicago: Pluto Press.

Gupta, A. and Ferguson, J. 1997: Culture, power, place: ethnography at the end of an era. In A. Gupta and J. Ferguson (eds), *Culture, Power, Place. Explorations in Critical Anthropology*. Durham, NC: Duke University Press, 1–29.

Hamilton, G. G. (ed.) 1991: *Business Networks and Economic Development in East and South-east Asia*. Hong Kong: Center of Asian Studies, University of Hong Kong.

Hefner, R. W. 1998: Introduction: society and morality in the new Asian capitalisms. In R. W. Hefner (ed.), *Market Cultures. Society and Morality in the New Asian Capitalisms*. St Leonards: Allen and Unwin, 1–40.

Huntington, S. P. 1971: The change to change. Modernization, development, and politics. *Comparative Politics*, 3 (3), 283–322.

Huntington, S. 1996: *The Clash of Civilizations and the Remaking of World Order*. New York: Simon and Schuster.

Kiernan, B. 1982: Pol Pot and the Kampuchean communist movement. In B. Kiernan and C. Boua (eds), *Peasants and Politics in Kampuchea, 1942–1981*. London: Zed Books, 227–317.

Kitching, G. N. 1982: *Development and Underdevelopment in Historical Perspective: Populism, Nationalism, and Industrialization*. London: Methuen.

Kjekshus, H. 1977: The Tanzanian villagization policy: implementational lessons and ecological dimensions. *Canadian Journal of African Studies*, 11 (2), 269–82.

Latouche, S. 1996: *The Westernization of the World. The Significance, Scope and Limits of the Drive towards Global Uniformity*. Translated by Rosemary Morris. Cambridge: Polity.

Lerner, D. 1958: *The Passing of Traditional Society. Modernizing the Middle East*. New York: Free Press.

Lever-Tracy, C., Tracy, N., and Ip, D. 1997: *The Chinese Diaspora and Mainland China: An Emerging Economic Synergy*. New York: St Martin's Press.

Levy, M. J. 1967: Social patterns (structures) and problems of modernization. In W. E. Moore and R. M. Cook (eds), *Readings on Social Change*. Englewood Cliffs, NJ: Prentice Hall, 189–208.

Leys, C. 1996: *The Rise and Fall of Development Theory*. Oxford: James Currey.

Long, S. 1997: Adjust to live good old times. *The Straits Times (Singapore)*, Sunday Review, October 12, 1997 (*Focus*, p. 9).

McClelland, D. C. 1964: Business drive and national achievement. In A. Etzioni and E. Etzioni (eds), *Social Change*. New York: Basic Books, 165–78.

McIntyre, K. 1996: Geography as destiny: cities, villages and Khmer Rouge orientalism. *Comparative Studies in Society and History*, 38 (4), 730–58.

Ogden, S. 1988: *China's Unresolved Issues: Politics, Development, and Culture*. Englewood Cliffs, NJ: Prentice Hall.

Pigg, S. L. 1996: The credible and the credulous: the question of "villagers' beliefs" in Nepal. *Cultural Anthropology*, 11 (2), 160–201.

Ponchaud, F. 1978: *Cambodia Year Zero*. New York: Holt, Rinehart, and Winston.

Rist, G. 1997: *The History of Development. From Western Origins to Global Faith*. London: Zed Books.

Schrijvers, J. 1994: *The Violence of "Development": A Choice for Intellectuals*. New Delhi: Kali for Women.

Scott, K. V. 1995: *Gender and Development: Rethinking Modernization and Dependency Theory*. Boulder, CO: L. Rienner Publishers.

Selden, M. and Lippit, V. (eds) 1982: *The Transition to Socialism in China*. Armonk, NY: M. E. Sharpe.

Smelser, N. 1964: Toward a theory of modernization. In A. Etzioni and E. Etzioni (eds), *Social Change*. New York: Basic Books, 268–84.

So, A. Y. 1990: *Social Change and Development*. Newbury Park: Sage.

Stewart, F. with Basu, A. 1995: Structural adjustment policies and the poor in Africa: an analysis of the 1980s. In F. Stewart (ed.), *Adjustment and Poverty. Options and Choices*. London: Routledge, 138–70.

Tan, Lek-Hor 1979: Cambodia's total revolution. *Index on Censorship*, 8 (1), 3–10.

Teo, P. 1994: The national policy on elderly people in Singapore. *Ageing and Society*, 14 (3), 405–27.

Warren, B. 1980: *Imperialism, Pioneer of Capitalism*. Ed. John Sender. London: New Left Books.

Weller, R. P. 1998: Divided market cultures in China. In R. W. Hefner (ed.), *Market Cultures. Society and Morality in the New Asian Capitalisms*. St Leonards: Allen and Unwin, 78–103.

Wuyts, M. 1994: Accumulation, industrialisation and the peasantry: a reinterpretation of the Tanzanian experience. *The Journal of Peasant Studies*, 21 (2), 159–93.

3 Globalization and the Politics of Representation

1 Introduction

This chapter examines a way of thinking about culture and development which has emerged since the 1980s. This deconstructionist approach to development draws on new initiatives in the social sciences and cultural studies, in particular, studies of globalization and postcolonial theory. In critiquing existing paradigms in development studies, it circumvents the theoretical impasse discussed in chapter 2 and places culture at the center of a new agenda for thinking about global inequality and social change.

Globalization studies has become a broad-based endeavor in the social sciences, producing a diversity of approaches. They tend to focus on the restructuring taking place in the larger economies of the world, or on the power of globalizing forces to homogenize culture, politics, and social life generally. In this manifestation, globalization studies can be seen as one step on from modernization. A more complex model of globalization is emerging from studies, particularly of cultural anthropologists, whose research often involves detailed study of local circumstances. It is this strand which has begun to theorize a more subtle relationship between the global and the local, and to tease out the implications of this for development studies. In this chapter we shall focus on this anthropology of globalization, rather than the more economistic and sociological studies that tend to ignore issues of global inequality and focus on the dominant economies of the West.

Postcolonial studies are not, as the name might indicate, studies of ex-colonies in the political sense. Rather, postcolonial studies is a term adopted by a diverse group of scholars to describe their efforts to engage with and destabilize the legacy of colonial rule, not only in terms of its political and economic aftermath, but also its cultural and intellectual consequences. In particular, a number of these scholars have been concerned to reveal and challenge a politics of representation which continues to use colonizing strategies in describing the Third World and problems of development.

In this chapter, we provide an overview of both globalization and postcolonial studies in order to contextualize the deconstructionist perspective on development. What does "deconstruct" mean here? In chapter 1, we outlined the constructionist approach to culture, which emphasizes how meaning is constructed through systems of representation. Deconstruction is the term applied to the process of revealing the ways in which particular meanings are constructed through specific systems of representation or discourses. In terms of development discourse, Jonathan Crush (1995: 3) describes this as challenging "the taken-for-grantedness" of the discourse by revealing the links "between the words, the practices and the institutional expressions of development; between the relations of power and domination that order the world and the words and images that represent those worlds" (Crush 1995: 6). This deconstructive effort has led some scholars to argue for a move beyond development discourse to a post-development praxis centered on local experiences and knowledges. The conclusion to this chapter will briefly consider how they see this shift emerging from the politics of new social movements, and evaluate the potential of this perspective to address global inequality.

2   Globalization, culture, and development

2.1   Snapshots of globalization

What is meant by globalization? The term refers to the intensification of global interconnectedness, particularly the spread of capitalism as a production and market system. It also refers to innovations in technologies of communication and transportation, which are reconfiguring social relationships spatially, temporally, and in terms of speed (McGrew 1992; Robins 1997; Tomlinson 1997). International divisions of labor operated by multinational corporations stretch the production and manufacture of commodities across regional and national boundaries. The car you drive may have been designed in Japan, with components manufactured variously in Brazil, Malaysia, or India, and finally assembled in Detroit, Adelaide, or Dagenham. Commodities are now often marketed globally.

An abiding image of the Gulf War in 1991 was of the displaced labor force of Kuwait. Stranded in the desert were poor peasants from Bangladesh, Filipina maids, Indian computer engineers, British, Indian, and Australian nurses and doctors. Individually and collectively, they represented the dimensions and diversity of the flows of people across national borders – economic migrants, expatriate professionals, refugees, dissidents, tourists, and students – that is such a feature of the last half of the twentieth century. Mass migration is not a new phenomenon. Poverty and persecution, as well as the imperatives of empire, saw millions uproot themselves from Europe during the nineteenth century to settle in North America and Australasia. The breakdown of imperial rule in China likewise saw significant overseas Chinese communities go on to become an economic force in Southeast Asia and elsewhere.

What is different about the flows of people in the latter part of the twentieth century is that they are engendered not only by war, dislocation, and poverty, but also by relations of production and consumption that generate a constant coming and going across borders, as the Gulf War example above demonstrates. But it is not only the changing geographies of work which contribute to the globalization phenomenon. Tourists map space and culture in new configurations: Japanese honeymooners hold a second "white" wedding in Bondi, Sydney; Australians go shopping in Malaysia; European holidaymakers seek sun and fun on the beaches of North Africa or Thailand; and North Americans retire to the balmy climate of the Caribbean.

Fueling such interconnections is a technological revolution in communications which built on earlier revolutions in transportation to shrink the world spatially and temporally. Telephones, satellite television, and now the internet, enable information, images, and emotions to be almost instantaneously transmitted around the globe. Chinese farmers use public telephone boxes to monitor agricultural prices locally, regionally, and even internationally, in order to make informed decisions about marketing their crops.

2.2 Charting globalization

Globalization is not new. New trade routes and innovations in shipping and navigational technologies in the early modern era fostered interconnections around relations of consumption and production between the erstwhile unconnected and distant worlds of imperial China and Western Europe. Prior to this, interconnections between societies were more regional in focus. One of the most sophisticated networks of economic, political, and cultural relations was sixteenth-century Southeast Asia under the aegis of the Chinese empire (Abu-Lughod 1989).

Institutional and organizational globalization received its major boost from European colonialism, in tandem itself with an emergent industrial capitalism which increasingly sought a global scope for its production and marketing capacities. Mercantile and administrative organizations such as the East India Company paved the way for colonial administrations and state structures that forged new kinds of connections between peoples, communities, and cultures. The late twentieth century witnessed an intensification of the processes of globalization, which are reworking space, speed, and communication in ways which undermine the modern configurations of the nation-state and its territorial and cultural integrity. The frequency and complexity of relations of connectedness which are global in scope, it is argued, push the contemporary consequences of globalization well beyond the existing conceptual and institutional framework of social life.

A question frequently posed by social scientists in relation to globalization is whether the world is becoming more homogeneous, more the same? For those influenced by modernization theory, the answer is most usually positive, with globalization seen as the outward flow of Western know-how, capital, and culture to the rest of the world. The spread of Western lifestyles, consumption patterns, and political and social values is taken as an indicator of growing prosperity and progress. This echoes Fukuyama's *End of History* thesis (1990) discussed in chapter 2. From a perspective more influenced by dependency theory, the appraisal is negative. Yes, the world is becoming more uniform, not under the benign march of progress, but as a consequence of the global hegemony of Western capitalism – the "McDonaldization" of the world is "constantly tending to push the meanings of various Third World cultures in a single direction" (Asad 1986: 163) – toward those of the West. An amalgam of both these approaches is the "Americanization" argument, which puts a negative twist into the modernization thesis. A good example of this is the way some Islamic states have identified "Americanization" as a threat hidden in development or modernization, and have sought to reject some aspects of globalization, for example banning satellite dishes, as in the case of Iran, in order to prevent their citizens from viewing American television, seen as an attack on the integrity of Iranian culture.

2.3   Globalization and difference

As Robins (1997: 12) points out, "Globalization is ordinary." It is not a macro structure out or up there, but something that intervenes directly into daily life, as our examples above indicate. Few of us, wherever we might live, escape some kind of connection with the global, whether it is through the ways we earn our living, the foods we eat, music we listen to, or the environment we inhabit. The parameters of our lived experiences are permeable as never before, in an ever-expanding awareness of "other" circumstances, experiences, images, and ways of living. This "ordinary" quality of globalization implicates it in the reworking of the "cultural." The idea of culture as a bounded, discrete entity cannot comprehend the fluidities of globalization where everyday lives and ways of thinking are structured within broad influences stretching well beyond the borders of language, territory, and belief of specific communities, societies, and states.

Both the modernization and dependency theorists operate with this view of culture as bounded. Their arguments for increased homogeneity hinge on a center–periphery model in which the globalizing forces of Western capitalist modernity penetrate and absorb peripheral cultures. However, as Arjun Appadurai points out, what both variants of the one-world thesis "fail to consider is that at least as rapidly as forces from various metropolises are brought into new societies they tend to become indigenized in one way or another" (1990: 295; 1996: 32). Jonathan Friedman's (1990: 315) study of *Les sapeurs*, a men's grouping in the People's Republic of the Congo in francophone Central Africa, is a case in point:

> *Les sapeurs* progress through a system of age grades which begins in Brazzaville with the acquisition of European ready-to-wear imports, and which then takes them to Paris where they accumulate, by any means available, famous designer clothes from France and highest ranked Italy at tremendous expense. [our italics]

On their return to Brazzaville, the men "perform the *danse des griffes*, with the great name labels that are sewn into the lapels of a jacket and displayed accordingly as part of the ritual status" (Friedman 1990: 315). Friedman's point is that this is not an example of the adoption of Western consumerism and its values by the periphery – in this case, the ranks of the urban poor in an impoverished Third World state. Rather, he argues, it is the incorporation of newly available means of self-definition – in this case, European high-fashion clothing – into existing Congolese ways of thinking about self and social status. The result is not without its consequences for Congolese cultural practices; the "lumpen-proletarian dandyism" of *Les sapeurs* is a potent threat to established norms of elite status in Congolese society (Friedman 1990: 318). It certainly locks the men into the global cultural economy, not only as consumers but as immigrant workers in Paris, where they live in squalor "eking out a bare subsistence, all and any cash is channelled into the instalment purchase of the great names in menswear" (Friedman 1990: 317). But it is not a straightforward example of westernization in either the modernization or dependency sense of that term; rather, it reflects precisely that process of indigenization that Appadurai refers to.

Instead of a core–periphery model in which the global is always incorporating and eclipsing the local, Appadurai draws a more complicated picture of globalization as "cultural flow" across five dimensions or "scapes":

1 **ethnoscapes**: the flows of people "having to move, or the fantasies of wanting to move." Even where stable communities and networks exist, they are "shot through with the woof of human motion" (Appadurai 1990: 297).
2 **technoscapes**: fluidities of global configurations of technology, moving quickly across previously impervious borders. (See figure 3.1.)
3 **financescapes**: the flows of capital in ever more rapid, complex, and opaque forms.
4 **mediascapes**: refers to both the distribution of technologies of information production and dissemination such as television, newspapers, and the images created by such media.
5 **ideoscapes**: the diaspora of political ideologies of democracy, originally part of the Euro-American Enlightenment world view, to different parts of the world where such ideas assume different meanings to those of their original context. (See figure 3.2.)

Figure 3.1   Technoscape in Ho Chi Minh City, Vietnam

These scapes form the building blocks of what Appadurai calls "imagined worlds" as against "imagined communities," in which the scope of people's lives – as groups and as individuals – is constituted across a global reach, much as *Les sapeurs* reconstitute themselves in terms of Congolese status hierarchies through the overlapping but disjunctive ethno-, finance, and media "scapes" which coalesce in the *danse des griffes* (see also Holton 1998).

The cultural flows which Appadurai describes do not just reconfigure local cultures in the periphery, but also upset "the cultural certainties and fixities of the metropole" (Gupta and Ferguson 1997: 38). Gupta and Ferguson quote a young white reggae fan in Birmingham, England: "There is no such thing as 'England' any more . . . welcome to India brothers! This is the Caribbean! . . . Nigeria!" (Hebdige 1987: 158–9, quoted in Gupta and Ferguson 1997: 38). He enthusiastically embraces the sweeping changes that migrants from the old British empire have brought to this part of the West.

In both the Congolese and the English examples, the connection drawn between a particular place and a particular culture is broken. But, as Gupta and Ferguson point out, "spaces have *always* been hierarchically interconnected," even if not in as many ways as they are today. Seen in this way, "cultural and social change becomes not a matter of cultural contact and articulation," as modernization theorists would have it, "but one of rethinking difference *through* connection" (Gupta and Ferguson 1992: 8). In other words, the greater connectedness fostered by globalization may actually produce more diversity, not less.

To illustrate this point, Appadurai uses the concept of "deterritorialization."

Figure 3.2   Ideoscape in Kerala, India

For those who move across borders, for whatever reason, there is often no longer a congruence between the spatial, cultural, and political aspects of their sense of identity and belonging. Often, the very act of moving to another place makes people more aware and committed to their erstwhile "local" community.

Thus globalization, despite, or perhaps because of, the ways in which it makes the boundaries of nation-states porous, may have the paradoxical effect of intensifying and reinvigorating nationalisms in multiple and complex ways. Appadurai takes the example of middle-class Indians who have migrated to the West, only to become passionate advocates of newly articulate religious and ethnic fundamentalisms which then take on an effect within the subcontinental political milieu. As he comments, "the problems of cultural reproduction for Hindus abroad has become tied to the politics of Hindu fundamentalism at home" (1990: 302). The paradox is that despite achieving and adopting many of the signifiers of late-twentieth-century American modernity, significant sections of this expatriate middle class feel more not less (Hindu) Indian in ways which serve to exaggerate the politics of difference and communalism in India rather than the West, where they live.

2.4   The local and the global

This complex dynamic between the global and the local is played out variously in numerous contexts. Janet Abu-Lughod (1991: 132) points out how the global flow is not simply from the global to the local, but also the reverse. World Music is a good example of this. Over the last decade of the twentieth century, non-Western forms of music and various blends of music and instruments became commercially successful in the previously monocultural world of Western popular music.

Richard Wilk (1995) puts a different spin on the question of power, hegemony, and globalization. He explores how the beauty pageant has operated in the Caribbean state of Belize to structure the politics of national identity in ways which have created a "local" within a global institutional framework. Precisely as Belizean society has become more cosmopolitan, so it has been able to produce a sense of a uniquely Belizean culture where little sense of such an entity existed before. Wilk's point, however, is not that a Belizean local emerges against or in spite of globalizing forces, but the reverse: "The new global cultural system promotes difference instead of suppressing it, but difference of a particular kind. Its hegemony is not of content but of form, global structures organize diversity, rather than replicating uniformity" (Wilk 1995: 118).

Wilk thus takes the notion of hegemony used in variants of dependency theory and twists it. The hegemony embedded in globalization is not one productive of sameness, but of difference – the power lies in the ways in which global institutions and structures, such as the beauty pageant, provide the boundaries within which difference is acknowledged, articulated, and played out. Thus the appearance of many diverse expressions of the local, and the apparent indigenization of global processes, commodities, and so on, does not necessar-

Figure 3.3   A billboard of Jamaican "Miss World 1993"

ily contradict a move to homogeneity or sameness, but it is a sameness predicated on the "organization of difference." To set up the global and local as a binary, external to each other, is, Wilk argues, to miss the ways in which the local, ethnic, and national are "essential constitutive parts of global culture" (Wilk 1995: 118).

Lila Abu-Lughod (1995) makes a similar point about the relationship between the local and modernity in her study of the cultural politics around Egyptian television. The conventional view of the local as the repository of tradition, essentially outside of modernity, runs deep within development theory. As we argued in chapter 2, studies of modernization provide the clearest example of this in their assumption that modernization is predicated upon the dislocation and disintegration of the "backward" and "traditional" local. In Egypt, this modernization ethos informed urban elite views of television as a powerful instrument with which to bring "modernity" to the masses.

However, the villagers who were intended as the recipients of these educational messages engage with television somewhat differently. Their favorite programs are not the Egyptian soap operas peddling a message of national modernity, but the apolitical American soaps which focus on the personal lives of the rich and beautiful. When they do watch the Egyptian programs, it is with a similar fascination about the personal aspects of the soap opera characters, rather than identifying with the characters as role models of an urban middle-class national modernity. Moreover, as Abu-Lughod points out, television and its content are not modern invaders into a backward world of tradition. The villagers of Upper Egypt have long been tied into national and transnational circuits of political economy and cultural interaction. Their response to the television programs is thus not because they are traditional and ignorant of modernity, "but because the ways they are positioned within modernity is at odds with the visions these urban middle-class professionals promote" (Abu-Lughod 1995: 191). The villagers of Upper Egypt experience their modern lives as "the modernity of poverty, consumer desires, underemployment, ill health, and religious nationalism," a far more common kind of modernity than that portrayed in the idealistic nationalism of the Egyptian soaps (Abu-Lughod 1995: 207).

2.5   Summary

The impasse in development theory, which we sketched in the second chapter, was during the 1990s side-stepped to an extent by the language of globalization. Globalization as a process and as a model of social change has challenged many of the key components of existing development theories, whether of the modernization or dependency schools. The binary models of modern/tradition, core/periphery collapse when confronted by the new patterns of interaction and movement generated by globalization. Most particularly, the fluidities of global cultural flows undermine the concept of culture as a distinct, discrete, and bounded entity – whether conceived of as local, regional, national, or global. Instead, "culture" is more accurately conceived as complex and multidirectional cultural interactions and re-combinations, weaving the local and global together in myriad patterns and configurations. Modernity becomes fluid and multiple rather than a coherent, singular endpoint – whether cast in terms of westernization or hegemonic capitalism. The consequences for development as a concept and set of practices will be taken up in section 3.

3 Postcolonial challenges

If globalization has reworked spatial relations and the material stuff of cultural practices and identities in Western and non-Western societies, postcolonial studies have challenged the underlying cultural representations of the Third World which had been established in the Western mind since the colonial era. In this section we are concerned primarily with identifying those aspects of postcolonial studies which are most relevant to the development context.

3.1 Shadows on Western self-perceptions of enlightenment

For most of the twentieth century, development thinking concerned itself with the task of closing the gap between the First and the Third World. While there were debates over the underlying causes of Third World underdevelopment, and how this could be remedied (see chapter 2), few disputed the reality of the divide – economic and cultural – between the two blocks. Neither was there much discussion in the academic or popular literature over which of the two constituted a higher level of development: the First World, or "the West," clearly represented the most advanced type of society on earth, and the greatest achievement of humanity.

On closer inspection, this comfortable self-image of the West was never accepted universally. The Second World War and its aftermath, specifically the Holocaust in Europe and the collapse of European empires, challenged Western claims to be the pinnacle of enlightenment and humanity. The Holocaust clearly demonstrated that it was possible for an economically advanced, democratic, civilized Western nation such as Germany to become the main perpetrator of genocide. Many commentators see the Holocaust as a failure, or rupture, of the civilizing process. Zygmunt Bauman, on the other hand, argues that the Holocaust merely uncovered the face of modernity: "[I]t was the spirit of instrumental rationality, and its modern, bureaucratic form of institutionalization, which had made the Holocaust-style solutions not only possible, but eminently 'reasonable' – and increased the probability of their choice" (Bauman 1989: 18). It can also lead to the silencing of morality as rules and laws are implemented. In Bauman's view, we must let go of the myth of Western society having emerged from prehistoric barbarity, and recognize that creation and destruction are inseparable aspects of every civilization.

The break-up of empires and the concomitant process of decolonization prompted a rewriting of the relationship between Western societies and the rest of the world. In contrast to imperial notions of colonialism as a civilizing mission, postcolonial critics argue from the outside, much as Bauman does from inside the European tradition, that Western colonialism was the dark side of modernity, and that the barbarity and traditionalism of the non-West were ideological constructions of the colonizers' imaginations. The arguments made by Bauman and the postcolonial critics about the dark side of modernity destabilize a central binary underlying many development theories: that the West is modern, civilized, and enlightened, and "the Rest" are traditional, barbaric, and ignorant.

3.2   Defining the postcolonial

The term "postcolonial" is interpreted in various ways and still attracts much debate. However, the crux of the concept and its use is the ways it focuses on the cultural as defining features of a politics which analyzes and contests colonial stratagems. Drawing on Ashcroft, Griffith, and Tiffin's (1998: 187) definition, we can identify five elements the term postcolonial embraces.

1   The study and analysis of European territorial conquests

This involves examining how European imperial aggression initiated a process of cultural change which has affected the colonized societies up to the present time (Ashcroft, Griffith, and Tiffin 1989). This process is more complicated than many dependency and modernization theorists would have it:

> colonialism is not best understood primarily as a political or economic relationship that is legitimised or justified through ideologies of racism or progress. Rather, colonialism has always, equally importantly and deeply, been a cultural process; its discoveries and trespasses are imagined and energized through signs, metaphors and narratives; even what would seem its purest moments of profit and violence have been mediated and enframed by structures of meaning. (Thomas 1994: 2)

2   The institutions of European colonialisms

The structures of meaning Thomas (1994) refers to in the quotation above were often based in the churches, administrations, schools, and other institutions which colonial powers established in the colonial territories. One example is the way the British monarchy was deployed in colonial territories as a parental figure who watches over its subjects with great concern and benevolence (Ranger 1983; see chapter 5).

3   The discursive operations of empire

Language is central to colonial domination. As Spurr (1993: 4) points out, "[t]he very process by which one culture subordinates another begins in the act of naming and leaving unnamed." Painting was also an important tool of representation, as Bernard Smith's analysis of the artwork of painters who accompanied Captain Cook on his South Seas voyages demonstrates. These paintings played an important role in shaping European ideas about the Pacific and its peoples. They worked as information and scientific description, at the same time as stereotyping the Pacific as an exotic and primitive place, and idealizing the European voyagers' explorations of the Pacific as peaceful and benevolent (Smith 1993).

The Rhetoric of Empire

In his book *The Rhetoric of Empire*, Spurr (1993) identifies thirteen key rhetorical devices in colonial and contemporary Western journalistic writing and in travel writing. He asks "[h]ow does the Western writer construct a coherent representation out of the strange and (to the writer) often incomprehensible realities confronted in the non-Western world? What are the cultural, ideological, or literary presuppositions upon which such a construct is based?" (1993: 3).

1 Surveillance – the power relation is evident in the act of looking. Describing colonized bodies and landscapes from a vantage point, the "commanding view."
2 Appropriation – refers to the colonizers "inheriting the earth." Natural resources of the colonized lands belong to "civilization." E.g. *Terra nullius* – the doctrine of "empty land" in colonial Australia.
3 Aestheticization – aesthetic transformation of social reality helps to maintain the distance between us and Third world reality. E.g. American journal *National Geographic*'s beautiful pictures of foreign lands and peoples (Lutz and Collins 1993).
4 Classification – "Western writing generates an ideologically charged meaning from its perceptions of non-Western cultures" (Spurr 1993: 62). E.g. nineteenth-century classifications of humanity into races which are hierarchically ordered, and naturally and permanently different. This supported the then predominant view that the white race never existed in the "purely primitive" state, and that black people were backward and uncivilized (see also chapter 1).
5 Modernization – "the order that classifies non-Western peoples according to the paradigm of modernization contains within it, already and as given, a judgement of their character" (Spurr 1993: 71; see also chapter 1).
6 Affirmation – the need for self-affirmation of colonialism leads to

presentations of a world in chaos and disorganization, waiting to be sorted out by the West.

7   Debasement – portrayal of the non-Western as filthy, inhuman, amoral. This involves attributing to the Other the dark side of the Western Self, which is feared and rejected.

8   Negation – the Other conceived as absence, emptiness, nothingness, death. E.g. Africa's alleged lack of history, and Africa as "the heart of darkness" in Joseph Conrad's (1973) novel, first published in 1902.

9   Idealization – idealizing the Other as noble savage, with a purity and simplicity which the West has lost. This makes it possible for the Other to be incorporated more readily into the fabric of Western values.

10 Insubstantialization – Western experience of the non-Western world as an inner journey, turning that world into a backdrop for the drama of the writer's self. E.g. Redmond O'Hanlon's (1986) travel writing.

11 Naturalization – non-Western people are perceived as being closer to nature, and are represented in terms of natural species or natural phenomena.

12 Eroticization – involves representing the relationship between colonial power and colonized in terms of a male–female relationship. E.g. Africa as a mistress, ready to be awakened or dominated by rational Western men/colonizers (Torgovnick 1990).

13 Resistance – the colonized mimic and mock colonial authority, appropriating terms of colonial discourse and turning it back against their source.

4   The subject construction in colonial discourse

This refers to the impact of cultural displacement under colonial rule on the sense of self of the colonized. Frantz Fanon's work on colonial Algeria explores the impact of French colonial rule on the colonized in psychological terms. Himself a black man from the Caribbean island of Martinique (also a French colony), he argues that the black man is enslaved by his skin, which is the signifier, from a white perspective, of savagery, brutality, ignorance, inferiority. The black man feels

> Shame. Shame and self-contempt. Nausea. When people like me, they tell me it is in spite of my color. When they dislike me, they point out that it is not because of my color. Either way, I am locked into the infernal circle. (Fanon 1968: 116).

This distinctive psychological impact of colonialism has led many postcolonial writers to stress the importance of retrieving and/or constructing a culture which offers a positive identity. Thus, During (1987: 33) points out "the need, in nations or groups which have been victims of imperialism, to achieve an identity uncontaminated by universalist or Eurocentric concepts and images."

5   Resistances to colonialism

Far from being all-powerful and uniform, "colonial rule was frequently haunted by a sense of insecurity, terrified by the obscurity of 'the native mentality' and overwhelmed by indigenous societies' apparent intractability in the face of government" (Thomas 1994: 15). This sense of insecurity, or instability, is a response to the resistance of the colonized. Resistance took a variety of forms, including overtly political nationalist movements as well as contestations over the character and meaning of cultural practices. Relations between colonizer and colonized transform both sides of the "colonial encounter." Hence, there is no uncontaminated identity outside the Western hegemonic system – Third World nations are the result of the international order established by European colonial power.

Postcolonial studies have put firmly on the agenda the issue of representation. By revealing how the Third World was produced out of the colonial experience, they destabilize a number of the binaries underlying the discourse of the West and the Rest. As well, they challenge the notion of an authentic tradition around which Third World societies can construct their own development models in the ways canvassed in chapter 2. At the same time, revealing the colonial production of the Third World calls into question the Enlightenment ideals of modernity as a progressive march toward emancipation and social well-being. Economic dependency and political repression have been the experience of many, if not most, ex-colonies. Postcolonial theorists argue that it is the cultural sphere which is central to the analysis of how the relationship between the First and Third Worlds has been constructed. It is also central in their analysis of where the resistances to this construction come from. Homi Bhabha has coined the term "hybridity" to grasp the inauthenticity of the contemporary Third World. One use of the term hybridity refers to the products of cultural mixing, for example, Creole and Pidgin languages. This draws on the horticultural usage of the term to refer to grafting or cross-breeding in order to produce a third species. Bhabha employs this sense of hybridity and modifies it to describe the products of the colonial relationship in ways that challenge the dichotomy that is usually seen as descriptive of the relationship colonizer/ colonized. Instead, he points to the mutuality of the colonizer and colonized, in the sense that the one cannot exist without the other. Take the civilizing mission as an example. In British colonial discourse, the civilizing mission superficially rests on an assimiliationary model of sameness; the brief is to Europeanize the native. This ambition took concrete policy form, the most famous example being Lord Macaulay's 1835 Minute to Parliament. It instituted a policy of creating an intermediary class of Indian men who were to be "brown Englishmen," fully versed in British culture and fluent in the English language. However, at the same time as the Minute appears to offer membership of the colonizers' club, its actual intention was "the desire for a reformed, recognizable Other, as a subject of a difference that is almost the same, but not quite" (Bhabha 1994: 86). Here we can see how both sameness and difference operate together in an ambivalence which limits the effect of each. It is out of this ambivalence that Bhabha theorizes the resistance to colonial power emerging.

Orientalism

The historical construction of Eastern cultures and people as "foreign," often alien or exotic objects of Western scrutiny or contemplation. The concept is associated with the influential work of Edward Said, who has identified Orientalism as a key feature of Western attitudes and writing about the Orient from the eighteenth century onwards. Orientalism is best understood as a discourse which both assumes and promotes a sense of fundamental difference between a Western or Occidental "us" and an Oriental "them" – the cultures and people of Eastern, Asiatic origins and traditions. Grounded in particular ideological assumptions held by Western writers, scholars, civil servants, and politicians, the discourse of Orientalism has been embodied historically in the complex social and political practice which Western societies have employed to dominate and gain authority over Eastern, Oriental cultures.

Orientalism should not be understood as crude racism or jingoism, although these may draw upon related values or assumptions. In Said's terms, it refers to those forms of communicative practice, such as serious travel writing or journalism, academic or political accounts, which seek to present objective analysis of Eastern phenomena to Western audiences. A characteristic of these accounts is their tendency to dehumanize the Oriental, presenting a fixed, unchanging Other, lacking subjectivity or internal variation and condensed in binary opposition to Western consciousness and culture. In these and other forms, Said argues that the discourse of Orientalism ultimately reveals less about the characteristics of the Eastern countries to which it refers than about the consciousness and culture of Western groups which have looked at them, studied them, and sought to exercise rule over them. As a historical set of ideas for making sense of the "unfamiliar" – the Orient – they reveal much about the preoccupations and structures of "our world" – Western European culture. Orientalism has emerged as a significant theme in recent discussions of reporting the Middle East, including the Gulf War and Islam, and in the analysis of contemporary travel and tourism writing (O'Sullivan 1994: 212; see also Said 1993 and 1995).

4 The deconstruction of development discourse

Drawing on globalization studies and postcolonial theory, some development studies scholars have opened up in new ways the question of what is meant by development and in whose interests it operates. Development, they argue, is not a means of addressing global inequalities and power differentials. Their rejection of modernization theory is total: "For instead of the kingdom of abundance promised by theorists and politicians in the 1950s, the discourse and strategy of development produced its opposite: massive underdevelopment and impoverishment, untold exploitation and oppression" (Escobar 1995a: 4). Unlike earlier critiques of modernization theory, such as dependency theory, this perspective does not see the answer in some alternative form of development – a "socialist" or "nationalist" path of development. Rather, as the quote above indicates, these scholars reject the very notion of "development" itself. Their search is for a "post-development" discourse (Escobar: 1995b), a discourse which will emerge outside of, and importantly, in resistance to Western modernity, to embrace the knowledges, ways of living, and aspirations of those "objects" of development discourse – the poor and dispossessed of the Third World.

4.1 Inventing the Third World

Arturo Escobar's influential book, *Encountering Development. The Making and Unmaking of the Third World* (1995a), is the most comprehensive exposition of this perspective to date. Escobar's aim is to deconstruct the concept of development in order to explain the "dream and how it progressively turned into a nightmare" (1995a: 4). Escobar demonstrates the representational power of development discourse in the way in which poverty was "discovered" and applied as a defining feature of the "Third World" in the post-Second World War period (1995a: 22). When the World Bank set the poverty indicator for nations at a national income level of $100 per capita, in 1948, "almost by fiat, two-thirds of the world's peoples were transformed into poor subjects" (Escobar 1995a: 23). The consequence of this act of definition was to entrench an economic model of poverty that implicitly took the materially "rich" West as the desirable endpoint, and depicted those regions of the world not conforming to this image of prosperity as deficient and requiring "development." The "Third World" is, in this sense, an invention of a Western discourse of development, defined by what it lacks – a material abundance – rather than by what those societies now represented as "poor" might have or value as measures of well-being. Poverty became solely a matter of inadequate income, the solution to which was also one-dimensional – economic growth, to be delivered through an infrastructure of "development" designed to bring the "poor" nations and peoples "up" to the levels of income of the West.

Development was – and continues to be for the most part – a top-down, ethno-centric, and technocratic approach, which treated people and cultures as abstract concepts, statistical figures to be moved up and down in the charts of "progress." Development was conceived not as a cultural process (culture was a residual vari-able, to disappear with the advance of modernization) but instead as a system of more or less universally applicable technical interventions intended to deliver some "badly needed" goods to a "target" population. (Escobar 1995a: 44)

Escobar emphasizes the ways in which this "development industry" operates to consolidate certain forms of knowledge as taken-for-granted truths (1995a: 45). Science and technology, planning, and management operate through the professional and institutional practice of "development" to displace and marginalize other modes of knowing and seeing the world (Escobar 1995a: 37); "even the most remote communities in the Third World are torn apart from their local context and redefined as 'resources'" (Escobar 1995a: 194). The "Third World" becomes a stereotype of the development industry's imagination, con-stantly reproduced through the lens of development discourse, much as Said documents the operations of Orientalism as a powerful discursive framework for imagining the non-West.

James Ferguson's (1994) deconstruction of a World Bank country report on Lesotho, a tiny kingdom encircled by the Republic of South Africa, gives an excellent illustration of how development discourse operates as a prism through which a development institution such as the World Bank constructs its own object – the underdeveloped country. Contrasting the report with academic studies of Lesotho, Ferguson reveals how the institutional context shapes the picture of Lesotho that emerges. Academic studies reveal a country which had, for a very long time, effectively operated as a de facto colony of, and labor reserve for, the South African economy. By contrast, the Bank's report describes a "traditional," "peasant," and "subsistence" economy, outside the framework of modern economic development. Lesotho emerges as a "less developed coun-try" or "LDC" in desperate need of precisely those development interventions the World Bank was established to provide: "the apolitical, technical 'develop-ment' intervention" (Ferguson 1994: 69).

The difference between these two representations is, according to Ferguson, the institutional contexts within which they are produced. The World Bank is charged with finding appropriate contexts within which to implement its stand-ardized development packages. It is strategies such as irrigation schemes and micro-credit programs that the Bank is geared to implement, rather than tack-ling issues of political economy such as Lesotho's complex relationship with South Africa. Thus, it is those representations of Lesotho that confirm and jus-tify this which appear most useful to the Bank.

The LDC as a stereotype

Ferguson outlines how a generic notion of an LDC, premised on four distinctive features, structures the representational framework of Lesotho as requiring "development":

> First, it must be *aboriginal*, not yet incorporated into the modern world, so that it can be transformed by roads and infrastructure, education, the introduction and strengthening of the cash economy (as against the "traditional subsistence sector"), and so on. . . .
> Secondly, it must be *agricultural*, so that it can be "developed" through agricultural improvements, rural development projects, extension, and technical inputs. . . .
> Thirdly, it must constitute a *national economy*, in order to support the idea of national economic planning and nation- and sector-based economic programs. . . .
> Fourthly, it must be subject to the principle of *governmentality*. That is, the main features of economy and society must be within the control of a neutral, unitary, and effective national government, and thus responsive to planners' blueprints. (Ferguson 1994: 71–2).

It is not only countries but also people who are transformed into objects of development by the representational power of development discourse. Nanda Shrestha (1995) recounts his experiences as a poor Nepalese boy who gains an education to eventually join the ranks of the "developed" as an academic in the USA. Drawing on postcolonial writers such as Fanon and Said, Shrestha reveals how a "colonial mindset" was embedded in Nepalese society through an elite identification with development or *bikas*, to use the Nepalese term, in ways which alienated him from his local context of class and culture:

> Increasingly, it has dawned on me that my own development odyssey served as an autopsy of how the imported discourse of development had possessed the mind of a national ruling class, and how such a mindset had, in turn, played a major role in deepening the social roots of poverty – all, of course, in the name of development. (Shrestha 1995: 266)

In a nutshell, then, the deconstructionist critique of the discourse of development is that it is part and parcel of "the globalization of Western state institutions, disciplines, cultures and mechanisms of exploitation" (Crush 1995: 11). Constructed within a Western-centric discursive framework, the concept of development is deployed within an institutional context – the "development machine" or "industry," as Crush and Escobar label it – which constantly reproduces the conditions for its own agency. Ferguson's account of the World Bank diagnosis of Lesotho's "underdevelopment" demonstrates that there is always a "crisis" that requires the external techno-fixes of "development" to right itself. In the process, the recipients of this "development" are positioned as passive beneficiaries of Western benevolence and expertise, or, in more critical evaluations of mainstream development, such as dependency theory, as helpless victims of capitalist development.

4.2 Local developments

While Escobar seeks to deconstruct hegemonic discourse, other researchers have focused on the ways in which this discourse is interpreted on the ground, either by development workers (Porter, Allen, and Thompson 1991; Ferguson 1994), states (Ong 1995), or by local communities (Pigg 1992 and 1996) or groups of people (Ong 1987; Nagata 1995; Stivens 1998). Drawing on cultural anthropology, these micro-level studies reveal the hybrid modernities which often result. In this sense, they complicate any simple model of colonization which sees a direct transference of Western imaginaries of development to the local context. Rather, as Pigg (1992: 492) succinctly states: "development fuses the local and the global" in ways which are profoundly cultural in their consequences and effects.

Shrestha's account of the alienation he experienced through being "developed" provides a very personal account of this process of fusion. Pigg's case studies of Nepal usefully build on this and explore in more detail the complexities of localizing "development." Her 1992 study focuses on the ways in which the Nepalese state's rural development plans invent the social category of "the village." Nepalese society and social relations are re-mapped around the degree of *bikas* a place, group, or individual is regarded as having, quantified in terms of things, such as videos, schools, new breeds of animals, electricity, and so on. The accouterments of "development" become the measure of *"bikas,"* and "the village" becomes the category identifying all those places seen to have little or no *"bikas."*

> The village crystallizes into a distinct social category in the context of this national project of development. Further, the conceptual joining of village, development, and nation reworks an abstract, internationalized development ideal, rendering it Nepalese. The nepalization of development concepts account for why the village becomes a marked category in a society in which the vast majority of people are villagers. (Pigg 1992: 492)

Pigg looks at images from Nepalese schoolbooks portraying national development. The effect is much as Shrestha documents: the lives of the villagers are recast as poor and backward alongside the ideal of the upper class present – educated, non-manual occupations, and lives lived in a harmony of cleanliness and order. Nepalese development workers thus distinguish themselves from the rural people their projects are designed to serve. They "speak of the village as a social world distinct and distant from their own" (1992: 503). Thus, on the one hand, *bikas* draws together an imagined national community of Nepal as an underdeveloped country forging a future modernity, while, on the other, it divides Nepalis between those with *bikas* and those without it. Even those who inhabit villages use the distinction between "the village" (as generic stereotype) and *bikas* to chart the social map of their place. Having *bikas* means not having to carry loads, an image expressive of the lack of mechanization in the hilly regions of Nepal, and the attractions of a development seen to reduce the demands of labor (Pigg 1992: 507).

This Nepalization of development is both connected to, and distinct from, the concept of development embedded in the global development industry. Ideas about modernity and progress informing *bikas* clearly derive from Western definitions and images of modernity. However, in a later study of villager beliefs about healing, Pigg argues that notions of modernity have permeated Nepali villagers' common sense, but have not totally taken it over. Rather, there is a "cosmopolitanism, a kind of cultural transivity, being produced out of the displacements the notion of the modern creates" (1996: 164). Her ethnography documents the different viewpoints expressed by shamans (the traditional healers), those using shamans, development bureaucrats, and health workers. Linking these people and their different viewpoints is a social order organized around national development, the agendas for which are set in Kathmandu, New York, Geneva. The government bureaucrat wants to use his local influence to promote a more rational kind of healing based on images of modern medical science. The development workers want bureaucrats to stop seeing culture as an obstacle, and instead to start using it as a tool for development. The villagers are not as depicted by either of the previous agents. They are not credulous or gullible; they neither dismiss nor leave unquestioned the shamans' authority. Finally, the shaman was well aware of people's skepticism from the outset.

> He knew he battled with witch-magic in a place where his clients also trot down the trail to buy medicines in the Bazaar, where relatives who think shamans are deceivers preying on people's superstitions may have just flown in from Kathmandu, where sophisticated local people invoke science to evaluate shamans' powers, and where an anthropologist might even show up to document his every move. (Pigg 1996: 171)

Pigg argues against a simple dichotomy of Western modernity taking over traditional cultures. Nor does she suggest that there exists a "coherent local counter-ideology that 'resists' modernity" (Pigg 1996: 192). Instead, the villagers express a complex cosmopolitanism in which awareness of wider worlds is a cultural capital capable of opening up the employment opportunities the "development industry" brings with it – more valued by the "locals" than any perceived or actual benefits wrought by its policies, programs, and projects. The production of this Nepalese version of modernity and development – *bikas* – is not a top-down process of Western development discourse trickling through national filters to displace or take over the local. Power, in this context, is the power of a network whose extensive reach depends on a web of linkages rather than its ability to be everywhere at once. The idea of the modern exists in a network of translatable social maneuvers that are not reducible to a single thing. . . . the explicit ideology of modernization . . . is neither the only source of local ideas of the modern nor the only form such ideas take . . . In order to account for the symbolic power, the social effects, and indeed the imputation of "Westernness" to the idea of the modern, we must begin by paying close attention to the specific ways this idea is alive in the world. (Pigg 1996: 193)

5   Problems of deconstruction

Pigg's model of the localization of development discourse as a complex fusing of the local and the global points to the pitfalls in some deconstructionist attempts to go beyond development discourse. As we indicated in the introduction to this section, Escobar, Sachs (1992), Rahnema (1997), and others look toward the emergence of such a discourse outside of the globalizing structures of Western modernity "in order to make room for other types of knowledges" than Western modes of knowing (Escobar 1995b: 216). This revaluing of non-Western, often indigenous, local knowledges sometimes comes dangerously close to romanticizing and essentializing indigenous ways of knowing and being. The binary drawn in development discourse between the global/local and modern/tradition is simply reversed; the local and the traditional become the valued authentic counterweight to a global modernity seen purely in negative terms. An example of this is found in some environmental/ecological critiques of development.

Vandana Shiva, an Indian scientist, has been a trenchant critic of what she calls the "maldevelopment" fostered by Western and elite Third World governments and institutions. In particular, she focuses on the ways in which a modern Western scientific rationality views nature as something to control, exploit, and consume, with disastrous ecological and social consequences. In contrast, Shiva argues, indigenous ways of knowing conceive of the relationship between nature and people as symbiotic and reflexive, such that "[t]reading gently on the Earth becomes the natural way to be" (Shiva 1997: 22). Drawing on Indian ways of thinking about this, she identifies a gendered quality in this relationship, such that women, because of their responsibilities for reproduction and nurturing of the young, are the main practitioners of "shakti" or the feminine principle, expressed in protective and sustainable ways of living in nature. By contrast, Western-inspired maldevelopment is patriarchal, both in its colonization of nature and in the ways it displaces women from their traditional roles at the center of social production. Drawing on the example of the women of Chipko, a tribal region in northern India, where women have been at the forefront of opposition to schemes to "develop" the forests they rely on for their spiritual and economic sustenance, Shiva argues that it is Third World women who are uniquely positioned to guide resistance to globalization and Western maldevelopment, and whose ways of living offer an alternative model of sustainable development based on a more reflexive, non-exploitative relationship with nature (Shiva 1989).

While valuing the emphasis Shiva places on the destructive aspects of Western scientific views of nature, and the consequent negative impact on the environment and people of much so-called "development," other feminist environmentalists have criticized her approach as overgeneralizing and romantic. Her view of Indian subsistence agriculturalists such as the Chipko women and the tribal people threatened by the World Bank-sponsored Narmada dam project in central India idealizes both their past and present. It ignores the often very oppressive class and caste relations within which this subsistence lifestyle and culture was and is placed (Braidotti, Charkiewicz, Häusler, and Wieringa 1997: 58). Subsistence communities have often had a long history of integration within market economies and commodity relations. The "local" in this sense has never been isolated from the "global." Their lifestyles and beliefs are as much a consequence of this history of connection as they are of any authentic "tradition." As Gita Sen (1995) points out, the tribal peoples threatened with displacement by the Narmada dam project are not so much against the dam or "development" as against even further impoverishment as a result of inadequate compensation or resettlement plans from the state for their loss of land and livelihood. Their opposition is thus derived not from some pure "traditional" subsistence ethos but from the pragmatics of desperate poverty and oppression.

Jonathan Rigg makes similar criticisms about the "local" in Escobar's work. He charges Escobar and other "post-development" writers of setting up the "local" as a generic category: "Terms like endogenous, indigenous and local pervade the material, and yet local histories and cultures are barely dissected" (Rigg 1997: 34). He accuses Escobar of overgeneralizing: "he paints all the countries of the developing world in a single shade of (largely Colombian) 'underdeveloped'" (Rigg 1997: 34). This ignores the experiences of other parts of the world, which differ considerably from that of the Colombian case study used by Escobar, Rigg argues, particularly the economies of Asia, which appear to undermine Escobar's thesis that development has produced underdevelopment and poverty rather than the opposite.

Moreover, Rigg asks, "when scholars ask for interpretations of development, history and culture to be rooted in, and based on local/indigenous visions and experiences, it is fair to ask 'which local?'" (Rigg 1997: 36). To illustrate his point, Rigg documents how representations of Thai identity and tradition have varied over time according to the political purposes of those groups with the power to shape the representation:

> To assume that there is one "natural" indigenous vision which can somehow be accessed to shed light on the reality of local places, and which at the same time truly represents the interests of the whole, is unlikely. Even local visions are unrepresentative, are subject to manipulation, have been created and moulded by powerful interest groups, and are subject to constant change. (Rigg 1997: 36)

Moreover, "local" knowledges are not necessarily outside of, or opposed to, development discourse and practices. In Southeast Asia, he points out, most people "have climbed aboard the modernization bandwagon, whether they be for or agin it" (Rigg 1997: 36). Peasants, urban businessmen, and low-wage workers all utilize the vocabulary of development and globalization to describe themselves and their contexts; "to a large extent the ethic of, and allegiance to modernity, consumerism, progress and development have been internalized. Development and alternative development, like development and underdevelopment, are two sides of the same coin" (Rigg 1997: 37).

Rigg's book was published before the so-called "Asian meltdown" of 1997–8. We might ask whether the majority of Indonesians who have slipped back below the poverty line they so diligently raised themselves above over the previous three decades of often spectacular "development" are still "aboard" the modernization wagon with any fervor. Nevertheless, Rigg's criticisms are important in pointing out the diversity and complexity of the "local" and the difficulties in building any overarching alternative to the "development machine" on the basis of local knowledges, cultures, and perspectives. In particular, he raises the important point that "locals," after decades of development discourse, agendas, and practices, may well be as desirous of the attributes of a globalized Western modernity based on material affluence as anyone else. To a degree, Rigg's account echoes Pigg's description of Nepalese engagements with development discourse and Western ideas of modernity. The point of difference between the two, however, is in how they view the nature of this engagement and its outcome. Rigg seems to see his Southeast Asian advocates of development as willing recruits to the Western vision of development as modernization. In contrast, Pigg highlights how the cosmopolitan fusions involved in Nepalese engagements with the global produce new versions of modernity which are not simply carbon copies of the global development vision. This is an important distinction, developed by Escobar in the notion of "hybrid cultures" to describe the ways in which modernity is being reinterpreted in the periphery out of this fusion between the "traditional" and the "modern," the global and the local. It is this notion of hybridity that allows Escobar to posit the possibility of going beyond "development" to "post-development," a move we shall explore in the final section below, as a prelude to reflecting on the charge laid at the deconstructionist door: their failure to provide practical alternatives to deal with the empirical problems of poverty and deprivation in the Third World.

6   Hybrid modernities and post-development discourse

Escobar develops his concept of hybridity through the Latin American example. Hybridity denotes a cultural mixing in which there are no sharp boundaries between old and new, tradition and modern, but "complex processes of cultural hybridization encompassing manifold and multiple modernities and traditions" (Escobar 1995a: 218). In the Latin American context this often means the coexistence of pre-modern, modern, anti-modern, and amodern cultural forms, a rich mix which undermines any straightforward displacement of the non- or pre-modern by the modern. Just as Appadurai charted the ways in which global "scapes" were creating new and often unexpected circuits of knowledge, power, and identity, so Escobar argues that Latin American popular cultures are fertile mixtures of transnational, indigenous, and local influences and practices. He cites the example of an indigenous community's use of video cameras and planes to protect their land and ways of life in the Brazilian rainforest (Escobar 1995a: 219). In Australia, remote Aboriginal communities, scattered over northern Australia, are using the latest communications technologies to communicate ancient cultural knowledges to a new generation of indigenous youth, thus rejuvenating ways of living and seeing the world previously on the brink of extinction after the onslaughts of colonialism and postcolonial "development."

What is modern and what is traditional in such contexts? Escobar's point is precisely that "many 'traditional cultures' survive through their transformative engagement with modernity" (Escobar 1995a: 219). Inventive and adaptive, these engagements undermine any notions of static categories of "tradition" and "modern." The "traditional," for example an indigenous art form, may in fact be an astute adaptation to a marketing opportunity rather than an "authentic" survival from the past. Yet this adaptive form may well serve as an effective emblem around which a new sense of indigenous identity emerges to articulate a resistance to conventional, elite, or non-indigenous-inspired "development." Escobar is, however, keen to point out that such hybridities do not necessarily challenge or overcome pre-existing hegemonies; they may even feed into the production of new forms of domination. However, he nevertheless argues that "[b]y effecting displacements on the normal strategies of modernity, they contribute to the production of different subjectivities" (Escobar 1995a: 220) that may be progressive or conservative in tone, but give their own twist to modernity. Appadurai's example, mentioned in section 3 of this chapter, of the "modern" expatriate Indian professionals and their allegiance to a Hindu nationalism based on a reinscription of religious identity is a good case in point of the contradictory and complex effects of hybridized cultures.

Hybridity has clearly long been a part of the development experience. In chapter 2 we looked at the Asian model of development, which in many ways would fit Escobar's definition of cultural hybridization. For example, in Singapore, a governing elite bent on successful modernization deployed an ancient philosophy of Confucianism to foster what it saw as "traditional" values complementary to its development agenda. In so doing, the Singaporean government explicitly inverted modernization theory to argue that Asian traditional values were superior to those of the modern West. The difference between this kind of hybridity and the forms which Escobar sees as possible generators of a post-development discourse lies in the identity of the social agents involved. Escobar's concerns are for those people whose views are rarely, if ever, incorporated in development discourse: "God forbid that a Peruvian peasant, an African nomad or a rubber tapper of the Amazons should have something to say in this regard" (Escobar 1995a: 194). Hence, he places a lot of emphasis on the possibilities of new social movements, such as the Chipko movement.

The deconstructionist approach to development does not reject change, or deny the need for change. Rather, it seeks to do two things. One is to reveal the politics of representation embedded in conventional development discourse, and the other is to problematize the institutional context of development. Taken together, they enable us to see how power and knowledge operate to distort the rhetoric of development which emphasizes the alleviation of poverty and global inequality. One criticism of this approach is that it does not offer any concrete suggestions for tackling the immediate problems that confront the Third World. Neither does it put forward alternative models with which to replace development. What it does do is challenge development practitioners to take the local and the cultural seriously, including the local and cultural lenses embedded in their own taken-for-granted assumptions and preconceptions.

7 Summary

The new ways of thinking about development that have emerged since the early 1990s challenged earlier models through their focus on culture, or more precisely, "the cultural." Anthropological studies of globalization reveal the ways in which the global and local fuse in complicated patterns of cultural effect. Appadurai's model highlights how straightforward dichotomies of core/periphery, tradition/modern, and global/local underpinning much thinking in development studies are unable to grasp the complexity of cultural flows within the context of globalization. Postcolonial theory likewise revealed the ways in which a politics of representation, formed within European/Western thought in the era of colonialism and empire, continues to inform contemporary Western writing and thinking about the Third World, replicating the stereotypes and power relations of colonialism. Bhabha's notion of hybridity is a way of depicting a postcolonial cultural politics that goes beyond and resists the colonizing relations embedded in contemporary constructions of the First/Third world relationship.

The deconstructionist school of development critics draw on both the anthropology of globalization and postcolonial theory to illustrate how "development" as a discourse, set of institutions, and process is implicated in the cultural effects of both globalization and colonialism. Demonstrating how development discourse powerfully constructs the "Third World" as the object of development, Escobar, Crush, and others argue for a "post-development" discourse which would inform a different politics of global inequality, one which builds on and recognizes the diversity and intrinsic worth of the "local" and actively resists the hegemonic Western authority embedded in contemporary notions and practice of development. However, as the case studies of Nepal and Thailand indicate, "post-development" may not necessarily mean no "development" in the sense of a modernist vision of a material progress.

The hybrid forms of cultural politics emerging out of the complex and sometimes jagged meshing of local, national, and international discourses about "development" suggest a complicated plurality of modernities and developments. Whether these are, separately or collectively, likely to displace the hegemonic dominance of Western development discourse remains to be seen, but it seems unlikely that "development" in some form or another will not continue to play a part in the cultural and political mappings of global inequality. Another challenge to the post-development critics of development discourse is to address the issues of policy and practice raised by their radical critique of development discourse. If the current "development industry" is simply reproducing the inequality it requires to legitimate its own existence, then how are the problems of worsening poverty to be addressed in concrete and practical terms? In chapter 4 we consider feminist interventions within development studies, concluding with feminist deconstructionist approaches that have gone some way toward addressing these issues of praxis.

References

Abu-Lughod, J. 1989: On the remaking of history: how to reinvent the past. In B. Kruger and P. Mariani (eds), *Remaking History. Dia Art Foundation Discussions in Contemporary Culture*, No. 4. Seattle: Bay Press, 111–29.

Abu-Lughod, J. 1991: Going beyond global babble. In A. D. King (ed.), *Culture, Globalization and the World-System*. Basingstoke: Macmillan, 131–7.

Abu-Lughod, L. 1995: The objects of soap opera: Egyptian television and the cultural politics of modernity. In D. Miller (ed.), *Worlds Apart. Modernity through the Prism of the Local*. London: Routledge, 190–210.

Appadurai, A. 1990: Disjuncture and difference in the global economy. In M. Featherstone (ed.), *Global Culture. Nationalism, Globalization and Modernity*. London: Sage, 295–310.

Appadurai, A. 1996: *Modernity at Large: Cultural Dimensions of Globalization*. Minneapolis: University of Minnesota Press.

Asad, T. 1986: The concept of cultural translation in British social anthropology. In J. Clifford and G. E. Marcus (eds), *Writing Culture: The Poetics and Politics of Ethnography*. Berkeley: University of California Press, 141–64.

Ashcroft, B., Griffith, G., and Tiffin, H. 1989: *The Empire Writes Back: Theory and Practice in Post-colonial Literatures*. London: Routledge.

Ashcroft, B., Griffith, G., and Tiffin, H. 1998: *Key Concepts in Post-colonial Studies*. London: Routledge.

Bauman, Z. 1989: *Modernity and the Holocaust*. Oxford: Polity/Blackwell.

Bhabha, H. 1994: *Locations of Culture*. London: Routledge.

Braidotti, R., Charkiewicz, E., Häusler, S., and Wieringa, S. 1997: Women, the environments and sustainable development. In N. Visvanathan et al. (eds), *The Women, Gender and Development Reader*. London and New Jersey: Zed Books, 54–61.

Conrad, J. 1973: *Heart of Darkness*. London: Penguin. First published in 1902.

Crush, J. 1995: Introduction. Imagining development. In J. Crush (ed.), *Power of Development*. London and New York: Routledge, 1–23.

During, S. 1987: Postmodernism or post-colonialism today. *Textual Practice*, 1 (1), 32–47.

Escobar, A. 1995a: *Encountering Development. The Making and Unmaking of the Third World*. Princeton, NJ: Princeton University Press.

Escobar, A. 1995b: Imagining a post-development era. In J. Crush (ed.), *Power of Development*. London and New York: Routledge, 211–27.

Fanon, F. 1968: *Black Skin, White Masks*. Translated [from the French] by Charles Lam Markmann. London: MacGibbon and Kee.

Ferguson, J. 1994: *The Anti-Politics Machine. "Development," Depoliticization, and Bureaucratic Power in Lesotho*. Minneapolis and London: University of Minnesota Press. First published in 1990. Oxford: Oxford University Press.

Friedman, J. 1990: Being in the world: globalization and localization. *Theory, Culture and Society*, 7, 311–28.

Gupta, A. and Ferguson, J. 1997: Beyond "culture": space, identity, and the politics of difference. In A. Gupta and J. Ferguson (eds), *Culture, Power, Place: Explorations in Critical Anthropology*. Durham, NC: Duke University Press, 33–51. First published in *Cultural Anthropology*, 7 (1), 1992, 6–22.

Hebdige, D. 1987: *Cut 'n Mix: Culture, Identity and Caribbean Music*. London: Methuen.

Holton, R. 1998: *Globalization and the Nation State*. New York: St Martin's Press.

Lutz, C. A. and Collins, J. L. 1993: *Reading National Geographic*. Chicago: University of Chicago Press.

McGrew, A. 1992: A global society? In S. Hall, D. Held, and T. McGrew (eds), *Modernity and its Futures*. Cambridge: Polity, 61–112.

Nagata, J. 1995: Modern Malay women and the message of the "veil." In W. J. Karim (ed.), *"Male" and "Female" in Developing Southeast Asia*. Oxford/Washington, D.C.: Berg, 101–20.

O'Hanlon, R. 1986: Amazon adventure. *Granta*, 20, 15–54.

Ong, A. 1987: *Spirits of Resistance and Capitalist Discipline: Factory Women in Malaysia*. Albany: State University of New York Press.

Ong, A. 1995: State versus Islam: Malay families, women's bodies, and the body politics in Malaysia. In A. Ong and M. G. Peletz (eds), *Bewitching Women, Pious Men: Gender and Body Politics in Southeast Asia*. Berkeley: University of California Press, 159–94.

O'Sullivan, T. 1994: Orientalism. In T. O'Sullivan, J. Hartley, D. Saunders, M. Montgomery, and J. Fiske (eds), *Key Concepts in Communication and Cultural Studies*. London: Routledge, 212.

Pigg, S. L. 1992: Inventing social categories through place: social representations and development in Nepal. *Comparative Study of Society and History*, 34, 491–513.

Pigg, S. L. 1996: The credible and the credulous: the question of "villagers' beliefs" in Nepal. *Cultural Anthropology*, 11 (2), 160–201.

Porter, D., Allen, B., and Thompson, G. 1991: *Development in Practice: Paved with Good Intentions*. London: Routledge.

Rahnema, M. 1997: Towards post-development: searching for signposts, a new language and new paradigms. In M. Rahnema with V. Bawtree (eds), *The Post-development Reader*. London: Zed Books, 377–403.

Ranger, T. 1983: The invention of tradition in colonial Africa. In E. Hobsbawm and T. Ranger (eds), *The Invention of Tradition*. Cambridge: Cambridge University Press, 211–62.

Rigg, J. 1997: *Southeast Asia. The Human Landscape of Modernization and Development*. London and New York: Routledge.

Robins, K. 1997: What in the world's going on? In P. du Gay (ed.), *Production of Culture/ Cultures of Production*. London: Sage/Open University Press, 11–47.

Sachs, W. 1992: Introduction. In W. Sachs (ed.), *The Development Dictionary. A Guide to Knowledge as Power*. London and Johannesburg: Zed Books in association with Witwatersrand University Press, 1–5.

Said, E. W. 1993: *Culture and Imperialism*. London: Chatto and Windus.

Said, E. W. 1995: *Orientalism*. London: Penguin. First published in 1978.

Sen, G. 1995: National development and local environmental action – the case of the River Narmada. In V. Bhaskar and A. Glyn (eds), *The North, the South, and the Environment: Ecological Constraints and the Global Economy*. New York: St Martin's Press, 184–200.

Shiva, V. 1989: *Staying Alive. Women, Ecology and Development*. London: Zed Books.

Shiva, V. 1997: Economic globalisation, ecological feminism, sustainable development. *Canadian Women's Studies*, 17 (2), 22–7.

Shrestha, N. 1995: Becoming a development category. In J. Crush (ed.), *Power of Development*. London and New York: Routledge, 266–77.

Smith, B. 1993: *Imagining the Pacific*. Melbourne: Melbourne University Press.

Spurr, D. 1993: *The Rhetoric of Empire*. Durham, NC: Duke University Press.

Stivens, M. 1998: Modernizing the Malay mother. In K. Ram and M. Jolly (eds), *Maternities and Modernities. Colonial and Postcolonial Experiences in Asia and the Pacific*. Cambridge: Cambridge University Press, 50–80.

Thomas, N. 1994: *Colonialism's Culture: Anthropology, Travel and Government*. Cambridge: Polity.

Tomlinson, J. 1997: Internationalism, globalization and cultural imperialism. In K. Thompson (ed.), *Media and Cultural Regulation*. London: Sage/Open University Press, 118–53.

Torgovnick, M. 1990: *Gone Primitive: Savage Intellects, Modern Lives*. Chicago: University of Chicago Press.

Wilk, R. 1995: Learning to be local in Belize: global systems of common difference. In D. Miller (ed.), *Worlds Apart: Modernity through the Prism of the Local*. London: Routledge, 110–33.

4 Feminism, Development, and Culture

Contents

1 Introduction

Long before development came to be analyzed as a cultural construct, feminist researchers had begun to open our eyes to the ways in which development thinking and practice were permeated by the gender factor. Since the late 1960s, feminist social scientists have been collecting empirical evidence that women were either ignored by the development process, or assigned roles which did not allow them to benefit from development as much as men. The lower status of women appeared to be a universal fact, visible in all societies to a greater or lesser degree. The dominant explanation for this, at the time, was biological determinism, which argued that the biological difference between men and women explained their different status. The work of feminist sociologists and anthropologists, such as Sherry Ortner (1974), challenged this view. They pointed the finger at culture, suggesting it was not biological difference in itself but how this difference was interpreted within culturally defined value systems.

In the early 1970s, British feminist sociologist Ann Oakley (1972: 16) expressed this as a distinction between sex and gender:

> "Sex" is a word that refers to the biological differences between male and female: the visible difference in genitalia, the related difference in procreative function. "Gender" however is a matter of culture: it refers to the social classification into "masculine" and "feminine."

Oakley's definition was an important innovation at the time in arguing against biological determinist assertions that gender inequalities in society were the natural and appropriate result of the biological differences between men and women. Her emphasis on the cultural origins of gender implied that the definitions of what it means to be masculine and feminine were variable across time, space, and location. As Sherry Ortner (1974: 67) pointed out, "the specific cultural conceptions and symbolizations of woman are extraordinarily diverse and even mutually contradictory," and the treatment of women, their status, and their contribution to society varied enormously from one culture to another.

As this chapter aims to show, the contradictory constructions of gender, particularly between Western culture and other cultures, have produced development failures which eventually forced gender on the agenda of mainstream development institutions. The International Women's Year (1975) and the Decade for Women (1975–84) constituted a highly public move by the United Nations which marked the beginnings of a watershed in development thinking and practice. Bringing gender into focus broadens "development" well beyond the technocratic understanding of development as primarily a basket of economic quick-fixes; a nuts-and-bolts affair to do with market mechanisms, industrialization, technology, and institution building, divorced from the intimacies and intricacies of relations between women and men. This chapter surveys feminist development theory, which has, in various guises, been the main advocate for placing gender as a category and issue on the development agenda. Particular attention is paid to the extent to which feminist thought about development has challenged the mainstream development paradigms outlined in chapter 2.

Feminist scholars' efforts in making visible how cultural constructions of femininity and masculinity shape development processes and interventions, and how ideas of gender equality and justice should be applied to the field of development, were important in forging new ways of thinking about culture and development. However, these efforts themselves became the object of critical analysis by postcolonial and poststructuralist feminisms emerging in the 1980s. Some critics, from postcolonial and Third World positions, exposed the cultural assumptions about non-Western women which haunted many of the Western feminist studies. Others, influenced by poststructuralism, began to dismantle the distinction between "sex" and "gender," arguing that the distinction assumes the body is outside of culture and hence fixed in terms of its meanings and how it is lived in social life. Instead, they maintained that the body is itself a cultural construction and "sex" is, therefore, also a social category like gender:

> Whether male or female, the human body is thus already coded, placed in a social network, and given meaning in and by culture, the male being constituted as virile or phallic, the female as passive and castrated. These are not the result of biology, but of the social and psychological meaning of the body. (Grosz 1989: 111)

In other words, "sex does not *describe* a prior materiality, but produces and regulates the *intelligibility* of the *materiality* of bodies" (Butler 1992: 17). This radical dismantling of biological essentialism, on the basis of which we see the world's population in two mutually exclusive groups of "women" and "men," has had the effect of blurring the lines between sex and gender once again. However, whereas biological determinism reduced gender to a natural *a priori* sex, poststructuralists bring the two together at the cultural level in the phrase "gender and sexuality," which indicates the conceptual distinction between the two at the same time as it recognizes their interrelatedness. This has been productive, for example, in the area of development and HIV/AIDS, where, in addition to gender relations between men and women, cultural constructions of the sexual body have been recognized as an important area of study (e.g. Campbell 1997; McNally 1998).

2   Women, development, and feminist development theory

"Women hold up half the sky" was a phrase originally coined by Mao Zedong (1893–1976), the revolutionary Chinese communist leader, to challenge Chinese cultural norms about the status and role of women in order for them to assume more significant roles in the national development effort. This and other similar Chinese revolutionary slogans, such as "Even chicken feathers can fly to heaven," argues Elizabeth Croll (1994: 205), challenged "the customary sexual division of labour whereby women were largely confined to the domestic inside," leaving the public sphere of government and economic production to men. The sentiment spread far beyond China and served as one of the slogans in the political struggle waged to place women on the international development agenda. Its imagery evoked the numerical presence of women in the world's population and emphasized their equivalent responsibility and effort in maintaining social life, as well asserting their entitlement to a fair share in the future – the heaven on earth to be constructed through revolutionary transformation by the people themselves. This promise only served to highlight the lack of attention being given to women in existing development discourse. Mounting statistical evidence that women and children made up a disproportionate number of the poorest of the poor in the Third World gave ready ammunition to feminist critics in their argument that this neglect was not benign but had a disastrous impact on women's lives (Buvinic, Lycette, and McGreevey 1983; Gulati 1982). Such awareness further fueled the urgency with which women's movements lobbied national governments and international development institutions for action to address the situation, culminating in the UN declaring 1975 as International Women's Year and the beginning of a whole decade for women.

The results of this conference, which brought women from the North and South together for the first time under the auspices of the UN, were mixed. On the one hand, it was officially recognized that women were not only critical in encouraging development but were disadvantaged in access to development initiatives and intentions and required specific policy attention to remedy this. On the other, the often heated debates at the International Women's Year Conference (1975) highlighted profound differences amongst women across the global divides of North and South as well as within the South and North along class and political lines. What were "women's issues," and to what degree did they differ from men's in terms of development? Was there one universal understanding of "development"? No easy compromise solutions emerged to such problems and divisions. As the extract by Domitila Barrios de Chungara (see Box below) indicates, for poor women from the South, economic exploitation and political oppression, as well as the provision of basic needs such as clean water and children's education, loomed larger on their horizons than the issues of sexual politics and gender oppression which often motivated Northern middle-class women to international activism.

Domitila Barrios de Chungara, a women's leader and miner's wife in Siglo XX, the most important tin-mining community in Bolivia, came to the International Women's Year Conference in Mexico (1975) with a long history of union struggles alongside her husband, and experiences of army massacres and a lifetime of work and poverty (see also Nash 1979). Her twenty-hour working day and the labor of her children, she argues, benefits mainly the mining company, because her husband's wage does not cover the necessities of the family. So she has to make small pies to sell in the street, and her children must help her by standing in line to get the supplies they need from the company store. She believes that

> the first battle to be won is to let the woman, the man, the children participate in the struggle of the working class, so that the home can become a stronghold that the enemy can't overcome. Because if you have the enemy inside your own house, then it's just one more weapon that our common enemy can use toward a dangerous end. (Barrios de Chungara 1982: 236)

Barrios de Chungara was invited by the United Nations to participate in the International Women's Year Tribunal, a forum for non-governmental organizations' representatives taking place simultaneously with the official conference. Many of the feminist concerns – about the rights of prostitutes, the rights of lesbians, and the scourge of patriarchy in general – gave her a "rude shock. We spoke very different languages, no?" Together with other Latin American representatives, Barrios de Chungara set out to make

> our common problems known, what we thought women's progress was all about, how the majority of women live. We also said that for us the

first and main task isn't to fight against our compañeros [meaning, in this context, husbands], but with them to change the system we live in for another, in which men and women will have the right to live, to work, to organize. (Barrios de Chungara 1982: 239)

This line of argument raised criticism from some North American feminists, who interpreted it as a sign of being manipulated by men and ignorance of women's problems. As well, Barrios de Chungara recounts how this also interconnected, from her point of view, with class differences among women from the South.

And a lady, who was the president of the Mexican delegation, came up to me. She wanted to give me her own interpretation of the International Women's Year slogan, which was 'equality, development, and peace'. And she said:

"Let's speak about us, señora. We're women. Look, señora, forget the suffering of your people. For a moment, forget the massacres. We've talked enough about that. We've heard you enough. Let's talk about us . . . about you and me . . . well, about women."

So I said:

"All right, let's talk about the two of us. But if you'll let me, I'll begin, Señora, I've known you for a week. Every morning you show up in a different outfit and on the other hand, I don't. Every day you show up all made up and combed like someone who has time to spend in an elegant beauty parlour and who can spend money on that, and yet I don't. I see that each afternoon you have a chauffeur in a car waiting at the door of this place to take you home, and yet I don't. And in order to show up here like you do, I'm sure you live in a really elegant home, in an elegant neighbourhood, no? And yet we miners' wives only have a small house on loan to us, and when our husbands die or get sick or are fired from the company, we have ninety days to leave the house and then we're in the street. Now, señora, tell me: is your situation at all similar to mine? Is my situation at all similar to yours? So what equality are we going to speak of between the two of us? If you and I aren't alike, if you and I are so different? We can't at this moment, be equal, even as women, don't you think?" (Barrios de Chungara 1982: 241) [punctuation in the original]

In the years since 1975 feminist engagement with mainstream development discourse has taken a variety of paths reflecting these differences between women. They range in scope from a call to include women in existing development approaches to policy and processes, to more radical viewpoints which challenge the very concept of development itself. In between these two points are a multitude of political positions, theoretical debate, and analytical framework. However, this diversity is commonly clustered into four broad perspectives, roughly chronological in terms of their emergence as components of feminist development theory since 1975. They are Women in Development

(WID), Women and Development (WAD), Gender and Development (GAD), and, most recently, poststructural and postcolonial feminism's critique of feminist development theory (Parpart and Marchand 1995). Starting with WID, each perspective has emerged out of engaged critique with those preceding it. In the rest of this section, we shall briefly outline each one and indicate the main points of contention between each, concluding with a summary of the ways in which feminist theory has impacted on development discourse.

2.1 Women in Development – WID

Frequently seen as a variant of the broader strand of "liberal feminism" (Bandarage 1984; Kabeer 1994), WID was the first coherent theoretical attempt by feminists to engage with mainstream development. It was the primary philosophy motivating the UN initiatives in 1975 and is still prevalent among women bureaucrats and politicians of international agencies and governments involved in development and aid issues. The core point of the WID approach was that development policies and programs had excluded women. Hence the primary goal was to include and integrate women into existing initiatives. Ester Boserup's pioneering book, *Woman's Role in Economic Development* (1970), exemplifies both the strengths and limitations of this approach.

Boserup's work was the first documented attack upon development's marginalization of women to achieve wide circulation. In particular, her environmental model of explaining the differences in the status and visibility of women in different agrarian systems cogently illustrated, first, that not all Third World societies' traditional mores were discriminatory toward women, and second, that both colonialism and postcolonial development had excluded women. In the case of many African women in "female farming" areas (Boserup's main example), the results of this exclusion were a new economic marginalization and exclusion from development benefits; and in male farming systems a worsening of the marginality and subordination of women.

Boserup does not, however, attribute this marginalization of women to development itself. Rather, she distinguishes between her perception of the beneficial process of "modernization" and the male bias which distorts this progress away from women. The problem, and the agenda for the future, thus becomes primarily educational. What was necessary was the changing of attitudes of male development officials and planners, and the education of Third World women for the new roles that integrated development will provide for them. These roles, in turn, were essentially reflections of women's roles in Western societies (Boserup 1970: 223–4). Thus, as Benería and Sen point out, patriarchal attitudes, not capitalist development, are the major barriers to women's equal participation in development processes from the WID point of view (Benería and Sen 1982: 161).

This emphasis on male bias was extended in Barbara Rogers's (1980) influential study of the institutional context of development planning and administration. Her survey of the Food and Agriculture Organization (FAO) head office found virtually no women in positions above that of auxiliary secretarial level, and no female field officers in the technical division. When challenged about this, most administrators cited Third World governments' traditionalism as making female appointments unacceptable or unworkable. Many of the FAO bureaucrats also openly expressed attitudes that such work would be either beyond the capacities of, or unsuitable for, women. Rogers concluded that the combination of male attitudes and women's absence from key administrative and policy areas was having a twofold effect. Not only were women excluded from planning and decision-making procedures, but the particular needs of women in any specific development process, or the ramifications of induced changes for existing situations of women in development projects, were being ignored or overlooked far more readily. This was compounded by the stereotyping of women as housewives, regardless of local circumstances, in data-collection procedures, thus undervaluing women's economic contribution. Similarly, households were always assumed to be headed by a male breadwinner, thus obscuring the realities in many countries of female-headed households, where women had the primary responsibility for income generation (Rogers 1980: 66). Moreover, Rogers argued, the initiatives undertaken by international and national development agencies since 1975 had, if anything, reinforced rather than dislodged such bias. Programs were small, ad hoc, and marginal to the overall operations of organizations, and continued to view women primarily as housewives reliant on a male breadwinner for income support. In parts of Africa, for example, where women are often the main food producers as well as traders, extension education programs offered to women were primarily in domestic science. Only 15 percent of programs in agriculture and none in commerce and trade were targeted at women (Rogers 1980: 88).

Both Boserup and Rogers blamed the influence of Western male bias and the imposition of Western gender stereotypes on Third World societies for women's marginalization in development. Embedded in development policies and programs was a taken-for-granted normative model of sex roles formalized in the functionalist model of the sociologist Talcott Parsons (1964: 58–60), in which the male breadwinning role was seen as functionally complementary to the female role of housewife and mother. In Third World contexts, Boserup and Rogers argued, this either compounded existing versions of patriarchal ideology and female dependence or ignored those contexts where women had long been involved in economic production. Hence Rogers's argument that development was actually "domesticating" women and entrenching economic inequalities between women and men, rather than fostering equality of opportunity between the genders. Echoing Boserup, Rogers's solution was to change male attitudes, tackle patriarchal ideologies, and bring women into the policy and planning processes of development institutions and agencies. Proponents of WID argued women would thus be able to be fully integrated into the modernization strategies of development processes as economically productive agents in their own right. Underlying WID approaches is a model of gender inequality as primarily cultural in character and origins. Development itself is seen as gender neutral. It is the vestiges of patriarchal culture, evinced in the sexist attitudes of Western bureaucrats and the "traditionalism" of Third World men (and often Third World women), that was the problem in preventing women's full participation in development. Such a view was vehemently rejected by anthropologists such as Eleanor Leacock (1983), whose research on "pre-capitalist" societies in Australia, the Americas, the Pacific, and Africa led her to argue that traditionally women and men were independent economic actors, and women only became subordinated to men in the process of colonization and capitalist development.

Efficiency replaced equity in WID discourses in the 1980s, indicating the reluctance at the official levels of international and national development agencies to accept the feminist critique of mainstream development culture. According to the WID efficiency approach, women deserve equal attention in development policies because they are evidently working as efficiently as men, or because they *could*, given equal opportunities, contribute to economic development as much as men. The focus on efficiency and productivity issues is already inherent in Boserup's and Rogers's work, but in the hands of the major development institutions, the task of enhancing women's role in production became depoliticized and turned into an economic development issue, leaving ideologies and practices of development bureaucracies unchallenged (Goetz 1994). In this sense, culture dropped out of the women in development equation.

2.2   Women and Development – WAD

A quite different set of arguments emerged out of the twinning of dependency and Marxist feminist theory. Turning the WID analysis upside down, WAD advocates argued that, in fact, women were already integrated into development processes and that it was precisely this integration which perpetuated and structured women's inequitable experiences of development strategies. From this point of departure, however, several schools of thought emerged within the WAD perspective, depending on where they placed their analytical emphasis. Using Naila Kabeer's typology, we can distinguish between "global capitalist patriarchy" and "dependency feminists" (Kabeer: 1994).

Dependency feminists

Dependency feminists, reflecting their political and theoretical allegiances, stressed that it was the capitalist nature of development, dictated by the imperatives of a world capitalist economy, that determined women's inclusion in the process of development in detrimental ways. Following dependency theory (see chapter 1), they saw mainstream development as part of Western capitalist neo-imperialism, designed to mold Third World economies to the needs and profits of Western-based global capital. Analytically, dependency feminists' innovation was to bring a specific focus on women and their labor to what was essentially a neo-Marxist analysis of capitalism and development. WID saw gender oppression as based primarily in the inequitable sexual division of labor within the private sphere of marriage and the family, particularly in female dependency on male breadwinners, and essentially outside of the sphere of production and economic activity. WAD, in contrast, extended their theoretical focus to reveal how the sexual division of labor was an integral component of the capitalist system of production and accumulation.

Maria Mies's (1982) now classic case study, *The Lace Makers of Narsapur*, described how poor women working from their homes under norms of *purdah*, or seclusion, in Andhra Pradesh, India, were directly linked into world market export production. The lace they made was exported to North America, Europe, and Australasia, where it was bought mainly by women. The lacemakers' labor was both underpaid and unregulated as well as continuing to be categorized as domestic labor and leisure activity. Here capitalism was not pulling down the walls of tradition and custom, as Marx predicted (see chapter 1), but reinforcing and benefiting from patriarchal customs. This also undermined the WID thesis that patriarchy was separate from development and, ultimately, was simply an issue of cultural change, particularly in respect of male attitudes and priorities. Mies's study also uncovered the ways in which the so-called "domestic work" of Third World women was directly appropriated by global capital for the consumption of affluent Western women.

A similar argument was made by those feminists who focused on Third World women's location in the new international division of labor researchers were identifying as having emerged since the 1960s. This new division of labor was based on the export of manufacturing employment from the West to the Third World, as transnational corporations (TNCs) moved offshore to access cheaper, more flexible, and often less unionized labor in so-called export processing zones (EPZs). Particularly in parts of South America and Southeast Asia, export-oriented development strategies adopted by national governments set up EPZs to encourage TNC investment. A distinguishing feature of this shift was the predominance of female workers in these new world market factories, especially in the electronics and clothing and textile sectors. These new employment opportunities were frequently hailed by WID development officials and politicians as examples of integrative development, liberating women through economic independence. However, dependency feminists painted a more complicated picture of very low wages, poor conditions, and few protections or rights. Linda Lim, one of the first to explore this phenomenon of the feminization of labor, points to the ways in which capitalism, imperialism, and patriarchy each combined to shape the exploitation of women workers in these factories.

> All workers employed in capitalist enterprises are exploited to produce profits for their employers, but the degree of exploitation differs among different groups of workers. In addition to being paid less than the value of the output they contribute, Third World women workers in multinational export factories are paid less than women workers in the multinationals' home countries and less than men workers in these countries and in their own countries as well, despite the

fact that in relocated labour-intensive industries their productivity is frequently acknowledged to be higher than that of either of these other groups. Thus, Third World women workers are the most heavily exploited group of workers, relative both to their output contribution and to other groups. Although all are subject to capitalist exploitation, Third World women workers are subject additionally to imperialist and to patriarchal exploitation. (Lim 1983: 80)

Nevertheless, Lim maintains, such employment opportunities do offer attractions for women workers. The pay and conditions in TNC factories are usually better than those of local employers. Moreover, such jobs are often preferable to the available alternatives: staying at home, manual labor, or unemployment. However, Lim argues, this raises dilemmas in terms of political action. Making the TNC employer the main focus of struggle will not dismantle patriarchy, as the corporation simply taps into pre-existing practices and ideologies. Yet attacking "traditional patriarchy" may simply invite a backlash, given the webs drawn between tradition and nationalism in many postcolonial societies (see chapter 5 for a discussion of this linkage). Lim advocates the necessity of a multidimensional struggle against all three exploitative relations, to be determined in its particular strategies by the specific context of time and place.

Global capitalist patriarchy

In her subsequent writings, Maria Mies has, in collaboration with others, built a strong sub-strand of WAD analysis focused on exploring precisely the patriarchal nature of contemporary global capitalism: "patriarchal violence is not a feature of some feudal past but the 'necessary' correlate of the so-called modernization process" (Mies 1986: 4; see also Mies, Bennholdt-Thomsen, and von Werlhof 1988). Uncompromising in its acknowledgment of the patriarchal power of white Western men, as the dominant "class" within contemporary global capitalism, this variant of Marxist-feminism also puts forward a thesis of the domestication of Third World women under Western capitalist development. Unlike Boserup and Rogers, however, it is not male attitudes alone which import ideologies of domesticity to the Third World, but the very economic logic of capitalism. "Women are the optimal labour force because they are now being universally defined as 'housewives', not as workers; this means their work . . . is obscured, does not appear as 'free wage-labour', is defined as an 'income-generating activity', and can hence be bought at a much cheaper price than male labour" (Mies et al. 1988: 116). As an analysis of capitalism, however, this model places much more weight on patriarchal relations of power than those of class. More recently, in conjunction with Vandana Shiva (see chapter 3), Mies has extended the model of patriarchal capitalism to embrace an environmental feminism which sets a rampaging global capitalism working in the interests of men, but especially white men, against an essentialized female world view in harmony and balance with the natural world (Shiva 1989; Mies and Shiva 1993). In many respects, this brings the argument full circle, back to a cultural emphasis in which women and men inhabit fundamentally different and opposed cultures, one based on exploiting nature, and one based on environmental harmony and sustainability, preserved in the ways of living and belief systems of Third World women. The danger in this model, as Naila Kabeer points out, is that "[a]ll men appear as monsters, their culpability is in direct inverse proportion to their location in the global patriarchal hierarchy; all women appear as their victims" (Kabeer 1994: 53).

2.3   Gender and Development – GAD

Dissatisfactions with both versions of WAD were increasingly expressed, particularly by socialist feminists. On the one hand, they were unhappy with the ways in which "patriarchy" became an ahistorical universal in the analysis of global capitalism. On the other: "The economistic categories of traditional Marxism were clearly inadequate to formulate, let alone explain, the dynamics of the gender relations we observed and experienced," wrote the editors of one seminal early collection of GAD analyses (Pearson, Whitehead, and Young 1988: p. ix). Moreover, the emphasis in the WAD perspectives on "women" as some kind of coherent and discrete social category could easily fall into the trap of seeing women as the problem: "No study of women and development can start from the viewpoint that the problem is *women*, but rather *men* and *women*, more specifically the *relations* between them" (Whitehead, quoted in Ostergaard 1992: 6).

GAD emphasized the interconnectedness of gender and class relations by distinguishing relations of reproduction from those of production.

> The various elements or "inputs" of any production process first have to be produced, and then replaced: that is, they require *reproduction* for production to continue in the future. The most vital element of the whole process – namely the producer – also needs reproducing. *Social reproduction* replaces the inert elements of the process. The "production of the producer" involves *biological reproduction* (childbearing), *generational reproduction* (childrearing) *and daily reproduction or maintenance* (provision of human needs like food, shelter, etc.). (Pearson 1992: 229)

Thus the sexual division of labor and relations between men and women were centrally connected to the capitalist sphere of production. Moreover, cultural constructions of gender and work were brought to the fore, challenging purely economistic explanations. A good example of this is the way in which GAD analysts challenged WAD explanations of female employment in global factories. Diane Elson and Ruth Pearson (1988) pointed to the cultural constructions of gender which informed the ability of global capital to draw on a female labor force. The stereotype informing employers' views was of a young, docile, easily managed, and highly dexterous worker who was basically seeking a secondary income until such times as she left work to marry and have a family. Elson and Pearson take this stereotype and reveal how it is based on gender ideologies and relations which are not "natural" but socially constructed.

> The famous "nimble fingers" of young women are not an inheritance from their mothers, in the same way that they may inherit the colour of her skin or eyes. They are the result of the training they have received from their mothers and other female kin since early infancy in the tasks socially appropriate to women's roles. (Elson and Pearson 1988: 21)

Teaching industrial garment-making to workers who already know how to sew can take as little as six weeks; how long would it take to train a male worker who had never held a needle or handled a sewing machine? The authors argue that it is women's subordinate location within gender relations which makes them available as a labor force subject to exploitation by global capital (or, for that matter, as Pearson (1992) points out, in smaller enterprises operated by local capital).

GAD's conception of gender as relational and involving both women and men provides for a more flexible and nuanced approach to gender inequality and the development process. Coupled with the emphasis GAD scholars place on the variability of gender relations in time and space, this mitigates against any *a priori* assumption of automatic male privilege in any given development context. Depending on the nature of the interactions between gender, class, and development processes, a variety of consequences is possible, even that women may benefit more than men in certain circumstances. At least potentially, it is possible to see (some) men as possible supporters of (some) women, much as Domitila Barrios de Chungara argued in terms of poor Bolivian mining communities in the extract above. Indeed, it was precisely the complaints voiced by poor Third World women such as Barrios de Chungara about feminist priorities and politics in the development sphere that motivated another aspect of the GAD perspective. One accusation leveled at WID approaches by GAD proponents was that WID was "about poor women of the Third World . . . not a force of those women themselves" (Bandarage 1984: 500). Reflecting this criticism, GAD has placed a lot more emphasis on listening and responding to the voices of poor Third World women and working with them in grassroots organizations and activism to effect real changes in their lives.

In part this agenda reflected and informed a new partnership between feminists in the First and Third Worlds, in order to overcome the ethnocentrisms and divisions that had plagued the international women's movement, with sometimes negative consequences on its ability to effect change in mainstream development circles. DAWN (Development Alternatives with Women for a New Era) was one such network that emerged out of this awareness. In what was essentially a manifesto for DAWN, Gita Sen and Caren Grown outlined a GAD approach based on the concept of empowerment of women. They argued for an approach which took as its starting point:

> the experiences lived by poor women throughout the Third World in their struggles to ensure the basic survival of their families and themselves that provide the clearest lens for an understanding of development processes. And it is their aspirations and struggles for a future free of the multiple oppressions of gender, class,

race, and nation that can form the basis for the new visions and strategies that the world now needs. (Sen and Grown 1987: 10)

Sen and Grown (1987: 82) outlined a vision of development which was based on and acknowledged that "'the basic rights' of the poor and the transformation of the institutions that subordinate women are inextricably linked. They can be achieved together through the self-empowerment of women." They envisaged a multifaceted approach which would work to transform development organizations from within, while also working outside the mainstream institutional framework to effect change. Importantly for them, empowerment meant not just a redirection of resources to the poorest, as the basic-needs approach intended, but empowering poor women's participation in the policy-making and implementation processes of development.

More recently, Naila Kabeer comments that empowerment is an alternative approach to development which has come from the grassroots.

It signals a recognition by those working at the local level that, despite the rhetoric of participatory development, the power to define priorities remains where it has always been, in the hands of a minority at the top. (Kabeer 1994: 223)

Figure 4.1 Women at water well in Udaipur, India

Her review of alternative NGOs in South Asia who have consciously attempted to implement empowerment approaches in their work with poor women demonstrates that the women are well able to analyze their situations in ways which often confound expert prescriptions. A quite different set of needs often surfaces which challenge the organizational structures of program and service delivery, particularly the "magic bullet" mentality, as Kabeer terms it, of many development planners, who think one "strategic intervention" will solve the knotty connections between gender and poverty. On the contrary, greater participation in the needs-identification process by the poor women themselves reveals the complex interdependency between different types of needs, in ways which break down any discrete set of "women's issues" that can be isolated from development issues in general.

Kabeer (1994) shows the interconnectedness of "women's issues" and development issues in an Indian case study:

> The other issue that has remained submerged until recently is that of domestic violence. Here again, deep-rooted beliefs about the sanctity and safety of the domestic sphere, the shame and blame that often attach to women who are beaten, and the male biases of most development agencies have long combined to ensure that this was an issue largely characterized by silence and non-decisionmaking. The significance of organizational practice in allowing domestic violence to surface within the decisionmaking agenda, is described in Price's (1992) case study of SUTRA, which began working in Himachal Pradesh in 1977. In its early years, SUTRA worked within the pre-existing government model of service delivery, concentrating on improving on the efficiency of government targeting and delivery of services and hoping thereby to encourage demands within the local population for improved services from the government. Its targeting practices displayed fairly conventional gender biases: the services for men aimed at improving agricultural production and enhancing market access, while those for women aimed at their familial and domestic roles. An internal review in 1984 raised fundamental questions about the nature of the organization and its achievements in bringing about social change. It was recognized that women expressed greater support for the organization because they saw it as providing a space of their own which was not permitted to them elsewhere in society. It was also recognized that merely offering more efficient replacement services had not resulted in villages putting pressure on the government to improve its delivery system. Consequently, SUTRA decided to concentrate on building up women's organizations as its main goal, with development implementation as a secondary one.
>
> What was interesting about the shift to this new agenda was the way in which it challenged earlier preconceptions and threw up previously submerged needs. When consulted, women expressed concerns over issues that had earlier been categorized as male areas of interest:

drinking-water supplies, irrigation schemes, teachers' non-attendance at schools, corruption among local officials. As the needs that the women members began to articulate expanded into areas of women's health, more women were recruited onto the hitherto largely male staff to cope with some of the cultural barriers entailed in dealing with such needs. The increased numbers of women staff in turn brought further problems out into the open, particularly domestic violence, rape and alcoholism. In the early phase of the organization's life, problems of violence against women had been generally shrouded in silence or denial: "Women felt the honour of the family was affected by such discussions, and if individual women were beaten or faced other difficulties, there was often a tendency to lay blame on the woman herself for not 'suffering in silence'" (p. 55). One of the factors that helped to break down this silence was that some of the women staff had also suffered from these problems. The sharing of these experiences helped to break down the "them" and "us" relation between the village women and staff members. Once the taboo on the subject was broken, action could be taken. An increasing number of women came forward on their own or others' behalf to explore ways in which these situations could be dealt with. Thus issues that had been previously defined as private acquired a public and political status in the eyes of the women. (Kabeer 1994: 233–4)

Both DAWN and Kabeer advocate a feminist development theory which is predicated on the experience and perspective of Third World women themselves. Adopting such a standpoint would "help to realign development paradigms more closely to the 'real order of things'" (Kabeer 1994: 81). Third World women would thus move from the margins to the center of development praxis, reorienting development discourse from its fixation with economic growth to one which prioritized basic needs and valued women's domestic, subsistence, and community labor. Such a perspective shifts GAD approaches well away from the WID priority on formal equality with men by bringing women into existing development paradigms. Combined with the GAD emphasis on gender relations as cultural constructions, this emphasis on the standpoint of Third World women also avoids some of the pitfalls of the gender dichotomy underpinning the significance accorded patriarchy in WAD perspectives. As the example of SUTRA in the box above indicates, women themselves do not operate with a binary view of gender relations, which sees all men as powerful and all women as victims. Rather, they articulate a shifting scenario in which women and men often share the same interests in struggling for the provision of clean water or better schools, at the same time as other issues such as employment opportunities, access to credit, or domestic violence may be specific gender issues. However, similarly to WAD, GAD strategies necessarily involve a broad conception of development as involving major structural and cultural transformations if poor men and women are to be the main beneficiaries of development.

2.4   Bending paradigms

The boundaries and divisions traced in feminist development theory above are malleable and alter as the debates and issues concerning feminist development theory shift. Increasingly, WAD is tending to be collapsed into GAD, while the work of Vandana Shiva, Maria Mies, and others is beginning to be known as the Women, Development, and Environment school (WDE). However, regardless of the titles and lines drawn between them, the basic differences in approach and emphasis outlined above still pertain. Mapped in relation to mainstream development theory, however, new axes of comparison emerge.

On the one hand, WID, WAD, and GAD mirror the political divisions between liberal and socialist/Marxist perspectives, which roughly correspond to the divide between modernization theory on the one hand, and Marxist and dependency approaches on the other. WID, by and large, endorses modernization theory's model of development as involving the transformation of the Third World into a version of the West, through a top-down approach based on economic growth. For women, this means ensuring full integration into development processes in ways which enable them to achieve parity with men in economic, social, and political terms. As we have seen, taken up and translated into policy terms by international development institutions and national governments, WID has increasingly been reduced to an "add-on" strategy, designed to make women more efficient units in economic growth models. This often confirms rather than challenges existing stereotypes of women's roles and activities. The "women and development" offices established within international and national-level organizations as WID initiatives are often reduced to underfunded marginal ghettos (Karl 1995: 100). As Caroline Moser points out, "women's participation is equated with equity for women" (Moser 1993: 69).

In contrast, WAD and GAD embed their analysis within a conceptual framework critical of capitalist development models as exploitative of the Third World. Much of their efforts have been directed at exploring the relationship between capitalist development and female subordination, and revealing how it is precisely the inclusion of women in capitalist development processes which explains their parlous state in the contemporary Third World. Given their critical stance toward global capitalist development, they have paid much more attention to alternative conceptions of development, and ways of enabling resistance and struggle against capitalist exploitation. As the discussion of DAWN and empowerment illustrated, development is redefined as a process involving the satisfaction of basic needs for all, in a context that values women's multiple labors within a non-exploitative, participatory model of political economy. In policy terms, the consequences of this critical approach have been varied. Those WAD writers who emphasize the patriarchal nature of existing development institutions and organizations were often reluctant to participate in any way in mainstream development processes, preferring instead to focus on separate women's organizations and groups. On the other hand, DAWN and writers such as Kabeer advocate a more pragmatic approach which emphasizes a long-term transformational goal, coupled with strategic short-term engagement with mainstream development in ways which channel its resources to the alleviation of the immediate issues confronting poor Third World women. As Kabeer's discussion indicates, this dual strategy relies on an active NGO sector to open up space for alternative ways of doing development for and with women to emerge.

Despite these differences, however, all of these variants of feminist development theory stay within the boundaries of development discourse. None reject "development" as an ultimate goal; rather, they seek to broaden existing notions, or to find alternative ways of doing "development." Their overall impact has been one we might term "paradigm bending" rather than paradigm shifting. The inclusion of women as a specific focus in liberal development theory, and the conceptual extension of "gender" as a term with equivalent analytical weight to those of class and race in dependency lexicons, has involved significant shifts in development studies. A narrowly economic focus which fails to take into account the ways in which women's locations in informal and non-market areas of social life are part of, and contribute to, development processes is now far less legitimate than it was three decades ago. The cultural context within which development processes impinge and occur is now more central to analytical frameworks, as theorists, policy makers, and planners struggle with the failures of past strategies to make substantial inroads into global poverty and the increasingly feminized character of the poorest of the poor. This does not always result in programs conducive to transforming women's lives. Feminist critiques of structural adjustment policies (SAPs), and neo-liberal theory more generally, have shown that mainstream development strategies are adept at harnessing women's multiple roles as homemakers, carers, and producers, and the ideologies that legitimate them. This facilitates restructuring of local, national, and global economies in the interests of a few, while compounding the burdens for most, and especially poor, women. Drawing on structural adjustment experiences in the 1980s in countries as culturally and economically diverse as Chile and Iran, Haleh Afshar (1994: 155) concludes that

> severe shortages of food, fuel and clothing, and the failure of the government to honour the allocation of rations, has meant that Iranian women, like Chileans, have to spend a great deal of time buying smaller quantities of poorer food and more time and energy processing it into acceptable means. The burdens of poverty and domesticity are as intense for the impoverished Iranian women, despite the rhetoric of the government, as they are for Chileans.

However, Afshar also points out that the impact of structural adjustment programs – similar as they are in design and intention – does not leave a uniform impression on each nation-state's human landscape. The presence of (ever-decreasing) government welfare provisions in Chile at least offers some relief to poor heads of household, who are often women, while in Iran, a lack of systematic welfare provisions means that "the rational choice for impoverished women was to get themselves jailed, since the best assistance was provided by the charity

which supports the dependants of prisoners" (Afshar 1994: 155). More important still, in contrast to their Chilean counterparts, poor women in Iran are barred
from many employment opportunities, due to the dominant religious ideologies that promise "glorified domesticity and motherhood" (Afshar 1994: 154).
Thus, even economic policy analysis is thrown back on questions of culture.

3   Postcolonial feminisms and feminist development theory

In 1984 Chandra Talpade Mohanty's seminal article, "Under Western eyes: feminist scholarship and colonial discourses," appeared and brought postcolonial
and poststructuralist (see chapter 3) scrutiny directly to bear on feminist development writings. Taking as her case study a series of books on Third World
women published by Zed Books, Mohanty revealed how their Western and feminist authors universalized their own particular perspectives as normative, and
essentialized Third World women as tradition-bound victims of timeless patriarchal cultures. In so doing, she argued, Western feminist scholarship reproduced and continued the colonial discourses of mainstream, male-stream
scholarship. What Mohanty terms the "colonialist move" (Mohanty 1991: 71)
comes about from the twinning of a binary model of gender, which sees "women"
as an *a priori* category of oppressed, with an "ethnocentric universality" (Mohanty
1991: 72) which takes Western locations and perspectives as the norm. The effect
is to create a stereotype: "the third world woman," which not only ignores the
diversity of Third World women's lives across boundaries of class and ethnicity,
as well as gender, but produces what Mohanty terms "third world difference."

> For in the context of a first/third world balance of power, feminist analyses which
> perpetuate and sustain the hegemony of the idea of the superiority of the West
> produce a corresponding set of universal images of the "third world woman," im-
> ages such as the veiled woman, the powerful mother, the chaste virgin, the obedi-
> ent wife, etc. These images exist in universal, ahistorical splendor, setting in motion
> a colonialist discourse which exercises a very specific power in defining, coding,
> and maintaining existing first/third world connections. (Mohanty 1991: 73)

Effectively, this also distinguishes the "third world woman" as Other to Western women, whose implicit self-representation in feminist discourse is as the
educated, modern, liberated individual who has escaped the bonds of tradition, still seen to bind her non-Western counterpart. Mohanty's unpacking of
Western feminist discourse about Third World women built on the work of
other Third World feminists and women of color, who had likewise identified
the ways in which much white Western feminist discourse was caught in imperialist traps. This discourse ignored the ways in which class and race
disaggregated any unitary category of "woman," and continued the privileging
of Western ways, values, knowledge, and power (e.g. Ong 1988; hooks 1984;
Spivak 1990; Trinh Min-Ha 1989).
    More recently, Uma Narayan (1997; 1998) has shown how feminist writings

about Third World women not only misunderstand and disguise the constructed nature of "tradition" (see chapter 5), but also fall into the trap of cultural essentialism. In trying to account for the differences between Western(ized) women and non-Western(ized) women (such as those illustrated by Domitila Barrios de Chungara in the box above),

> Seemingly *universal* essentialist generalizations about "all women" are replaced by *culture-specific* essentialist generalizations that depend on totalizing categories such as "Western culture," "Non-western cultures," "Western women," "Third World women," and so forth. . . . The resulting portraits of "Western women," "Third World women," "African women," "Indian women," "Muslim women," or the like, as well as the pictures of the "cultures" that are attributed to these various groups of women, often remain fundamentally essentialist. They depict as homogeneous groups of heterogeneous people whose values, interests, ways of life, and moral and political commitments are internally plural and divergent. (Narayan 1998: 87–8)

The consequence is "an ongoing practice of 'blaming culture' for problems in Third-World contexts and communities" (Narayan 1997: 51). As the Egyptian feminist Nawar El Saadawi put it: "They tend to depict our life as a continual submission to medieval systems" (Saadawi 1980: xiv). A good example of this is the ways in which Western feminists have taken the practice of veiling as a straightforward demonstration of the oppression of women in Islamic societies.

As the box below illustrates, in many feminist texts the veil has become synonymous with Islam as a religion uniquely forceful in its oppression of women; a perspective reiterated many times over in Western representations more generally of Islam and of veiling, notably in the media. As Nancy Hirschmann (1998: 345) argues, "[t]his belies a great diversity in the practice [of veiling] . . . and completely ignores the fact that many Muslim women not only participate voluntarily in veiling, but defend it as well, indeed claiming it as a mark of agency, cultural membership and resistance." Moreover, collapsing veiling and Islam into each other denies both the historical and regional distinctions between the practice and the religion, at the same time as it tends to "blame" them for women's oppression. Throw the veil off and disavow Islam and women's liberation would be achieved, is the subtext of many Western feminist and non-feminist perspectives alike. Such arguments ignore the empirical evidence that "it is not the veil per se that indicates whether women are free or not; rather, it is the patriarchal use of the veil to control women that indicates women's freedom and agency or lack thereof" (Hirschmann 1998: 354). The consequence is that the veil attains a symbolic power in bolstering Islam's integrity against a perceived Western Christian cultural assault, and as a practice which preserves and maintains cultural autonomy and religious purity.

The Taliban regime's current draconian laws regarding women's veiling and public visibility in Afghanistan are a good example of this. Under a religious rubric, control of women has become a central feature of the struggle for

Geraldine Brooks, an American journalist, went to Iran in 1989 to cover the funeral of the country's religious and political leader, the Ayatollah Khomeini, and, as she states, to understand this man's role in persuading women

> that the wearing of a medieval cloak was a revolutionary act. Something in his message had brought thousands of women into the streets to face the shah's army and risk their lives calling for the return of a code of laws that allowed child marriage, polygamy and wife beating. . . . Khomeini's daughter Zahra invited me to a conference sponsored by the Women's Society of the Islamic Republic of Iran titled "Aspects of His Highness Imam Khomeini's Personality." I studied the title with bemusement. The only aspects of His Highness Imam Khomeini's personality I was familiar with were his penchants for condemning novelists to death, dispatching young boys to the war front as human minesweepers and permitting little girls to be married off at the age of nine. . . . The party dress code was basic black – layers of it. Chadors were only the finishing touch over long pants, socks, calf-length tunics and hoods called *magnehs* – a circle of fabric like a nun's wimple that falls over head and shoulders, leaving just a hole for the face. As the black-cloaked figures milled around me, I began to feel I'd been locked up by mistake in some kind of convent from hell. (Brooks 1995: 16)

Brooks traces the *hijab* to the Prophet Muhammad's household, where his wives were secluded behind curtains in order to preserve their purity. Other women were given more general instructions to "lower their gaze and be modest, and . . . to draw their veils over their bosoms" (Brooks 1995: 21). She points out that the dress code for Muslim women varies greatly, but the "veil" (as the headdresses came to be unanimously called) became a symbol of Islamic revival from the late 1960s onwards. After some probing of what is beneath these "concealing devices," Brooks (1995: 32) comes to the conclusion that

> under all the talk about *hijab* freeing women from commercial or sexual exploitation, all the discussion of *hijab*'s potency as a political and revolutionary symbol of selfhood, was the body: the dangerous female body that somehow, in Muslim society, had been made to carry the heavy burden of male honor.

national power between competing groups of men. This is reinforced by the way the seclusion and veiling of women also feeds into the regime's claims to be resisting Western influences. This situation, however, is in stark contrast with the voluntary adoption of the veil by many educated, professional middle-class women in societies such as Egypt, Malaysia, and Indonesia, precisely as a marker of what they see as an Islamic modernity (e.g. Hoodfar 1997; Ong 1995). This confounds a number of assumptions in both mainstream and feminist development theory. Implicitly, both work with a model of development as progress toward a secular modernity (see chapter 1). Moreover, as the discussion in section 2.1 above indicated, feminist development theory has often assumed that once women are educated and enter paid work, their new-found economic autonomy would automatically encourage the kind of enlightened views and aspirations about individual achievement and freedom that Western feminism has held in such high esteem. This vision is rudely ruptured when it is precisely the most "modern" women from some of the more successful "developing" societies who are adopting veiling. Either way, whether it is the Taliban's authoritarian and oppressively violent policies toward women, or the examples of women redefining their own modernity in Malaysia and elsewhere, both challenge the "blame the culture" thesis, which portrays Third World women as passive victims of unchanging traditions. The Taliban's repression is more about reworking Afghani patriarchies than it is about an unchanging Islam, while adopting the veil is often indicative of women's own agency within complex contexts of rapid social and economic change, rather than any straightforward indication of oppressive tradition or "retreat" from modernity.

The veil in different cultural, political, and socio-economic contexts

Malaysia

Anthropologist Aihwa Ong begins her account of the contradictory social and cultural effects of recent developments in state policies and Islamic revivalism in Malaysia by describing how the same urban middle-class women have shifted in their use of the *hijab* over time:

> In the summer of 1990, on my annual visit to Malaysia, I noticed that many young Malay women had traded in their black Islamic robes (*hijab*) for pastel colored ones, and that their headcloths (*mini-telekung*) were now embroidered with flowers. The effect was rather like seeing a black and white film in color. In the late 1970s and early 1980s, when Malaysian campuses were the hotbeds of Islamic resurgence, female students shrouded in black robes and veils sometimes appeared like phalanxes of Allah's soldiers. Now university women were dressed in *Hijab* outfits that had been transformed by color and more subtle touches in cut, style and decoration. As they walked around campus, many attracted the eyes of young men, who were sometimes rewarded with subdued giggles and responsive glances. The Islamic resurgence of the 1970s, emerging in its black female garb and fiery criticism of

> Western consumerism, official corruption, and the spiritual hollowness of modern life, had settled down as a normalized cultural practice in which people carried on the daily affairs of life of an affluent, developing country. (Ong 1995: 160)

Egypt

Homa Hoodfar (1997) focuses on the veiling movement among educated women in Cairo, whom she describes as lower income and employed mainly in government or other public sector offices and workshops.

> In Egypt's past, as for many other Muslim societies, a manifestation of the increased status of a household was often the total veiling and more restrictive seclusion of women – in emulation of upper-class traditions. However, in more recent years the upper classes have worn a rather modest version of the western type of clothing. Until recently, this practice was closely followed by the middle classes and those inspired by middle-class values. The 1980s, however, witnessed a new phenomenon in that educated and lower-middle-class women returned to the veil.
>   This modern veil is a style of dress very different in appearance from clothing worn by more traditional *balady* (urban lower classes) or *felaheen* (peasant) women. The most popular version of the modern veil is an outfit consisting of a long, western-style dress or skirt worn with a kind of turban or a scarf. (Hoodfar 1997: 321–2)

Hoodfar finds out that one key factor in educated women returning to the veil is that it allows them to work outside of their home and at the same time be accepted as a good wife and daughter-in-law:

> The veil communicates loudly and clearly to society at large and to husbands in particular that the wearer is bound by the Islamic idea of her sex role. A veiled woman indicates that despite her unconventional economic activity she respects traditional values and behaviour. By wearing the veil women lessen their husbands' insecurity; they convey to their husbands that, as wives, they are not in competition, but rather in harmony and cooperation with them. Further, wearing the veil puts women in a position to expect and demand that their husbands honour them and recognize their Islamic rights. Husbands should not claim their wives' wages and they should fulfil their duty of providing for the family to the best of their ability. (Hoodfar 1997: 324)

Within the context of development policy and planning, the colonial move embedded in feminist development theory takes on a structural imperative as well. As Anne Marie Goetz (1994: 33) points out:

the body of information and knowledge produced in the WID movement has been shaped by the power dynamics of the North–South system of which it is a part, assigning a highly problematic epistemic superiority to the knowledge Western women produce about women in development.

To the extent that WID has been successful in getting women placed on the official development agenda, this has simply served to reinforce the authority of this particular point of view, in terms of being noticed and taken seriously by development organizations and institutions. Goetz gives the example of Bangladesh, where every WID text has either been sponsored by Western donors to explicate specific aid programs, or through Western research institutions, to illustrate how the effect is to exclude indigenous views and privilege those of external WID experts. The knowledge thus produced is either restricted to those areas relevant to the specific program goals of the funding agency, or reflects the colonial gaze of the outsider. Thus women's fertility assumes an overwhelming prominence as it reflects donor concerns with population and food provision. "Also, many observers fixate on the practice of *purdah*, or female seclusion, as the main feature of women's disadvantage, whereas local scholars argue that poverty and violence are the primary constraining features of local patriarchy amongst poor women" (Goetz 1994: 33).

Not only WID is caught within the colonizing boundaries of Western modernist discourses about development. Mitu Hirshman (1995) argues that even the DAWN manifesto's laudatory call to revision development with poor women as the starting point, as outlined by Sen and Grown (1987), shares some of the assumptions of WID about "development" and "women." While they acknowledge the diversity of experience and location amongst women, Sen and Grown nevertheless predicate a sameness linking women globally, through the ways in which the sexual division of labor operates to structure gender oppression through the exploitation of women's labor. In Hirshman's view, this simply universalizes concepts which are rooted in the culture of Western capitalism and modernity, and hence ignores their potentially limited valency in "other" contexts. Recently, feminist anthropologists of Southeast Asia, for example, have argued that indigenous gender systems are not predicated on a dichotomous gender hierarchy privileging men over women, but on a notion of gender bilateralism:

> the need to maintain social relationships through rules of complementarity and similarity rather than hierarchy and opposition, and the need to reduce imbalances in power through mutual responsibility and cooperation rather than oppression and force. (Karim 1995: 16)

They argue that Western feminism "cannot envisage a situation where male and female relations are managed in a way as flexible and fluid as they are in Southeast Asia" (Karim 1995: 26; see also Stivens 1992).

Moreover, Hirshman argues, it locks Western feminist analysis within the bounds of mainstream development discourse, including Marxist variants, with its emphasis on production as the core realm of social activity. Drawing on anthropological ethnographies and indigenous perspectives, she also charges DAWN with continuing the features of the "missionary position," because despite their focus on bringing poor women into a participatory framework of development practice, the main agency in this context is that of progressive development activists who will help poor Third World women to liberate themselves. Echoes of this are also evident in Kabeer's more recent elucidation of a GAD empowerment approach. Her emphasis on consciousness-raising amongst poor women also assumes a benchmark of gender awareness external to their lives, and one outside experts will help them reach. Ultimately, as Kabeer makes clear, while GAD theorists acknowledge diversity and difference between women in terms of class, race, ethnicity etc., gender is accorded a privileged significance as "the most pervasive form of inequality" (Kabeer 1994: 81) embodied in the archetypal "poor Third World woman."

Jane Parpart and Marianne Marchand (1995) summarize what is required of a feminist development theory that transcends the colonizing boundaries of modernist discourse in terms of a three-pronged strategy. Awareness of difference needs to be fully recognized, particularly the multiplicity of axes and identities which shape women's lives, such that there is no figure of "the Third World woman" stalking feminist approaches to development. A feminist development practice needs to rethink its approach around a partnership with women at the grassroots level, as Sen and Grown (1987) and Kabeer (1994) propose, but in ways which do not continue hierarchies of knowledge/power that privilege the expert/outsider. This will, thirdly, undermine "Northern universalism, whether based on liberal or Marxist assumptions, and provides the intellectual basis for a new understanding of global diversity" (Parpart and Marchand 1995: 19). There are clear parallels here with the post-development and anthropology of modernity approaches discussed in chapter 3, and their models of local hybrid cultures, which challenge the orthodoxies of development discourse and potentially point to a post-development framework. Feminist critics of Western-centric modernist discourse also place their emphasis on bringing local knowledge and experience to the fore, in ways which dismantle the *a priori* categories of existing feminist development theory. However, as Parpart and Marchand themselves point out, there are dangers in such an approach for feminism. Dangers other feminist writers have felt limit the insights and usefulness of this critique for a specifically feminist perspective on development. In the next section we shall look at some of these dangers and the concerns they have raised, before considering how some feminist writers are attempting to resolve the tensions and dilemmas in new ways of conceiving a cross-cultural feminist politics of development.

4   "Chucking the baby out with the bath water": counter-arguments

As we discussed in chapter 3, the postcolonial critique of "development" as a particular vision of Western modernity radically questioned the possibility of a singular universally applicable notion of development or progress. For feminists, this critique had a particularly challenging relevance. Feminism is itself a social movement predicated on an aspiration for social justice, most usually couched in terms of gender equity, however this is conceived of amongst the various strands of feminist thought. Feminist development theory assumed this emancipatory goal within the context of conventional meanings of "development." "Development" was bringing women into the mainstream, or meeting the needs of, and empowering, poor women. Either way, "development" was a concept around which a shared perspective and basis for action could coalesce. Raising the possibility of multiple meanings of "development," and even "post-development," radically challenged one of the key foundations of feminism as a social movement and political perspective. This was compounded by the postcolonial feminist dismantling of the notion of universal gender oppression, and their emphasis on the differences between women internationally, regionally, and locally. "Woman" could no longer operate as a taken-for-granted category of the "second sex," always and everywhere subordinate to "man" in a binary construction of gender relations. Moreover, revealing the colonizing quality of the relationships between feminists and Third World women further seemed to undermine the possibility of any collective basis for feminism across the boundaries of global power inequalities. On what basis could a global feminism engage with issues of power, inequality, and poverty? Responses to this question have varied, but three broad schools of thought can be identified.

The first of these might be termed the "Poverty is Real" school. While taking on board the thrust of the postcolonial critique of feminist development theory as colonizing, they reject the emphasis on difference and discourse, and what they identify as a "turn towards culture" in feminism and away from material conditions (Barratt 1992, cited in Jackson 1997: 147). In her scathing critique of "postist" feminist understandings of poverty and gender, "where culture, ideas and symbols are discursively interesting and constitutive of power, whilst materiality is of questionable status, and at least suspect," Cecile Jackson argues that poverty "becomes largely a state of mind" rather than a matter of mind and body struggling for survival (Jackson 1997: 147). Real women and their circumstances get lost in a welter of image, text, and representation. Mridula Udayagiri (1995) makes a similar point, arguing that such critiques fail to engage with the moral underpinnings of development policy and practice, for example providing basic health care or literacy programs. She fears there is a danger of "chucking the baby out with the bath water" (Udayagiri 1995: 164), as prior GAD analyses which emphasized political economy are condemned by postcolonial feminists for stereotyping Third World women as passive victims. Moreover, "[i]f there is no connectedness between the two realms, 'us' and 'other,' then how is it possible to form strategic coalitions across class, race, and national boundaries?" (Udayagiri 1995: 166); alliances necessary to effect change in the South.

Another set of responses has been labeled "cultural relativist." Reacting to the charges of universalism and imperialism leveled at feminism and development discourse, some feminists argue that the solution is to respect each other's differences in a plurality of identity politics. In this way, they hope to avoid the problematic affirmations of universal sameness (Code 1998) which have plagued both Western feminist development theory and development discourse more generally. Couched in terms of respect for cultural difference, this stance offers little assistance in terms of dealing with some of the complex issues confronting the international feminist movement. Refusing to theorize domination, relativists implicitly evaluate all cultural positions as equal. This gives them no basis for making moral judgments about social justice in terms of feminist aspirations to deal with gender inequality and patriarchal power (Goetz 1991: 145). It also ignored the differences between women within specific cultural locations. Domitila Barrios de Chungara (in the box above) pinpoints one difference dividing women in the Third World, that of class; other lines of division may be regional, religious, and ethnic. Does "respect for cultural difference" mean having no moral or political position? How do cultural relativists distinguish between those African women who argue female circumcision is an important culturally specific part of being a woman in those cultures where it is practiced, and those African women who argue that it is a dangerous and damaging patriarchal practice? Also, as Nancy Hirschmann (1998: 345) comments, "the 'culture' that is often preserved through such respect is a patriarchal one that preserves male privilege at women's expense." At the International Women's Conferences held under UN auspices, "official" feminism, often allied to, or representing, national governments and their political agendas, has often been able to use the "cultural respect" argument to ward off more radical challenges emanating from "unofficial" feminists, less tied to the national and international status quo. It has also been used to legitimate development bureaucracies' inaction and neglect of issues relevant to women (Goetz, 1991: 146).

5 Building bridges

As Uma Narayan has pointed out, feminist relativists can find themselves with some strange and uncomfortable bedfellows: "forms of cultural relativism have an important place in the tool-kits of local masters" (1998: 101–2). Underlying the relativist argument is a view of cultures and identities as bounded, coherent, and autonomous. This replicates the notion of culture informing conservative fundamentalisms in a variety of contexts, who use these same arguments to cast patriarchal practices as essential to cultural preservation, as the Taliban example discussed earlier indicated. It can also feed into the stereotyping of feminism as a specifically Western knowledge, and hence leave Third World feminists vulnerable to the charge of being cultural traitors. Moreover, replacing "universal sameness" with cultural difference does not dislodge colonial legacies of cultural imperialism, Narayan argues, as colonial discourses relied on both sameness (the "civilizing mission") and difference, which denied any possibility of the colonized Other becoming the same (Narayan 1998: 100). In Frantz Fanon's (1986) famous words, the colonized has always a "black skin" – the unchangeable mark of difference – under her "white mask" – the European clothes, forms of behavior, language, and education which are the only hope to prove herself equal to white, civilized Westerners. Lata Mani illustrates this by describing an incident at the North American university where she works:

> It is dark and pouring with rain and I curse, unprepared as I am for the downpour and for the fact that buildings on campus are locked at 5.00 p.m. for reasons of safety. I am keeping a colleague waiting and there is no phone nearby. I decide to knock on the window of the office closest to the entrance. The gentleman, white and in his mid forties, is on the phone and gestures impatiently for me to wait. Although he is less than a minute, it feels much longer and I hop from foot to foot in the vain hope of dodging the raindrops. Placing the receiver on the cradle, he comes to the door. Opening it a crack, he asks me irritatedly what it is that I want. Surprised that he needs an explanation, I ask to be let in, stating that I am to meet someone in the building and had forgotten that the doors were locked at 5.00 p.m. Refusing to open the door any further, he states flatly that he cannot let anyone in off the street, god knows what I might do. I stand there gaping at him, shocked and taken aback. (Frankenberg and Mani 1993: 296)

Mani's colleague took her race as a clue that she could not have any legitimate business in the university at this time of the day, despite other outward signs to the contrary, such as her clothes and books. No matter how she defines her own position in society, there is always a possibility of "elements of the discourse of slavery or of the Other as a trespasser or potential thief" erupting "in unexpected places" (Frankenberg and Mani 1993: 297).

Instead of cultural relativism, a third possibility emerging from these debates over cultural imperialism within feminism is one that attempts to retheorize the universal in postcolonial ways. Anne Marie Goetz (1991: 149) states the problem in the following way:

> How can we start to see, responsibly and respectfully, from another's point of view, and yet at the same time find answers for an active feminism determined to make a difference?

Her answer is a perspective which combines both the material and the symbolic, and encourages the building of coalitions across differences. The new "universal" would be a contingent and contextual negotiation which measured competing claims on a gauge made up of two components:

1   A materialist analysis "to point to the consequences and inter-relations of different sites of oppression: class, race, nation and sexuality" (Goetz 1991: 151).
2   A recognition of the partial and situated quality of knowledge claims. Thus, Western feminist knowledge must see itself as simply another partial, local knowledge; one among many others, constrained by the boundaries of its viewpoint from a particular location. All such knowledges are contestable and open to revision. Hence, no one partial knowledge can claim an overall objectivity for their particular perspective. "And it is precisely because of the knower's partiality that she will be able to see with others without claiming to be them, or forcing them to see her way" (Goetz 1991: 151).

At the same time, by emphasizing the contestability of all knowledges, none escape external scrutiny, thus avoiding the hands-off "respect" of the cultural relativists.

> Thus while certain issues of sexist oppression may unite women cross-culturally, women of different nations within these broad alliances may be involved in struggles for racial justice or national liberation in which they will have to confront women from oppressor nations. Or third world women may struggle for freedom from personal oppression within the family while at the same time engaging in a common project with their menfolk to protect the integrity of their traditional economies. (Goetz 1991:153)

Goetz thus combines the GAD empowerment perspective, with its strong political economy and emphasis on local knowledge and experience, with a postcolonial and poststructuralist dismantling of an all-knowing universal. As Geeta Chowdhry (1995: 39) states, in this way, "Third World women become participants in, rather than recipients of, the development process."

Ann Ferguson (1998) attempts to theorize a new "ethico-politics" for feminist development practitioners from the North and South, working with such a modified empowerment model of development. The problem they confront is an ethical one. They are often funded by organizations caught in the very global relations of power the practitioners aspire to change, and hence there is "the danger of colluding with knowledge production that valorizes status quo economic, gender, racial, and cultural inequalities" (Ferguson 1998: 95). This is compounded, even for those who are funded by NGOs, by the "expert" trap, which authorizes the practitioner in terms of their supposed more objective knowledge. Through what she terms "building bridge identities," Ferguson attempts to overcome these problems by including self-reflexivity as a necessary aspect of any practitioner approach to participatory development processes. "[T]he first step for those in dominant positions who wish to be allies against the oppression of target groups is to make a critique of the hitherto negative aspects of one's social identity; that is, a devaluation of one's assumed moral superiority" (Ferguson 1998: 105). This means confronting the dominant aspects of one's own identity, and revealing its "horizons of ignorance," as a prelude to according a critical authority to "other" knowledges to "talk back" in ways which give full meaning to participatory democratic development processes. In this way, an ethical underpinning to feminist development becomes a "solidarity between women that must be struggled for rather than automatically received" (Ferguson 1998: 109; see also Barker 1998). This does not mean generalizations cannot be made; rather, it puts the emphasis back on how they are made. Explains Narayan (1998: 104),

> it seems arguably true that there is no need to portray female genital mutilation as an "African cultural practice" or dowry murders and dowry related harassment as a "problem of Indian women" in ways that eclipse the fact that not all "African women" or "Indian women" confront these problems, or confront them in identical ways, or in ways that efface local contestations of these problems.

Postcolonial and poststructuralist feminist approaches to development thus arrive at a similar point to that of the "post-development" theorists discussed in chapter 3, to the extent that they both emphasize the necessity to particularize and localize the theory and practice of development. This involves relativizing the "West" in terms both of feminist and development knowledge, as simply one "situated knowledge," rather than universally relevant. However, feminist writers such as Narayan, Goetz, and Ferguson, to name only those discussed here, are moving beyond deconstructing the discourses of Western feminism and development. Unpacking the binary oppositions still embedded in feminist and development thought, they do not simply reverse the binary by revaluing the female (as the WED school led by Mies and Shiva tend to do) or by valorizing the non-Western local (as Escobar, Sachs, and others sometimes do). They are embarked on a more comprehensive project to reforge a conceptual framework capable of embracing a global politics of social justice in ways which avoid the "colonizing move." Importantly, as Ferguson's article indicates, this involves addressing the issues of location and power embedded in the practice of development, including the nature of "partnership" forged between practitioners positioned awkwardly across the divides of cultural, political, and economic hegemony.

6 Summary

This chapter has surveyed the range of feminist interventions within development studies. All the various positions outlined here, from WID to postcolonial feminists, have contributed to challenging the mainstream notions of "development" as primarily about economic growth. The reason why the feminist focus on women, and latterly gender, brings culture into the center lies partly in the ways in which women have been associated with "culture" in both non-modern and modern societies. However, at the same time feminist theory has unsettled this binary woman/culture within development studies by demonstrating that women, and indeed gender, are central to the economic and political processes of development. It is no longer possible to ignore or elide issues to do with gender when dealing with the "hard" issues of development.

By focusing on the constructed nature of gender, in conjunction with the issues of power and difference between the West and the Rest, postcolonial feminists have also called into question the coherence of the category "woman." This reflects precisely the definition of culture outlined in chapter 1 (section 3.4) developed in cultural studies: Culture "is a network of representations – texts, images, talk, codes of behaviour, and the narrative structures organising these – which shapes every aspect of social life" (Frow and Morris 1993: viii). The main contribution of cutting-edge feminist development thinking is to bring together the theoretical insights of postcolonialism and postmodernism in regard to power/knowledge, with the imperatives of constructing an international feminist politics for addressing the dire material circumstances of poor women. By focusing on the praxis of development in terms of refiguring the partnership between development practitioner and beneficiaries, new possibilities emerge for a participatory development which empowers Third World women for themselves, rather than being empowered by others.

References

Afshar, H. 1994: Women and the state: some considerations of ideological and economic frameworks in engendering policies. In I. Bakker (ed.), *The Strategic Silence. Gender and Economic Policy*. London: Zed Books in association with The North–South Institute/Institut Nord–Sud, Suite 200, 55 Murray Street, Ottawa, Canada KIN 5M3, 152–57.

Bandarage, A. 1984: Women in development: liberalism, Marxism and Marxist-feminism. *Development and Change*, 15, 495–515.

Barker, D. 1998: Dualisms, discourse, and development. *Hypatia, Special Issue: Border Crossings: Multicultural and Postcolonial Feminist Challenges to Philosophy, Part 2*, 13 (3), 83–95.

Barrett, M. 1980: *Women's Oppression Today: Problems in Marxist Feminist Analysis*. London: Verso.

Barrios de Chungara, D. 1982: At the International Women's Year Tribunal. In H. Johnson, H. Bernstein with R. H. Ampuero and B. Crow (eds), *Third World Lives of Struggle*. London: Heinemann Educational Books in association with the Open University, 233–42.

Benería, L. and Sen, G. 1982: Class and gender inequalities and women's role in economic development – theoretical and practical implications. *Feminist Studies*, 8 (1), 157–76.

Boserup, E. 1970: *Woman's Role in Economic Development*. London: George Allen and Unwin.

Brooks, G. 1995: *Nine Parts of Desire. The Hidden World of Islamic Women*. New York: Anchor Books/Doubleday.

Butler, J. 1992: Contingent foundations: feminism and the question of "postmodernism." In J. Butler and J. W. Scott (eds), *Feminists Theorize the Political*. New York: Routledge, 3–21.

Buvinic, M., Lycette, M. A., and McGreevey, W. P. (eds) 1983: *Women and Poverty in the Third World*. Baltimore: The Johns Hopkins University Press.

Campbell, C. 1997: Migrancy, masculine identities and AIDS: the psychological context of HIV transmission on the South African gold mines. *Social Science and Medicine*, 45 (2), 273–81.

Chowdhry, G. 1995: Engendering development? Women in development (WID) in international development regimes. In M. H. Marchand and J. L. Parpart (eds), *Feminism/Post-Modernism/Development*. London: Routledge, 26–41.

Code, L: 1998: How to think globally: stretching the limits of imagination. *Hypatia, Special Issue: Border Crossings: Multicultural and Postcolonial Feminist Challenges to Philosophy, Part 1*, 13 (2), 73–86.

Croll, E. 1994: *From Heaven to Earth. Images and Experiences of Development in China*. London: Routledge.

Elson, D. and Pearson, R. 1988: The subordination of women and the internationalisation of factory production. In K. Young, C. Wolkowitz, and R. McCullagh (eds), *Of Marriage and the Market. Women's Subordination Internationally and its Lessons*. London: Routledge, 18–40.

Fanon, F. 1986: *Black Skin, White Masks*. London: Pluto Press. First published in French by Editions du Seuil in 1952.

Ferguson, A. 1998: Resisting the veil of privilege: building bridge identities as an ethico-politics of global feminisms. *Hypatia, Special Issue: Border Crossings: Multicultural and Postcolonial Feminist Challenges to Philosophy, Part 2*, 13 (3), 95–114.

Frankenberg, R. and Mani, L. 1993: Crosscurrents, crosstalk: race, "postcoloniality" and the politics of location. *Cultural Studies*, 7 (2), 292–310.

Frow, J. and Morris, M. (eds) 1993: *Australian Cultural Studies: A Reader*. St Leonards: Allen and Unwin.

Goetz, A. M. 1991: Feminism and the claim to know: contradictions in feminist approaches to women in development. In R. Grant and K. Newland (eds), *Gender and International Relations*. Bloomington: Indiana University Press, 133–57.

Goetz, A. M. 1994: From feminist knowledge to data for development. The bureaucratic management of information on women and development. *IDS Bulletin*, 25 (2), 27–36.

Grosz, E. 1989: *Sexual Subversions. Three French Feminists*. St Leonards: Allen and Unwin.

Gulati, L. 1982: *Profiles in Female Poverty. A Study of Five Poor Working Women in Kerela*. Oxford: Pergamon Press.

Hirschmann, N. J. 1998: Western feminism, Eastern veiling, and the question of free agency. *Constellations*, 5 (3), 345–68.

Hirshman, M. 1995: Women and development: a critique. In M. H. Marchand and J. L. Parpart (eds), *Feminism/Post-Modernism/Development*. London: Routledge, 42–55.

Hoodfar, H. 1997: Return to the veil: personal strategy and public participation in Egypt. In N. Visvanathan (co-ordinator), L. Duggan, L. Nisonoff, and N. Wiegersma (eds), *The Women, Gender & Development Reader*. London: Zed Books, 317–25.

hooks, b. 1984: *Feminist Theory from Margin to Center*. Boston: South End Press.

Jackson, C. 1997: Post-poverty, gender and development? *Institute of Development Studies (IDS) Bulletin*, 28 (3), 145–53.

Kabeer, N. 1994: *Reversed Realities. Gender Hierarchies in Development Thought*. London/ New York: Verso.

Karim, W. J. 1995: Introduction: genderising anthropology in Southeast Asia. In W. J. Karim (ed.), *"Male" and "Female" in Developing Southeast Asia*. Oxford/Washington, D.C.: Berg, 11–34.

Karl, M. 1995: *Women and Empowerment. Participation and Decision Making*. London: Zed Books.

Leacock, E. 1983: Interpreting the origins of gender inequality: conceptual and historical problems. *Dialectical Anthropology*, 7 (4), 263–84.

Lim, L 1983: Capitalism, imperialism and patriarchy: the dilemma of Third World women workers in multinational factories. In J. Nash and M. P. Fernandez-Kelly (eds), *Women, Men and the International Division of Labour*. Albany: State University of New York Press, 70–91.

McNally, S. 1998: Bia Om and karaoke: HIV and everyday life in urban Vietnam. Paper presented at the Vietnam Update 1998: Everyday life and cultural change in urban Vietnam, December 3–4, 1998, Canberra.

Marchand, M. H. and Parpart, J. L. (eds) 1995: *Feminism/Post-Modernism/Development*. London: Routledge.

Mies, M. 1982: *The Lace Makers of Narsapur. Indian Housewives Produce for the World Market*. London: Zed Books.

Mies, M. 1986: *Patriarchy and Accumulation on a World Scale. Women in the International Division of Labour*. London: Zed Books.

Mies, M., Bennholdt-Thomsen, V., and von Werlhof, C. 1988: *Women: The Last Colony*. London: Zed Books.

Mies, M. and Shiva, V. 1993: *Ecofeminism*. Melbourne: Spinifex Press.

Mohanty, C. T. 1991: Under Western eyes: feminist scholarship and colonial discourses. In C. T. Mohanty, A. Russo, and L. Torres (eds), *Third World Women and the Politics of Feminism*. Bloomington and Indianapolis: Indiana University Press, 51–80. Earlier versions were published in *Boundary 2*, 12 (3) / 13 (1) (Fall/Spring 1984) and in *Feminist Review* 30, 61–88 (Autumn 1988).

Moser, C. O. N. 1993: *Gender Planning and Development. Theory, Practice and Training*. London: Routledge.

Nagata, J. 1995: Modern Malay women and the message of the "veil." In W. J. Karim (ed.), *"Male" and "Female" in Developing Southeast Asia*. Oxford/Washington D.C.: Berg Publishers, 101–20.

Narayan, U. 1997: *Dislocating Cultures. Identities, Traditions and Third World Feminism*. New York: Routledge.

Narayan, U. 1998: Essence of culture and a sense of history: a feminist critique of cultural essentialism. *Hypatia, Special Issue: Border Crossings: Multicultural and Postcolonial Feminist Challenges to Philosophy, Part 1*, 13 (2), 86–107.

Nash, J. 1979: *We Eat the Mines and the Mines Eat Us. Dependency and Exploitation in Bolivian Tin Mines*. New York: Columbia University Press.

Nash, J. and Fernandez-Kelly, M. P. (eds) 1983: *Women, Men and the International Division of Labour*. Albany: State University of New York Press.

Oakley, A. 1972: *Sex, Gender and Society*. London: Temple Smith.

Ong, A. 1988: Colonialism and modernity: feminist representations of women in non-Western societies. *Inscriptions* 3/4, 79–104.

Ong, A. 1995: State versus Islam: Malay families, women's bodies, and the body politic in Malaysia. In A. Ong and M. G. Peletz (eds), *Bewitching Women, Pious Men. Gender and Body Politics in Southeast Asia*. Berkeley: University of California Press, 159–94. An earlier version appeared in *American Ethnologist* 17 (2), 1990, 258–76.

Ortner, S. 1974: Is female to male as nature is to culture? In M. Rosaldo and L. Lamphere (eds), *Women, Culture and Society*. Stanford: Stanford University Press, 66–87.

Ostergaard, L. (ed.) 1992: *Gender and Development. A Practical Guide*. London: Routledge.

Parpart, J. L. and Marchand, M. H. 1995: Exploding the canon: an introduction/conclusion. In M. H. Marchand and J. L. Parpart (eds), *Feminism/Post-Modernism/Development*. London: Routledge: 1–22.

Parsons, T. 1964: *Social Structure and Personality*. London: The Free Press/Collier-Macmillan.

Pearson, R. 1992: Gender and industrialization. In T. Hewitt, H. Johnson, and D. Wield (eds), *Industrialization and Development*. Oxford: Oxford University Press in association with the Open University, 222–47.

Pearson, R., Whitehead, A., and Young, K. 1988: Introduction: the continuing subordination of women in the development process. In K. Young, C. Wolkowitz, and R. McCullagh (eds), *Of Marriage and the Market. Women's Subordination Internationally and its Lessons*. London: Routledge, ix–xix.

Price, J. 1992: Who determines need? A case study of a women's organization in North India. *Institute of Development Studies (IDS) Bulletin*, 23 (1), 50–7.

Rogers, B. 1980: *The Domestication of Women: Discrimination in Developing Societies*. London: Tavistock.

Saadawi, N. El 1980: *The Hidden Face of Eve: Women in the Arab World*. Translated and edited by Sherif Hetata. London: Zed Books.

Sen G. and Grown, C. 1987: *Development, Crises and Alternative Visions. Third World Women's Perspectives*. New York: Monthly Review Press.

Shiva, V. 1989: *Staying Alive. Women, Ecology and Development*. London: Zed Books.

Spivak, G. C. 1990: *The Post-colonial Critic: Interviews, Strategies, Dialogues*. Ed. S. Harasym. New York: Routledge.

Stivens, M. 1992: Perspectives on gender: problems in writing about women in Malaysia. In J. S. Kahn and F. Loh Kok Wah (eds), *Fragmented Vision. Culture and Politics in Contemporary Malaysia*. Sydney: Asian Studies Association of Australia (ASAA) in association with Allen and Unwin, 202–24.

Trinh Min-Ha 1989: *Woman, Native, Other. Writing Postcoloniality and Feminism*. Bloomington: Indiana University Press.

Udayagiri, M. 1995: Challenging modernization: gender and development, post modern feminism and activism. In M. H. Marchand and J. L. Parpart (eds), *Feminism/Post-Modernism/Development*. London: Routledge, 159–77.

Visvanathan, N. 1997: Introduction to Part 1. In N. Visvanathan (co-ordinator), L. Duggan, L. Nisonoff, and N. Wiegersma (eds), *The Women, Gender & Development Reader*. London: Zed Books, 17–32.

Visvanathan, N. (co-ordinator), Duggan, L., Nisonoff, L., and Wiegersma, N. (eds) 1997: *The Women, Gender & Development Reader*. London: Zed Books.

Young, K., Wolkowitz C., and McCullagh, R. (eds) 1988: *Of Marriage and the Market. Women's Subordination Internationally and its Lessons*. London: Routledge. 1st edition 1981, 2nd edition 1984.

5 Inventing Traditions, Constructing Nations

1 Introduction

Development studies, in the 1950s and 1960s, imbibed almost unconsciously the belief in the sturdiness of the nation-state which prevailed in these post-war decades. Many took the Third World nation-state as the unit of analysis in their research of processes of modernization and development. By becoming independent and sovereign, the former colonies had now found their place in the modern political world order, able to govern their own processes of modernization and development. However, as Crawford Young (1993: 3) points out, by the 1990s, at the latest, "the comfortable certainties" concerning the nation-state had evaporated in the light of deepening cultural cleavages in many countries, and global economic and political liberalization. Both of these processes have revealed the glue which holds nation-states together to be rather less than permanent. Many countries are plagued by civil wars, repressive governments, or are torn apart by ethnic separatist movements, cultural fundamentalism, and anti-modern or anti-Western strands of politics. If we unpack the nation-state, we are invariably confronted with culture and power as the basic ingredients in the construction of national identity. Anticolonial independence movements were, in many instances, trying to forge a nation based on indigenous popular culture and traditions, which marked its difference from the culture imposed by the colonial power. At the same time, their claim to national sovereignty was thoroughly modern, founded on the principles of the European Enlightenment. These principles gave anticolonial nationalists the justification for self-government in the language of Western modernity, but it also meant sweeping aside indigenous models of governing. Those aspects of cultural practices and traditions which did not fit the emerging hegemonic nationalism were reinterpreted, marginalized, or suppressed by the new Third World rulers. As a result, some groups of people were pushed to the margin of "their" nation-state: examples are nomadic communities who do not fit into the modern patterns of land ownership and use, ethnic communities whose cultural practices differ from those endorsed by the national elite, or indigenous leaders who had retained or gained authority under colonial rule. When we look at a nation-state, writes Yuval-Davis (1997: 41), we see the cultural stuff that has survived, but we cannot know for sure how much cultural stuff has not survived historical change.

Some argue that the cause of the nation-state's problems lies at the heart of postcolonial nationalism itself: the unresolved tensions between the claims of nationalism – that the ex-colony is essentially different from, and at the same time equal, if not superior, to the West – and nationalism's justificatory structures, which are firmly rooted within Western conceptions of universal rationality (Chatterjee 1986). A national identity must be established which unites the people and distinguishes them from outsiders. National identity is often based on shared history and experience, cultural practices such as language, religion etc., and/or common origin and descent. Hence, Anthony Smith asserts that all nations have an ethnic character (Smith 1995), and the legitimacy of the nation-state rests at least in part on the strength and coherence of national identity. At the same time, the nation-state's legitimacy rests on its claim to represent all its citizens, whatever their cultural practices, and on universally accepted norms – such as the right to self-determination. Furthermore, in identifying this tension between cultural distinctiveness and universal principles at the heart of nationalism, it is no longer possible to maintain the distinction, made most strongly by modernization theorists, between "rational" and "modern" nation-building on the one hand, and "irrational" and "traditional" ethnic ties on the other. Michael Freeman (1998: 18) argues that it is "precisely the instability of the conceptual boundaries between ethnicity, nation, and state that constitutes an inherent weakness in the structure of the contemporary political world." Section 2 of this chapter explores the concepts of nation and ethnicity in more detail, using tradition as a key concept which enables us to bring together the divergent literatures on nationalism and ethnicity. It goes on to explore modernization approaches to tradition as they have been expressed in scholarly writings or in political discourse.

The conventional academic distinction between "good" national and "bad" ethnic identity is particularly difficult to sustain when explored from a constructionist perspective. As outlined in chapter 1, such a perspective holds that social groups coalesce around a variety of circumstances that form the basis of a sense of shared identity, the most important being the categories of class, gender, sex, "race," and nation. These categories are actively created through cultural practices, and therefore individuals do not naturally *belong* to a particular "race" or nation, but rather *come to see* "race" or nation as places of belonging. In other words, we ourselves are involved in creating these categories, and have some choice in our degree of identification with them. Chapter 1 also pointed out, however, that Michel Foucault's (1980; 1986) work on power and representation was concerned with the relations of power underpinning the production of meanings and the processes by which certain meanings were rendered "true." Some individuals or social groups have more influence than others on deciding which cultural practices are most representative of a nation, a "race," or an ethnic group. However, it is important to remember that Foucault envisaged power not as deployed from above to exploit and oppress those below, but rather as circulatory, pervasive, and multicentered, operating through discourse in ways which imbue all social actors with degrees of agency – and complicity – within the effects of power/knowledge (Foucault 1980). This means that identities, whether national, "racial," or ethnic, cannot be enforced in the longer term, and neither are they fixed.

Some postcolonial scholars (Fanon 1967; Ranger 1983; Chatterjee 1986) have made important contributions to constructionist perspectives on ethnicity and nationalism. In the early 1960s, Fanon observed the "passionate search for a national culture which existed before the colonial era" among anticolonial intellectuals, to fend off "a Western culture in which they all risk being swamped," and to conjure from the mists of a glorious past a way out of the miserable present (Fanon 1967: 168). However, Fanon also noted that decades or centuries of colonial rule had changed indigenous culture such that it was no longer possible to go back to its authentic roots. Furthermore, in many cases the colonial boundaries cut through the territories of indigenous communities, and threw together peoples with different traditions. One common response to these predicaments is to invent traditions. Section 3 of this chapter focuses on the invention of tradition in the construction of identities. It challenges conceptions, outlined in the second section, of tradition as fixed and essential features of a nation, seen either as protection against, or stumbling block to, a fast-changing, rootless modernity. Terence Ranger's (1983) work on invented traditions in Africa shows that many African ethnic collectivities (or "tribes") originated in the heads of colonial administrators, while Partha Chatterjee's (1986) discussion of Indian nationalism discusses how particular traditions have been enshrined in national culture and nationalist ideology to represent the nation.

In the fourth section, we draw on postcolonial research in Asia and Africa to provide examples of how traditions, and by extension, nationalist discourses, have been contested, and how such contestations may provide spaces to imagine different communities and futures. Some contestations manifest themselves with such violence that any optimism about a brighter future seems frivolous. They appear to reinforce the Western politics of representation in which the non-Western is cast as the barbaric, uncivilized Other who is in need of Western intervention. This raises the question, which is also applicable to less destructive forms of contestation, what kind of ideological resources are required in order to forge a future that can avoid the traps of Western modernity (in its contemporary version of good governance and free market), as well as preventing self-destructive events such as the genocidal killings in Rwanda in 1994?

The final section discusses the impact of globalization on cultural identities, whether buttressed by new or by old traditions. We ask the question how Third World governments manage the ambiguous and porous line between fostering a national identity, and the quest (or push) to globalize. Developing countries in particular face increasing pressures to open themselves up to a global economy which exposes not only their oil, coffee, and textiles to international competition, but also the very stuff which makes cultural identities: music, language, belief systems, land, and so on. In this fifth section, we explore the contradictory impacts of globalization on cultural identities by using case studies from Thailand, Nigeria, and South Africa.

2   Fixed traditions?

2.1   Defining state, nation, and ethnicity

In this section we argue that traditions are an indispensable component of the nation-state. However, many studies distinguish between "good" and "bad" traditions, taking as a yardstick their usefulness in a modern society. A similar value judgment can be observed in the literature in relation to national and ethnic identities, whereby national identity is seen to be a proper, almost natural, sense of belonging to the nation-state, while ethnic identities are regarded with suspicion. These issues are some of the most hotly debated in development studies and cultural studies, reflecting their prominence in contemporary global politics. The starting point of this chapter is to clarify the ways in which state, nation, and ethnicity are variously defined in the literature. The remainder of this section turns to the ways in which modernization theorists and modernizing Third World governments have argued the distinction between "good" and "bad" traditions in the construction of a modern national identity.

Many commentators bemoan a lack of clear definitions that could be used to mark off the concepts of "state," "nation," and "ethnicity" against each other. Of the three terms, "state" is the most straightforward because it identifies "the political entities that are the principal legitimate actors on the world stage" (Eller 1999: 16). States are what we see on a political map, and if we look at different times we also see that the shape of states can change as a result of historical and political processes. States are not natural entities but created. One useful definition of the state is as "a body of institutions which are centrally organized around the intentionality of control with a given apparatus of enforcement (juridical and repressive) at its command and basis," whereby the relationship between control and coercion varies from one type of state to another (Anthias and Yuval-Davis 1989: 5, quoted in Yuval-Davis 1997: 14).

Despite the common use of the term "nation-state," states and nations do not refer to the same thing. A nation can be part of a state, or incorporate several states, or parts of them. Nation is a diffuse term, subject to different definitions and theoretical debates. One definition, by Anthony Smith (1991: 40, quoted in

Eller 1999: 17), holds that a nation is "a named human population sharing a historic territory, common myths and historical memories, a mass, public culture, a common economy and common legal rights and duties for all members." A human population with these attributes is called a nation even if it is not recognized as a political entity. Furthermore, some point out that Smith's list of criteria is not independent of human interpretation; rather, nationhood, and "the specific markers and elements" of nationhood, "may be imagined, interpreted, or even '"invented'" (Eller 1999: 18). While Smith stresses the ethnic component of nation, Yuval-Davis (1997: 19) points out that "common destiny" is a crucial glue of nations, particularly in postcolonial states which do not have a shared myth of common origin.

Ethnicity is perhaps the most confusing of the three terms, and has been applied to a wide range of contexts and types of human communities. There are many similarities between definitions of "nation" and those of "ethnic group," with perhaps the only distinction being that the national project claims separate political representation. The following definition shows up the similarities between nation and ethnicity:

> "Ethnicity" is often defined as a consciousness of shared ethnic origin. Ethnic origin is thought to be objective, but the strength of the shared sentiment is highly variable, being the product of an interaction between within-group feeling and the degree of institutional recognition accorded by the political environment. (Banton 1998: 993)

This definition alludes to primordialist notions of ethnicity as an inherited, "given" characteristic, but it also presents ethnicity as created, imagined, and felt by a group of people *in interaction with* their surroundings. It exemplifies the third of three main theoretical approaches on ethnicity – instrumentalism, which combines the other two within itself. The instrumentalist approach assumes that ethnic difference is "always there" (primordial) but becomes a conscious identity and political issue when the members of the group "are dissatisfied with the way others are treating them or with the degree of autonomy allowed them" (Banton 1998: 993). Primordialists identify ethnic groups by markers such as ancestry ("blood"), territory ("soil"), "native" language, and religion – characteristics that are passed on from generation to generation. Primordial definitions often liken ethnic groups to families or kinship groups, which are commonly bound by blood ties rather than by voluntary, rationally founded linkages.

In recent years constructionist perspectives on ethnicity have gained currency. The main point here is that the constructionist, unlike the other two approaches, does not assume a pre-existing ethnic identity or consciousness. Instead, ethnicity is seen "as the product of human agency, a creative social act through which such commonalities as speech code, cultural practices, ecological adaptation, and political organization become woven into a consciousness of shared identity" (Young 1994: 79–80, quoted in Yeros 1999: 4). Similarly, Comaroff (1995: 249–50) argues that ethnic identities are relations, their content "wrought in the particularities of their ongoing historical construction."

He elaborates that "ethnicity typically has its origins in relations of inequality"; their construction involves struggle and contestation; and that once constructed, ethnic identities *appear* to be natural, primordial, essential. Constructivist approaches such as Norval's do not argue that ethnic markers are imagined, or "picked and chosen as if from a supermarket shelf" (Norval 1999: 86). Rather, they direct attention to the processes through which markers such as skin color and language become "material" as a result of political practices, and how ethnicity becomes a significant site of identification.

2.2   Backward traditions, desirable traditions

What is tradition? Raymond Williams calls it "a particularly difficult word." He explains that "[t]radition survives in English as a description of a general process of handing down, but there is a very strong and often predominant sense of this entailing respect and duty" (Williams 1988: 318). However, only some traditions, or parts of them, "have been selected for our respect and duty" (Williams 1988: 319). On the one hand, it takes only two generations to make a tradition, but on the other, the concept of tradition evokes age-old, immemorial practices. Within some forms of modernization theory, "tradition and especially traditional are now often used dismissively, with a similar lack of specificity" (Williams 1988: 319). Tradition, in this dismissive sense, signals resistance to innovation.

The *Concise Oxford Dictionary* (1995: 1478) lists the following meanings of "tradition":

1 **a** a custom, opinion, or belief handed down to posterity esp. orally or by practice.
   b this process of handing down.
2 an established practice or custom (*it's a tradition to complain about the weather*).
3 artistic, literary etc. principles based on experience and practice (*stage tradition; traditions of the Dutch School* [of painting]).
4 *Theol.* doctrine or a particular doctrine etc. claimed to have divine authority without documentary evidence, esp.: **a** the oral teaching of Christ and the Apostles. **b** the laws held by the Pharisees to have been delivered by God to Moses. **c** the words and deeds of Muhammad not in the Koran.
5 *Law* the formal delivery of property etc.

The contradictory perceptions of tradition which Williams identifies are long established in Western modernity, as we pointed out in chapter 1. While the Western European countries underwent rapid social, economic, and political changes during the industrial revolution, cultural movements emerged which romanticized "traditional" rural life (e.g. some strands of German Romanticism). In relation to the Third World, these dichotomous perspectives have manifested themselves in, among others, modernization studies on the one hand, and anthropological studies on the other – the former identifying non-Western tradition as obstacle, and many of the latter being devoted to recording and thus maintaining them. In chapter 2, we introduced Daniel Lerner's (1958) modernization study of the Turkish village of Balgat in the 1950s. Lerner focuses on the differences between the "traditional world view" of the village chief, and the modern values and aspirations of his sons. While tradition involves passing down from one generation to the next property, knowledge, skills, and values, modernization disrupts and revolutionizes knowledge, values, and social relations. As Lerner puts it, modernization "spells the passing of traditional society and defines the policy planning of social change" (Lerner 1968: 388). Modernization and tradition cannot coexist, in this view, and any nostalgia for the "good old days" is more than compensated for by modernization's promises of a better, more enlightened life.

Contrast this with the portrayal of non-Western ways of life in the television documentary series *Millennium* by anthropologist Maybury-Lewis. In the book accompanying the television series, Maybury-Lewis (1992) declares his disagreement with the modernization theorists' proposition that the "march of progress" will inevitably wipe out traditional societies. He elaborates that

> It's a popular misconception that societies pass through an inevitable series of stages, that they move from one phase to another unavoidably and that everybody has to pass through them. It is also a popular misconception that we are the most advanced people on earth and that tribal societies are either cases of arrested development – people who haven't got there yet – or people who have quite simply failed, flunked the test, been left behind. (Maybury-Lewis 1992: 268)

Rather than viewing Western modernity as a desirable way of being, Maybury-Lewis suggests that Western societies have suffered great losses in terms of their sense of community, identity, and meaning of life in the process of becoming modern. His documentaries are part of a mission to rediscover what the West has lost, and to incorporate some of the more enviable features of tribal societies into our modern way of living. As in some post-developmentalist approaches, indigenous traditions are perceived here as a resource to tap, in order to solve contemporary problems caused by modernization and development – problems such as environmental destruction and loss of community.

Despite the obvious differences in Lerner's and Maybury-Lewis's projects, there are important similarities (table 5.1; cf. chapter 2, table 2.1). Both view non-Western societies as being traditional, and both contrast tradition with modernity. As we argued in chapter 1, the disparaging view and the idealizing view of non-Western cultures have both been present in colonial representations of non-Western societies – those which Edward Said described as "Orientalism." Lerner's and Maybury-Lewis's work shows that their various echoes are still being heard today.

Table 5.1 Maybury-Lewis's traditional–modern dichotomy

Features	Traditional societies	Modern societies
Economic framework	operate a moral economy where exchanges define personal relationships, social relations between members of the society	operate an amoral economy: the impersonal market place which is concerned with economic transactions between members of the society
Trade	exchanges are not for financial gain or simply survival	exchanges are based on economic rationality and profitability
Social relations	social system depends on trust, complementarity, interdependence	"driven economy," "restless society," creation of new needs to ensure that economy grows
Overall goal	seeking stability	seeking competition, dynamism, and producing insecurity and uncertainty
Human development	relationships between people are carefully tended; people are a valuable resource	individualism – but human beings are robbed of their human dimensions; humans become disposable – things are valuable
Identity	well-developed spirituality; strong connection to the natural world; have a sense of place (even if separated from their lands)	emotional refugees, alienated; loss of community and a sense of connection; things and people are reduced to their economic role

Source: adapted from Maybury-Lewis (1992).

2.3 Third World elites on tradition

The dichotomy of traditional and modern is also evident in the work of Third World intellectuals and governments. On the one hand, Third World elites adopted the dim views of their own traditions which colonial administrations had held. Sumit Guha (1998: 423) turns to geological terminology to describe the way in which Indian elites viewed their "tribal" countrywomen and men as never changing. According to this view, "they merely accumulated, with the latest addition to the population overlaying its predecessors, much as geological strata did." The work of Indian anthropologists shows the influence of British colonial ethnographers, such as Charles Grant, who explained the marginalization of the aboriginal tribes of central India as a "natural" consequence of their subordination by the racially superior Aryans some two thousand years ago. Post-independence accounts revert but do not challenge the prejudice: aboriginal tribes are portrayed as "primitive" hunter–gatherers who have resisted subordination and modernization, and who live in harmony with the forests (Guha 1998), or as "post-primitive" shifting cultivators and laborers, who see themselves as "different from their neighbours" (Roy Burman 1979: 102). The Indian constitution makes provision for a ministry devoted to the welfare and "uplift" of "backward classes," in which the Scheduled Tribes, as the indigenous peoples are called, are included (Government of India 1982: 143). The Backward Classes Commission recommended in 1955 that "we offer certain concessions and help to the Scheduled Tribes in their effort to come up to the general standard." While the state should help tribal people to modernize, it should also bear in mind that they have "certain good things to offer to us" – such as "folk-dances, folk-songs and many customs" (Government of India 1982: 257–8). Clearly, the Commission held a view of culture as separate from social and economic change, as a feature that can be brought out on particular occasions or paraded in front of tourists.

On the other hand, however, Third World nationalist elites did not simply write off the traditions of their countries as outmoded, or at best quaint and harmless practices, and embrace the Western model of modernization. In the struggle against the colonial rulers, it was necessary to distinguish the colonized self from the colonizer, to search for one's own cultural roots, and to reaffirm indigenous cultural practices and traditions. In the 1950s Frantz Fanon analyzed the urge of Third World intellectuals to discover something beautiful and dignified beneath the misery of colonial everyday existence, something which could rehabilitate the colonized nation and give it hope for the future. Part of this effort of rehabilitation involves actively revaluing a precolonial history which had been represented by colonialism as barbaric and degraded, as having brought out the "evil instincts" of the native population. Third World nationalist intellectuals, in order to counter the argument that colonial rule was holding these "evil instincts" at bay and taming them with the help of a variety of civilizing institutions (Fanon 1967: 170), had to reinterpret local history and culture in more positive ways.

2.4   Women as keepers of tradition

Indian historian Partha Chatterjee (1986; 1992; 1993) provides an excellent analysis of the ways in which these contradictory perspectives on tradition are played out in India's nationalist movement during the late nineteenth century and up until the early postcolonial period. He describes the influence of Orientalist thought on Indian nationalists, who accepted the colonialist critique of India as "a society fallen into barbarism and stagnation, incapable of progress or modernity," while at the same time affirming "the superiority of the East's spiritual heritage" (Chatterjee 1992: 194–5). Chatterjee points out that "a central element in the ideological justification of British colonial rule was the criticism of the 'degenerate and barbaric' social customs of the Indian people, sanctioned, or so it was believed, by the religious tradition" (1993: 117–18). The treatment and representation of Indian women played a pivotal role in both the British justification of colonial rule and the Indian nationalists' claim to cultural difference and superiority. "By assuming a position of sympathy with the unfree and oppressed womanhood of India," Chatterjee (1993: 118) observes, "the colonial mind was able to transform this figure of the Indian woman into a sign of the inherently oppressive and unfree nature of the entire cultural tradition of a country." Traditions such as child marriage and *sati*, the burning of widows on the funeral pyre of their husbands, were branded by colonial administrators as barbaric and were legislated against. The nationalist response to the critique of Indian tradition also focused on the figure of the Indian woman, but in a very different way. Women came to represent the realm of the home which, according to Chatterjee (1993: 120), stands for "one's inner spiritual self, one's true identity." In the colonial situation

> The material/spiritual dichotomy, to which the terms world and home corresponded, had acquired . . . a very special significance in the nationalist mind. The world was where the European power had challenged the non-European peoples and, by virtue of its superior material culture, had subjugated them. But, the nationalists asserted, it had failed to colonize the inner, essential, identity of the East, which lay in its distinctive, and superior, spiritual culture. . . . The subjugated must learn the modern sciences and arts of the material world from the West in order to match their strengths and ultimately overthrow the colonizer. But in the entire phase of the national struggle, the crucial need was to protect, preserve, and strengthen the inner core of the national culture, its spiritual essence. No encroachments by the colonizer must be allowed in that inner sanctum. (Chatterjee 1993: 121)

While men have the task of adjusting to, and participating in, the changes occurring in the external world of material activity which produce a modern society, women are responsible for protecting and nurturing the spiritual quality of the national culture: "No matter what the changes in the external conditions of life for women, they must not lose their essentially spiritual (that is, feminine) virtues; they must not, in other words, become essentially Westernized" (Chatterjee 1993: 126). This does not necessarily mean that women have to remain more traditional than men, but their modernity must be different from that of men (see also Sunindyo 1998). As Yuval-Davis argues, placing the "burden of representation" of the collectivity's identity and future destiny on women does not necessarily increase women's status in society. To the contrary, it often legitimizes the control and oppression of women, and constructs them as passive bearers of the nation's essence and honor, rather than as subjects with an agency of their own (Yuval-Davis 1997: 45–7). It is ironic that for all their centrality to the nation's (or ethnic collectivity's) identity, women may come to see themselves as marginal to, or even excluded from, the nation.

2.5 Summary

From this discussion of the meanings and roles of tradition, it can be seen that on both sides of the colonial divide, tradition is seen as part and parcel of culture. Furthermore, both concepts are defined by their separation from the economic and political spheres. Lowe and Lloyd (1997: 23) argue that "Orientalist definitions of modernity suggest that modern societies 'have' culture, while nonmodern societies 'are' culture" – in other words, they are "traditional." In the nationalist discourses, the separation between culture and political economy is maintained, but instead of denigrating indigenous culture, parts of it are elevated to the core of the emerging nation. Around that untouchable cultural core of national identity, modernization is allowed to take place in the political and economic spheres, transforming the society from one that is traditional into one that has culture.

However, there is another view of culture, one that views it as linked to, rather than separated from, the economic and the political. Lowe and Lloyd (1997: 26) argue that this linkage becomes particularly evident in the contemporary period of globalization, in which transnational capitalism commodifies everything, including culture and traditions. Furthermore, they point out that the political has never been a discrete sphere of practice within the nation-state: "'politics' must be grasped instead as always braided within 'culture' and cultural practices." Yuval-Davis (1997: 67) gives primary importance to power relations and social, economic, and political activities, but accords culture a crucial role in "the continuous (re)construction of collectivities and collective identities and the management/control of their boundaries." The next section probes deeper into the linkages between the cultural and the political, and thereby challenges conceptions of tradition as fixed and essential features of a nation, in opposition to a fast-changing, rootless modernity, which have been put forward by both Western colonialists and modernization theorists, and by some Third World nationalist elites.

3 Inventing traditions

Conceiving tradition as something invented, actively created, contradicts what we have identified as the modernization perspective on tradition in the previous section. This conceptualization draws on the work of English Marxist historians Eric Hobsbawm (1983) and Terence Ranger (1983), which has been debated and elaborated by various students of ethnicity and nationalism. Eller (1999: 29–30) argues that ethnic groups are "virtually unthinkable" without a memory of their cultural past or tradition, adding that in "the most extreme cases the tradition may even be a fabrication, an invention." In Ranger's (1983) influential paper on invented traditions, he identifies ethnicity in Africa as invention of the colonial period. But what does invented tradition mean? According to Hobsbawm (1983: 1–2)

"Invented tradition" is taken to mean a set of practices, normally governed by overtly or tacitly accepted rules and of a ritual or symbolic nature, which seek to inculcate certain values and norms of behaviour by repetition, which automatically implies continuity with the past. In fact, where possible, they normally attempt to establish continuity with a suitable historic past. . . . However, in so far as there is such reference to a historic past, the peculiarity of "invented" traditions is that the continuity with it is largely factitious.

Hobsbawm (1983) points out that traditions are different from customs in that the former are meant to remain fixed, while the latter are to a certain degree open to change (for example, English judges follow a *tradition* in wearing a wig and a black robe, but their judgments are based on Common Law *custom*). Tradition is also different from routine or convention in that the latter have no symbolic or ritual function (for example, the conventions followed by a government bureaucracy).

The past two hundred years have been marked by an increase in invented traditions because societies have been experiencing more rapid change. Modernization "weakens or destroys the social patterns for which 'old' traditions had been designed, producing new ones to which they were not applicable" (Hobsbawm 1983: 4–5). While some traditions were swept aside by forces of change, others were deliberately rejected "as obstacles to progress, or, even worse, as its militant adversaries" (Hobsbawm 1983: 8). Both scenarios can lead to the invention of new traditions. These invented traditions, while usually drawing on the past, tend to be less specific and less binding than their "old" predecessors. They are important in public life, but occupy a much smaller place in the private lives of people than the old traditions did.

Hobsbawm distinguishes three overlapping types of invented traditions in the period since the industrial revolution:

1   traditions which establish or legitimize institutions, status, or relations of authority;
2   traditions which establish or symbolize social cohesion of communities (e.g. national communities);
3   traditions which serve to socialize, or inculcate, beliefs, value systems, and conventions of behavior in a population.

In the remainder of this section, we want to explore each of these three types of invented tradition. For the first type we examine the role of invented traditions in legitimizing British colonial rule in Africa. The second type is illustrated by returning to Partha Chatterjee's analysis of Indian nationalism. Then we look to Singapore to explore how traditions are invented to socialize a population.

3.1   Invented traditions to legitimize colonial rule in Africa

Colonial administrations at the height of colonial expansion were neither willing nor able to rule by military force alone. In many territories, colonizers were

vastly outnumbered by indigenous people, and thus relied on their collaboration in the colonial economy and acceptance of the administration. While British administrators seeking to legitimize their position in India were able to
draw on the complex traditions of previous rulers and well-established hierarchies of caste, ethnicity, and religion, their counterparts in Africa were faced
with indigenous political traditions that were very different from their own.
Terence Ranger (1983: 215) explains invented traditions in Africa with the

> desperate need in the last decades of the nineteenth century to make European
> activity in Africa more respectable and ordered. . . . With the coming of formal
> colonial rule it was urgently necessary to turn the whites into a convincing ruling
> class, entitled to hold sway over their subjects not only through force of arms or
> finance but also through the prescriptive status bestowed by neo-tradition.

One way for the British colonizers to establish themselves as a ruling class, in
their own eyes and those of their African subjects, was to set up in Africa repli-
cas of institutions whose traditions validated the British governing class. One
example of such an institution is Kenya Public School, built to replicate Eton,
an exclusive private school in England. Neo-traditionalist British school education was also offered to some of the children of the indigenous aristocracy, to
mold them such that they could function as part of the governing colonial elite.
However, in the feudalistic style of governance fostered by the British, Euro-
pean-style education was beyond the reach of the vast majority of African colo-

Figure 5.1   Edward, Prince of Wales, at Freetown, Sierra Leone (1925)

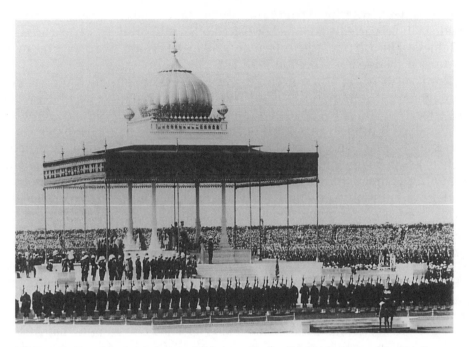

Figure 5.2 The Durbar amphitheater at Delhi (December 12, 1911)

nial subjects. As Ranger (1983: 227) stresses, "European invented traditions offered Africans a series of clearly defined points of entry into the colonial world,
though in almost all cases it was entry into the subordinate part of a man/
master relationship."

Thus, the main purpose of European invented traditions in colonial Africa,
according to Ranger (1983: 221), was to define a hierarchical society within "a
shared framework of pride and loyalty." Imperial monarchy was at the heart
of this shared ideology. Ranger (1983: 230–1) argues that the British monarchy
was built up by colonial administrations into a mystical figure, "almost divine;
omnipotent, omniscient and omnipresent." He somewhat mischievously describes a royal visit in the interwar period:

> When the Prince of Wales visited southern and eastern Africa in 1925, his notori-
> ous dislike of ceremony was overcome by the entreaties of colonial administra-
> tors who told him that if he did not appear in full scarlet before the assembled
> African masses it would be better for him not to appear at all. The effect was
> properly gratifying. "The Prince's arrival was a splendid affair," reported the *Daily
> Telegraph* from Basutoland; "His Royal Highness was ablaze with medals, a sight
> which deeply impressed the great, silent masses." (Ranger 1993: 232)

According to one British historian's adulatory account of the Prince of Wales'
royal tour of Southern Africa in 1925, the Prince's efforts to cut an impressive

figure paid off. In a tribute paid to him by the Zulu Chiefs, they are reported as having wholeheartedly accepted British colonial rule: "Having experienced the mildness of British rule," they allegedly said to the Prince, "we rejoice the more because it subdued us" (Bolitho 1937: 82).

Royal visits being a rare event, it was necessary to sustain the royal cult through invented tradition. Edward Twining displayed great talent in inventing a local version of the English coronation ceremony in 1937 for celebrations in Uganda. He proudly recounted having invented the "combined Tattoo and Firework Display" and adapted English traditions to local conditions with the help of leopard skins and ostrich feathers (Ranger 1983: 234). Ranger comments that British administrators took their own invented traditions very seriously, and proved resistant to attempts to change them, and hostile to any challenges. While there is evidence that some of these traditions appealed to African imagination, it is difficult to assess how Africans perceived them.

Its scant attention to African perceptions and agency left Ranger's work open to the criticism that his concept of invented tradition was too static and hierarchical, as he himself acknowledged (Ranger 1993). In particular, it did not do justice to African anticolonial political agency, and failed to address their reinvention of African identities and traditions after the demise of colonial rule. Is it not racist, asks his critic Adrian Hastings (1997), to assume that African ethnic identities were invented by Europeans, as if Africans were incapable of creating such bonds on their own? In his response Ranger points out that the inventionist approach aimed "not to deny identity to Africans but to liberate them from the assumption that African identities always have been and still are 'tribal'" (Ranger 1999: 134). Furthermore, he shows that precolonial identities in Africa were many and varied, and often difficult for European observers to comprehend. Ethnicity was only one among the possible ways of conceiving collective identities: "What one can still call colonial invention of ethnicity was a matter of selecting from among the elements of identity in a situation, and then privileging the elements selected at the expense of others" (Ranger 1999: 140).

3.2   The invention of tradition in the construction of Indian nationalism

Perhaps the key area where invented traditions are at work is in the construction of national identity. If colonial administrations directed their ingenuity to fostering a sense of belonging to the empire among their subjects, the task of anticolonial nationalists was both similar and different. They, too, had to invent traditions that would bind the population into a new national community, but at the same time they had to establish that these traditions were, in fact, much older, and therefore more persuasive, than the colonial traditions constructed by their opponents. As Eric Hobsbawm points out,

> modern nations . . . claim to be the opposite of novel, namely rooted in the remotest antiquity, and the opposite of constructed, namely human communities so

"natural" as to require no definition other than self-assertion. (Hobsbawm 1983: 14)

However, many Third World nations have no natural shape or shared culture. Their boundaries are determined by the vagaries of colonial conquests, and their indigenous cultural practices have been disrupted and emaciated by decades, or even centuries, of imperialist exploitation: "what we find are the dregs of culture, its mineral strata" (Fanon 1967: 191). Even colonies such as British India, whose well-established cultural practices and traditions were recognized as belonging to an ancient civilization by the colonial administration, were faced with the problem of how to forge a national community out of the disparate and vast array of local histories and cultures.

While many political theorists, particularly in nineteenth-century Europe, have defined nationhood in terms of "objective" criteria, such as linguistic uniformity or democratic governance, a subjective approach has emerged in recent decades which defines nations in terms of the perceptions of nationalists. This is evident in Ernest Gellner's (1964: 169) declaration that "[n]ationalism is not the awakening of nations to self-consciousness: it invents nations where they do not exist." Benedict Anderson's concept of nations as "imagined communities" expresses a similar sentiment. In his view, any community larger than can be experienced through face-to-face contact is imagined. What distinguishes nations from other communities is how they are imagined. Thus, nationality and nationalism "are cultural artefacts of a particular kind" (Anderson 1991: 4), and we can analyze them as systems of cultural representations:

> National cultures construct identities by producing meanings about "the nation" with which we can identify; these are contained in the stories which are told about it, memories which connect its present with its past, and images which are constructed of it. (Hall 1992: 293)

Many of the stories, memories, and images through which a national culture instills in us a sense of national identity or sense of belonging are invented traditions. Who invents these traditions through which we identify as a community? Anderson (1991: 140) argues that the early advocates for anticolonial nationalism were the intelligentsia – those "natives" who had been invited by the colonial state into schools and offices. They had access

> to models of nation, nation-ness, and nationalism distilled from the turbulent, chaotic experiences of more than a century of American and European history. These models, in turn, helped to give shape to a thousand inchoate dreams.

In the following case study of Indian nationalism, we look at the consequences of the educated middle class playing a dominant role in the construction of national culture. Returning to Partha Chatterjee's work, we see that their experiences of culture are enshrined in the dominant forms of nationalist culture and social institutions, while other groups' cultural practices, memories, or stories are subordinated, or excluded altogether.

From the late nineteenth century onwards, an emerging middle class in colonial India played an important role in creating the dominant forms of nationalist culture and social institutions. It was subordinated to the British colonial elite politically and economically, but it contested this relation of subordination on the basis of its cultural leadership of the indigenous colonized people:

> The crucial break in the history of anticolonial nationalism comes when the colonized refuse to accept membership of [the colonial] civil society of subjects. They construct their national identities within a different narrative, that of the community. They do not have the option of doing this within the domain of bourgeois civil-social institutions. (Chatterjee 1993: 237)

One of the ways in which the indigenous intelligentsia claims cultural leadership is through incorporating the popular into national culture. While the popular is taken to be "the repository of natural truth, naturally self-sustaining and therefore timeless," it must be mediated by an enlightened leadership so that "all marks of vulgarity, coarseness, localism, and sectarian identity" can be removed. Thus the popular can be controlled, and "its capacity for resolute endurance and sacrifice and its ability to protect and nourish" can be harnessed (Chatterjee 1993: 73).

This construction of tradition is evident in Gandhi's writings. His critique of civil society and his vision of an independent India returning to "the simple self-sufficiency of 'traditional' village life" were based on the idea that Indian civilization "had found the true principles of social organization" (Chatterjee 1986: 103), and therefore had no need for modernization and change. Gandhi consciously sought to bring the "whole people" within the political nation, by denying caste divisions the status of truth:

> Caste has nothing to do with religion. It is a custom whose origin I do not know and do not need to know . . . But I do know that it is harmful both to the spiritual and national growth. (Gandhi, quoted in Chatterjee 1986: 95)

This version of nationalism squarely contradicts another influential version, which argues that caste is an essential element of Indian society, one that distinguishes it from the West. In this "traditionalist" version, the caste system produces a stable and harmonious social order, in which each individual has its appropriate place (Chatterjee 1993). The nationalist elite's construction of national culture reflected their own social position and cultural experiences. They mobilized the Indian peasants as an anticolonial force, but remained "suspicious of their supposed ignorance and backward consciousness," and kept them at a distance from the institutions of the state (Chatterjee 1993: 160). And while the newly independent Indian state adopted the Western liberal critique of caste as contravening the principles of democracy and equality, its newly formed institutions explicitly acknowledged the reality of castes as part of the "given cultural material" with which the nation was constructed (Chatterjee 1993: 198). Despite its claims to involve the whole people, Indian national culture is the culture of the new middle class – other groups are merely represented. Thus Chatterjee concludes that

> the story of nationalist emancipation is also a story of betrayal. Necessarily so. Because it could only confer freedom by imposing at the same time a whole set of new controls, it could only define a cultural identity for the nation by excluding many from its fold, and it could only grant the dignity of citizenship to some because the others always needed to be represented; they could not be allowed to speak for themselves. (Chatterjee 1992: 214)

Does this mean that some social groups are forever condemned to a passive role in the processes of imagining and inventing the nation? Some, like Homi Bhabha (1994), suggest that such marginalized groups are in a privileged position to question dominant traditions, as they are not able to fully identify with the dominant cultural project. More radically, they could come to challenge the concepts of nation-state as homogeneous cultural units and of national and ethnic identity as pure and self-evident. These ideas are further discussed in section 4.

3.3 New traditions to inculcate values and beliefs

While Indian nationalists were able to draw on a complex mosaic of cultural practices to construct a national culture, other states are built almost entirely around values that have been created through the invention of new traditions. One such country of obvious invention is the city-state of Singapore. Established under the auspices of British colonial rule, it was initially part of the Malaysian Federation. It only achieved independence with the break-up of this Federation in 1965. The question Singapore's political leadership was then facing was how to become viable as an independent state (Ang and Stratton 1995), because the city-state lacked the conventional resources for the construction of a national "imagined community" as it has no precolonial past to draw on.

Under the leadership of Lee Kuan Yew, Singapore has led the way in advocating Asian values as a distinctive Asian way of life, different from the West (see chapter 2). Asian values are also promoted to instill a sense of national identity and social and cultural cohesion among the multicultural population of Singapore. What links these constituent ethnic groups are the shared values established by the government, which are defined as quintessentially Asian (see chapter 2). Singapore has a mature economy which is in many ways comparable to that of Western societies. Its role as a globalized city has raised the specter of cultural westernization undermining "Asian values." The government's response to Singapore's rapid economic and social change was to reassert "Asian values" in a white paper on *The Shared Values* in 1991. According to this paper, Singapore's national ideology rests on five core values:

1   ethnic and religious tolerance;
2   commitment to consensus decision making;
3   putting the needs of society before the needs of the individual;
4   upholding the family as the core unit of society;
5   regard and community support for the individual.

In his interpretation of this policy paper, John Clammer (1993: 45) argues that it seems "to be recommending an ideology which is statist, patriarchal, Confucian and conservative." It draws selectively on the cultural values and beliefs of Singapore's ethnic groups by asserting that the Singaporeans share the core values of hard work, thrift, and sacrifice characteristic of the Japanese, Koreans, and Taiwanese, and ignoring any values that the Malays, Eurasians, Arabs, and Indians may have to offer. In promoting these values in schools and through the media, the Singaporean government assumes that a change in values will bring about corresponding changes in social practice – reflecting "a basically Chinese cultural bias" (Clammer 1993: 37). The Singapore example illustrates how even an apparently free-standing national identity that is obviously invented still calls on a specific ethnic self-awareness. This clearly begs the question whether this particular ethnic identity is capable of including Singaporeans from other backgrounds. It is, however, important to bear in mind the point, suggested by Yuval-Davis, that a common destiny shared by the members of a nation could compensate for the lack of common origin or ethnicity. In this sense, Singapore's successful pursuit of modernization and economic development helped to galvanize the ethnically diverse population.

4   Contesting traditions

Neither "old" nor "new" traditions are immune to contestations. As Hobsbawm points out above, traditions can become redundant, or inappropriate to the new social patterns emerging out of the constant and increasingly rapid processes of modernization. Furthermore, the very act of inventing tradition, as in the construction of a national culture, involves a struggle over whose cultural practice is selected to represent the nation, and whose perspective on this practice is enshrined as the truth. One recent example of contested tradition is the conflict between Muslim and Hindu religious groups over a sacred site in Ayodhya, Northern India. On December 6, 1992 a group of Hindu fundamentalists demolished the 550-year-old Babri Masjid mosque and erected in its place a makeshift temple to mark the place where, according to them, the Hindu god Rama was born, and a temple had previously existed. The conflict over which religious tradition should be visible is connected to contemporary efforts by Hindu nationalist political parties to reinforce a particular version of Indian history, and marginalize the role which the Muslim minority has played in it (Rao 1994).
    This section explores some of the ways in which traditions become a site of

conflict and struggle, not only between different groups of indigenous people, but also along the West–Rest faultline. On the one hand, such struggles can open up a space for new ways of thinking about culture, identity, and intercultural relationships. In other words, they can give rise to new traditions which fit contemporary cultural needs better. On the other hand, however, struggles over traditions can also be destructive, leading to a hardening of opposing positions, or even to genocidal acts against the others. The section will explore whether modernity offers a way out of these dilemmas, or merely exacerbates them. It also considers whether Homi Bhabha's (1994) concept of hybridity helps us to throw a new light on cultural contestations.

4.1   The contentious tradition of widow immolation in India

Under colonial rule, indigenous cultural traditions are contested. In extreme cases, colonial administrations sought to destroy them on the grounds that they are remnants of an inferior culture. Frantz Fanon observed two different reactions among indigenous intellectuals, on the one hand, to adopt the culture of the occupying power and criticize their own national culture, and, on the other, to passionately defend the claims of that culture (Fanon 1967: 190). Putting the issue in this way leaves the colonial and the indigenous culture as fixed, homogeneous, mutually opposed entities, a view that does sit well with constructionist perspectives on culture. What happens under colonial rule, according to Bhabha (1994), is that both cultures are transformed in the colonial and postcolonial process, and therefore share, in different ways, in the condition of cultural hybridity.

This can be observed in one debate about tradition in India which has recently been revived: *sati*, whereby a widow is immolated along with her husband on his funeral pyre. Some Hindu nationalists consider *sati* as a religious tradition and argue that the practice should not have been outlawed. The abolition of *sati* by the British administration in 1829 followed a debate initiated by colonial officials who had recorded more than eight thousand instances of *sati*, mainly among upper-caste Hindus, and mainly in the eastern state of Bengal. This debate forced even those critical of colonialism to acknowledge the positive consequences of colonial rule, and gave rise to critical examinations of other Indian traditions.

However, Lata Mani (1987) has argued that the debate was actually about what constitutes authentic tradition, and which of the many traditions coexisting in India represented Indian society. She distinguishes three positions within the debate – the British official position and two indigenous positions, one progressive and the other conservative. Mani argues that the British official argument for the abolition of *sati* was not primarily concerned about its cruelty or barbarism from a Western perspective. It maintained that *sati* should be abolished because upper-caste Brahman scriptures required it to be a voluntary self-sacrifice by devoted wives, but in reality Indian women were not capable of consenting, and therefore had to be protected from pundits and crowds who might force them into *sati*. Uma Narayan (1997: 66) points out, following Mani's analysis, that the British (and Indian) participants in the debate distinguished between voluntary "good" *sati*, and involuntary "bad" *sati*, with "bad" *satis*, in the British view, being the more common. In pursuing this argument, the British administration elevated the scriptures to greater authority than they had previously held, and ignored the great variety in Hindu customs practiced in different regions and places. In other words, it simplified and generalized the complex set of traditions, beliefs, and customs of Hinduism in India.

The indigenous progressive discourse also criticized *sati* on the basis that the scriptures did not unequivocally command or condone this practice, particularly not if it was forced. Indian progressives such as Rammohun Roy argued that *sati* was a Bengali tradition because in this region women had inheritance rights to their husband's property, and *sati* was a way of denying widows these rights. Based on a different set of Hindu scriptures, conservative Indian intellectuals claimed that widows perform *sati* of their own accord and pleasure. According to their interpretation, *sati* was a great privilege as it bestowed on the widow the status of a goddess.

All three positions have in common that they sought to define a particular localized tradition as a timeless and structuring principle of Indian society. *Sati* became a powerful symbol of India because this debate took place "at an historical moment when 'shared national traditions' . . . became crucial components of political struggles for independence from colonial rule" (Narayan 1997: 67). In doing so they ignored other Hindu customs, as well as the secularist, rationalist Muslim rule prior to British colonization. Excluded are the women who are at the center of the debate about *sati*; not only have they no voice or agency, but they are "the site on which tradition is debated and reformulated" (Mani 1987: 153). Mani concludes that the conception of tradition emerging from this debate reinforces patriarchal notions of women as pure, weak, and submissive (Mani 1987). However, it can also be observed that the three positions outlined above differ in their construction of *sati*. Different scriptures are used to legitimize their claims to truth. Furthermore, it could be argued that both the British administration and the progressive Indian position operate in a space of cultural hybridity, where each seeks to incorporate aspects of the other's culture.

This controversy has been reignited in the 1980s, with the apparent revival of *sati* in parts of northern India. The ensuing debates are framed by the earlier colonial debate sketched out above. Much of the public condemnation in the Indian media, writes Narayan (1997: 68), "did not question or challenge *sati*'s status as 'Tradition' or as a 'Hindu ritual,' casting *sati* rather as a 'religious tradition,' that no longer deserved the endorsement of 'modern' right-thinking Hindus and Indians." Some Hindu fundamentalist groups, in contrast, sought to restore *sati* to the status of a national tradition. What is different about the contemporary debate is that feminist groups have challenged the traditional/ modern dichotomy underpinning it, arguing that "thoroughly modern motivations" explain the revival of *sati* (Narayan 1997: 71). There are the local

Figure 5.3 Map of *sati*-related sites in Rajasthan

economic motives of in-laws wishing to retain the widow's dowry, and to make financial profit out of her immolation by turning it into a focus for "religious tourism" (Narayan 1997: 70). At a broader political level, feminist analysis reveals that *sati* serves to reinforce patriarchal notions of Indian femininity, which we have already identified as central to Indian nationalist discourse. This two-pronged feminist challenge, according to Narayan (1997: 76), has been crucial in "generating widespread public concern over recent incidents of *sati*." She explains that

> Pointing to the mercenary economic and political motivations of many who "assisted" the *sati* suggests reasons to believe that outright coercion of the woman was involved. It helps to cast doubt on the "purity" or claimed religious motivations on the part of those whose "assistance" was crucial to the carrying out of a complicated public ritual. . . . Challenging the "ideal" of *sati* is a more difficult political move. . . . Questioning the validity of the stereotypes of wifely femininity that constitute the content of the "ideal of *sati*" is politically facilitated if the history and politics of *sati*'s tenuous status as an "Indian tradition" can be publicly articulated and widely communicated. (Narayan 1997: 76–7)

The crux of the general argument presented in this case study, then, is that traditions, whether "old" or "invented," must be understood as changing practices which can be imbued with different meanings and employed to serve a variety of purposes and interests. Rather than taking them to be fixed and sacred, they should be investigated, and, if necessary, contested. But Western perspectives on Third World traditions often remain caught within the dichotomy of traditional and modern, arguing either for respecting traditions that are seen as distinctively and essentially non-Western, or criticizing traditions for their role in legitimizing the oppression of particular social groups, e.g. women, in the case of *sati*. Thus, Western critics of Third World traditions should seek to establish a dialogue with their Third World counterparts whose familiarity with debates at the national level helps them to better understand the complicated politics of tradition (Narayan 1997).

4.2 Genocidal conflict over traditions in Central Africa

In many countries, conflict over tradition has expressed itself in widespread violence, such as the Hindu–Muslim riots in India following Ayodhya, or the civil war massacres in the Central African states of Rwanda and Burundi. Edward Said (1990) argues for a distinction to be made between a stable identity offered by affirmative agencies such as education, tradition, and the violent patriotism which alienated forces advocate. In other words, Said distinguishes between "good" and "bad" nationalism, but Chatterjee (1992) questions the Western liberal position from which this distinction is usually made. Instead, he suggests that we analyze these tensions and conflicts in terms of "the forcible marginalization of many who were supposed to have shared in the fruits of liberation" promised by anticolonial nationalism (Chatterjee 1992:

216). In the following paragraphs we look at genocide as an extreme form of marginalizing, or, in Malkki's (1995: 257) words, "one of the most extreme ways in which humanness and subjectivity can be denied to a social collectivity."

The post-independence conflicts between Tutsis and Hutus in Central Africa are taken here as a case study to explore this argument. Already under German and Belgian colonial rule (1900–62), the Tutsi minority was employed to extract surplus from the majority of Hutu agriculturalists in Rwanda-Urundi, as it was called then. But Liisa Malkki (1995) argues that it was competition for political power, rather than tribalism, that divided the population of the emerging states of Rwanda and Burundi into two opposing ethnic categories and rendered other social divisions less meaningful.

Burundi political leaders were drawn from the Tutsi minority, which also dominated the army. Several Hutu uprisings in the 1960s culminated in a "selective genocide" in 1972 of an estimated 150,000–200,000 Hutus by the army. Malkki's (1995) study focuses on the Hutus who had subsequently fled across the border to Tanzania. In comparing the understandings of nation and history of Hutus who had settled in refugee camps, and of those who had assimilated into Tanzanian towns, she traces the emergence of radically different traditions. Among camp refugees,

> exile was part and parcel of a more overarching historical trajectory of the Hutu as "a people," a trajectory which was traced back to the misty origins of the autochthonous nation of Burundi. The 1972 massacres which catapulted the Hutu into exile were seen as a moment of illumination and, also, of the violent, productive rupture of relations with the Tutsi. The beginning of asylum in Tanzania was, in the mythico-history, the "first birth" of a nation in exile. The culmination of exile was necessarily the future return to the "homeland." The realization of this millennial return was considered to depend on the way in which exile was lived by the collectivity of the Hutu. In this sense, exile represented a period of tests and lessons, a process of purification, which would make the Hutu as "a people" worthy of regaining the homeland. (Malkki 1995: 221–2)

Thus in the camps, Hutu refugees have reconstructed their national identity in ways which construct the Tutsi as outsiders. In contrast, town refugees tended to relegate the 1972 massacres and their own escape to the past, claiming that it was not relevant, or that it was not a problem in their present lives. They saw the camp refugees as living in the past, rather than adjusting to normal life in Tanzania and the new opportunities which it offered. In their own lived experience, the collective histories of the Hutu as a people did not make sense. Consequently, town refugees would also see less need to paint Tutsis as the outside enemy. The common experience which caused their exile is interpreted in conflicting ways by these two groups, with one nurturing racist definitions of Hutu nation, and the other regarding it as a "disabling variety of parochialism" (Malkki 1995: 233).

Malkki's study throws an interesting light on Homi Bhabha's concept of cultural hybridity. Both groups of Hutu refugees are displaced from their home country, forced to live in another land. It is from "borderlines" such as this, argues Bhabha (1994: 4), that challenges to dominant definitions of tradition and modernity, and to primordial identities, are launched, opening up "the possibility of a cultural hybridity that entertains difference without an assumed or imposed hierarchy" (Bhabha 1994: 4). What the discussion above shows is that marginalized groups such as the Hutu refugees in Tanzania do not necessarily become progressive challengers of primordial identities and imposed hierarchies; in fact, the opposite happened with camp refugees, whose reaction to their experience of repression and exile has been to construct an exclusive Hutu identity.

5   Globalization and the politics of identity

The recent re-emergence of violent ethnic conflict between Hutus and Tutsis in Rwanda brought to world attention the continued struggles about cultural identity and power in Third World countries. The First and Second Worlds have not been immune to violent eruptions of racial and ethnic conflict, as exemplified in the Los Angeles riots in 1992, and in the ethno-nationalist wars in former Yugoslavia in the 1990s. John Comaroff (1995: 244) confesses to feeling

> painful humility in the face of the sheer complexity of ethnic and nationalist struggles in the late twentieth century. Painful humility in the face of the terrifying violence, the homicide and genocide, committed in the name of the politics of identity across the great ethnoscapes of the planet. Humility, too, in the face of the banality of theory – of social scientific theory, that is – as it reduces an escalating world-historical reality to bloodless abstraction.

Social theory has not only been prone to banality, according to Comaroff (1995), but also to faulty analysis. European and American historians, as recently as Fukuyama and his thesis of the "end of history" (Fukuyama 1990; see chapter 2), have predicted that cultural pluralism will wither, making place for universally shared values. Sociologists predicted that societies will become color-blind melting pots into which ethnic and racial differences will gradually disappear. The process of decolonization, which was expected to reduce ethnic conflicts, only seems to have exacerbated cultural forms of consciousness and identity which – as most agree – have been invented by colonial powers. What explains the resurgence of the politics of identity in the late twentieth century?

In the previous two sections, we have explored the power and the vulnerability of invented traditions. These traditions are powerful when they successfully pass themselves off as being rooted in a distant past, are supported by influential social groups (i.e. colonial or nationalist elites), and at the same time incorporate popular cultural practices, which give meaning to the lived experience of ordinary people. But invented traditions are also vulnerable: to forces of modernization and globalization, which change people's lives and thus render invented traditions superfluous, parochial, or inadequate; and to challenges by social groups whose cultural practices had been excluded. At the level of social theory as well as social practice, the very notion of invented tradition undermines the power of traditions to shape coherent identities. In other words, traditions may lose their effectiveness when they are revealed to be invented.

At least, this is the case with the ways invented traditions are used by colonial administrations and nationalist elites, respectively to more effectively subjugate non-Western societies, and to galvanize a culturally heterogeneous population for the arduous and often painful task of modernization and development. As we have shown in the example of the "tradition" of widow immolation in India, colonial and nationalist elites often share invented traditions, despite their political antagonism. Indeed, nationalism – a modern European phenomenon – proved to be the most effective form of resistance against the colonizers, and we often find in local acts of resistance "the terms and categories of the colonizers, indeed turned back upon them but operating nonetheless to expand a powerful and inescapable colonial discourse" (Kaplan 1995: 13).

The resurgence since the 1980s of culture as a focus of political conflict in the Third World could therefore be attributed to invented traditions having a limited life expectancy. When the political, social, and economic conditions under which they made sense change, they no longer adequately perform the task of forging community and shared identity. According to one perspective, then, processes of globalization, both economic and cultural, have transformed Third World countries so fast and so much that the recently forged national identities no longer fit. The rise of "ethnic nationalisms" in East and Central Europe, "communalisms" in Asia, "tribalisms" in Africa, as well as racial, ethnic, and religious movements in other parts of the globe, including North America, Australia, and Western Europe (Kahn 1998: 1), could be interpreted as a variety of responses to globalization. These responses may on the one hand emphasize local cultural difference, and on the other plug into discourses of identity which transcend local and national boundaries.

A different perspective, put forward by some protagonists of the modernization school, looks at the resurgence of cultural politics as a sign of incomplete modernization. What justifies this view is the focus of many contemporary political movements on old primordialisms, such as race, ethnicity, and religion, which in a modern, enlightened society are firmly subordinated to universal values and national loyalties. The terms by which the politicization of culture is referred to in various world regions – ethnic, tribal, and communal in Europe, Africa, and Asia, respectively – reinforce the image of these movements as being pre-modern. We should remember, though, that these diverse terms, which supposedly refer to primordial sources of identity buried deep underneath the more modern national identity, in fact identify communities which were also imagined. Tanzania's tribes, for example, are largely the product of British colonial invention and active social engineering, as historian John Iliffe reveals. "The British wrongly believed that Tanganyikans belonged to tribes," and more generally, "that every African belonged to a tribe, just as every European belonged to a nation" (Iliffe 1979: 318, 323; see also Watts 1992 for Nigerian invented tribes). Accounts of "tribal" conflicts in Africa must therefore be approached with some degree of skepticism, as must references to racial/ethnic conflicts in Asian countries as "communal" violence. The races and ethnicities in multiracial Singapore, for example, were first codified by British colonial administrations. Today, the government of Singapore essentializes race "as an unchanging feature of the population" by insisting that a citizen's culture is determined by her or his race which is passed through the paternal line. The government reinforces racial identity "through compulsory school instructions in a 'mother tongue' language" additional to English (Chua 1998: 34, 35). Such government "inscription of communitarianism," as Chua (1998: 45) calls it, is also observed, in different ways, in other Asian countries.

Therefore, if contemporary cultural politics revolve around "primordial" notions of ethnicity, race, and tribe, we should be aware that these primordialisms "cannot be understood merely as premodern leftovers in a then emerging global order of 'rationalized' nation-states" (Kahn 1998: 24). Kahn points out that nationalism contains two apparently contradictory languages – a universal language of rights, national sovereignty, and citizenship, and a particularistic language of blood and territory, which often involves primordial concepts of race and ethnicity, or "the idea of a pure, original people or 'folk'" (Hall 1992: 295). Kahn (1998: 19) suggests that perhaps the problematizing of cultural identities in theory is part of a more general process of what might be loosely termed "post-nationalization," described as a situation where universalist and/or "blood and territory" elements of national identity are being challenged to the point of breakdown. As many scholars have pointed out, national boundaries are criss-crossed by the processes of globalization, and the relationship between universalist and particularist aspects of national identities is shaped by these processes. According to Stuart Hall (1992: 300), the impact of globalization on identities can take three contradictory forms:

> National identities are being *eroded* as a result of the growth of cultural homogenization. . . .

> National and other "local" or particularistic identities are being *strengthened* by the resistance to globalization.

> National identities are declining but *new* identities of hybridity are taking their place.

We can observe in the discussion about the fate of national identities in the face of globalization the same positions emerging as in the discussion about the impact of colonialism on the culture and tradition of the colonized (see e.g. Kaplan 1995 and discussion above). Kahn (1998) thus asks whether there is anything new about the cultural resurgence, and whether we need to look to globalization, postcolonialism, and/or postmodernism to understand it. On the other hand, Robins (1991: 41) asserts that "[c]ontinuity and historicity of identity are challenged by the immediacy and intensity of global cultural confrontations," and wonders whether it is "at all possible, in global times, to regain a coherent and integral sense of identity." One explanation for this difference in views is that Kahn's focus is on Southeast Asia, a region which has been shaped by global movements of goods, people, and ideas for centuries, while Robins is looking at Britain, which had transformed other parts of the world for centuries but maintained a "centred and 'closed' identity" (Hall 1992: 309) until very recently. Fragmented and hybrid identities are not a new phenomenon in Southeast Asia, neither is the return to "roots" or the embrace of new values. Indeed, as we have pointed out above, Third World governments have, in different places and different times, actively helped to engineer all or any of these three responses to change.

5.1 Globalization's impact on national identity

Discussing cultural identities in Thailand, Craig Reynolds (1998) stresses the long tradition of cosmopolitanism in Thailand. He notes that traditional Thai manuals "on such matters as astrology, medicine, and grammar had a capacity to absorb new material while appearing to remain unchanged," and that their fragmented, repetitive, and unsystematic character stemmed from the integration of foreign cultural elements (Reynolds 1998: 124). Openness also characterized Thai attitudes toward Western knowledge, values, and abilities, although in the early twentieth century Thai monarchs warned against "slavish copying of the West," for fear of losing national identity and sovereignty. However, Reynolds (1998: 134–5) argues that

> In the globalizing epoch of post-nationalism, when telecommunications are breaking down older forms of loyalty to national communities, it is culture, rather than sovereignty, that is increasingly one of the irreducible "givens" that identifies and differentiates a community. . . . The extensive Tai diaspora in northern Southeast Asia has become of great interest to Bangkok-based intellectuals and culture managers, because the Tai peoples scattered throughout the region offer an answer to the dilemma of how it is possible to remain Thai/Tai in the globalizing age.

If cultural tourism to ethnic Tai communities in neighboring countries is one novelty made possible by globalization, the international marketing of Thainess to bring tourists into the country is another.

> The international tourism campaigns are often coupled with domestic cultural themes, so that a kind of feedback mechanism operates which confirms that local identity is shaped in part by how the country is being sold to foreigners. What has been commodified for the international tourist may be consumed by the Thai national, whether that something is a self-image or a handicraft. (Reynolds 1998: 135)

Another feature of globalization is that national borders become increasingly porous. In the case of Thailand's borders, this process is encouraged by the

Thai government's decentralization policy, which aims at developing the "remote" regions of the country, and the Thai military's economic interests in the resource-rich border regions which reach into neighboring Cambodia and Myanmar. The danger to national identity, as Reynolds suggests, is that people in these flourishing "border zones may not only develop economically but also culturally and politically 'away' from the citizenship into which they were born" (Reynolds 1998: 117). In conclusion, he argues that different constituencies in Thailand contest and appropriate globalization for a variety of purposes, and are engaged in the search for new identities and ways of looking at the world.

5.2   Counter-hegemonic critiques of globalization

Not all societies have founded their sense of identity on openness and adaptation, however. As Kahn (1998: 25) reminds us, "[a]ppeals to blood, territory, race continue to characterize cultural conflict at all levels in Southeast Asia and beyond." He suggests these conflicts can be traced to critiques of an old universalism, or rejections of new kinds of cosmopolitanism that some scholars embrace. Anti-modernist Third World movements perceive universalist and newer cosmopolitan sets of values as predominantly Western, and fear that they will undermine their cultural identities and traditions. Kahn is sympathetic to this view, and points out that

> a close reading of much of what now passes for globalization theory can be seen to be a defence of at least certain dimensions of the American dream. In this, Appadurai is himself a significant figure, arguing that the particular relationships being forged among diasporic communities in the United States might be the model for the world in the future. This subtle re-insertion of the United States back into the world sounds suspiciously . . . like those older arguments for the superiority of Britain, Holland and France, based on the universality of their value systems when compared to the parochialism and particularisms of Asia. (Kahn 1998: 25)

A slightly different argument is put forward by Michael Ignatieff (1993), who argues that today only the privileged can be cosmopolitan, while the rest has little option but to cling fiercely to blood and territory. He argues that "[g]lobalism in a post-imperial age permits a post-nationalism consciousness only for those cosmopolitans who are lucky enough to live in the wealthy West," and, one could add, in wealthy enclaves of the rest of the world. "It has brought chaos and violence for the many small peoples too weak to establish defensible states of their own" (Ignatieff 1993: 13). In other words, how globalization influences people's cultural identities depends a great deal on their class position, with groups that are disadvantaged by the processes of globalization being more likely to uphold or revive particularist traditions.

Islamic fundamentalism is an often cited example of a local (and at the same time global) movement which invokes ancient traditions to resist the intrusion of modern Western cultural values on Muslim communities. One manifestation of Islamic politics of identity occurred in the Nigerian city of Kano in the late 1980s. The following case study of the so-called Maitatsine insurrection in Kano draws on Michael Watts's (1992) insightful analysis of the intersection between class and culture, and local and global change. He paints a picture of Kano as a "bustling, energetic city forged in the crucible of seventeenth- and eighteenth-century trans-Saharan trade," which "developed as West Africa's preeminent entrepot" during the sixty years of British colonial rule. Then the oil boom in the 1970s transformed Kano "seemingly overnight, from a traditional Muslim mercantile center of 400,000 into a sprawling, anarchic metropolis of over 1.5 million" (Watts 1992: 26). The boom was shortlived, and by the mid-1980s, government overspending, widespread corruption, and collapsing oil prices had led to a crippling foreign debt. The structural adjustment program prescribed by the International Monetary Fund (IMF) to put Nigeria's economic house in order created "massive retrenchment and economic hardship" (Watts 1992: 27). The IMF's intervention hit particularly hard the lower-income groups, which had benefited little from the oil boom. Already in 1981, Dudley Seers, a scholar who headed an International Labor Organization mission to Nigeria, had found that rural and urban poverty had worsened despite an average annual increase in government revenue of 40 percent in the 1970s.

It is in this context, argues Watts (1992), that the emergence of an Islamic movement in Kano should be understood. The movement's followers came from a disenfranchized segment of the popular classes, consisting of predominantly young, single male, dry season migrants, who had become semi-permanent city residents working in the construction sector, or as lowly service workers. Another social stratum was rooted in the "koranic networks," which brought rural students into the city to study with lay clerics during the dry season. "These networks were sustained by a sort of urban moral economy – begging and almsgiving as part of a normative set of relations between rich and poor – which served both to extend Islam into the countryside and to provide a measure of social and ideological integration for Hausa society as a whole" (Watts 1992: 41–2). What galvanized these strata was a charismatic figure, Maitatsine, who interpreted the Qu'ran (the holy book of Islam) with direct reference to their experience of the oil-based capitalist development taking place in Kano. Maitatsine challenged the materialist values which Kano's ruling classes had embraced, denouncing the modern accouterments that the oil boom had brought, such as "bicycles, apparel, cigarettes, buttons, cars, and so on" (Watts 1992: 22), and asked his followers to rid themselves of money, and instead trust in Allah to provide for them. Watts (1992: 58) explains the appeal of this movement by "[t]he fantastic intermingling of the old and new that Maitatsine wove from certain Muslim texts and the experience of oil-based capitalism" which shaped "new personal and collective identities, and in so doing fashioned a curious and ambiguous sort of Muslim modernity."

By the late 1970s the movement had grown large enough to cause concern to Kano's authorities, and a decade later the police were finally sent in to dissolve Maitatsine's community. Fierce resistance led the army to intervene and bombard the area where Maitatsine's followers had retreated. An estimated 10,000 people were killed in the fighting, some 100,000 more were rendered homeless, and the city sustained serious physical damage.

The Maitatsine movement can therefore be interpreted as a local, class-specific response to Nigeria's globalization via the international economy of oil. Against the emerging cosmopolitanism of the Kano elites it offered a "counter-hegemonic image of community imagined from within Islam itself," drawing on selected traditions (Watts 1992: 30). In this sense, Islam, rather than constituting a monolithic source of identity which is by default anti-modernist, is itself a focus of struggle over the definition and interpretation of Muslim tradition (Watts 1992).

5.3   Witchcraft and development in Africa

In this final section we examine how a particular group of globalizing agents, the international development institutions, contributed to reinforcing supposedly "traditional" practices in Africa. We focus on witchcraft, a long-standing obstacle to development and change in Africa, in the views of many modernizing outsiders. Its resurgence in recent years has been interpreted as one example of a more general retreat of Africans to their "age-old traditions" – precolonial traditions, that is (Chabal 1996: 32). The belief in witchcraft is widespread, according to Kohnert (1996: 1348), who notes its prevalence among poor and rich, illiterate and Western-educated alike, and among various religious affiliations. While witchcraft occasionally has been used by poor people in their struggle against oppression – for example, in order to discredit individuals who have enriched themselves through development projects – Kohnert argues that it serves mainly to legitimize oppression and exploitation. Since most belief systems involving witchcraft rely on secrecy and hierarchical systems of knowledge, one could assume that "the promotion of transparency and the democratization of decision-making processes . . . in politics, as well as in society and economy, . . . would also most likely contribute to the gradual eradication of witchcraft beliefs" (Kohnert 1996: 1352).

But the policies of good governance and democratization, pushed by the World Bank in recent years, seem to have underestimated the adaptability and power of traditional belief systems and relations of power which they legitimize. "Even Western-educated, high-ranking African politicians with excellent international reputations," says Kohnert (1996: 1353) could "feel a pressing need for protection against the menaces of occult powers," which have to be assuaged by serving "the interests of patronage and local solidarity first," before the interests of the nation. In the eyes of the international donor community, this means falling prey to corruption and/or nepotism, punishable by withdrawal of development assistance. Kohnert's analysis fits comfortably within a modernization approach, as far as his assessment of witchcraft as a traditional African belief system is concerned, although he does understand that cultural change does not occur from one day to the next.

However, Kohnert also suggests that development projects themselves, which often carry explicit political goals, such as the empowerment of women or of poor people, put increasing stress on the balance of power in the project area. The favoring of some groups at the expense of other (elite) groups triggers witchcraft accusations which could have serious detrimental effects on the project. In another study, Adam Ashforth (1996: 1200) makes the point that jealousy is the "most commonly cited source of the hatred driving the desire to inflict harm through witchcraft." In Soweto, where witchcraft, according to Ashforth (1996: 1191) is "of concern to everyone," jealousy is widely discussed in terms of achievement, success, and generally progress. He interprets jealousy as a result of feeling inferior and the real experience of underprivilege, as well as expressing the desire for equality. In this study, witchcraft is the weapon of the weak:

> Anyone who progresses sufficiently to arouse jealousy . . . knows that they can be a target for witchcraft aimed at bringing misfortune, disease, and death upon their house. They thus must ensure their protection through both social and spiritual means. They must redistribute enough through feasts and charity to ensure that they are well-liked and respected by their relatives (both living and dead) and neighbours; they must be able to command sufficient military force (in the absence of effective policing) to defend their property and their women; and they must employ witchdoctors powerful enough to repel witchcraft. (Ashforth 1996: 1202–3)

This rather more positive view of witchcraft, as a gauge of social strain which helps to keep inequalities in wealth and power under control, is tempered by evidence of increasingly violent ways of punishing people suspected to be witches. Furthermore, Ranger (1996: 276) points out that the postcolonial revival of witchcraft in Africa is reminiscent of witchcraft in colonial Africa. In both cases, "violent insecurity led to great outbursts of witch-finding." In colonial times, these outbursts were caused by the destruction of tradition by colonial agents, while in postcolonial times, it is the lack of a new common tradition and purpose. To push Ranger's point a little further, it can be argued that the structural adjustment programs which have been imposed by the international development institutions on many African countries constitute a new round of colonization: imposing new structures of government and turning people's lives upside down, spreading insecurity, and disrupting traditional ways of coping with poverty (e.g. Stewart with Basu 1995). The resurgence of witchcraft, then, is not so much the antithesis of or obstacle to modernization, but one of its effects.

6 Summary

This discussion on tradition and its relationship to modernization and development has come full circle. It started by arguing that tradition, rather than being age-old practices that stand in the way of modernization, is often invented by colonial or postcolonial government bureaucracies to facilitate government and modernization. Invented or selectively retrieved traditions can become the focus of modern economic activities, employed to bring tourist dollars into the country. The last section has shown that such traditions are also used to make sense of, or even galvanize resistance to, the failed promises of development. The chapter has also paid attention to struggles over traditions, for example, struggles between interest groups wanting to assert their power over the nation, or struggles waged by those who have been marginalized in the construction of the dominant culture. We have argued that traditions, as cultural resources, play a crucial role in nationalist and ethnic politics, although in most "ethnic" struggles, other interests – social, economic, political – may be the driving forces.

There remain important questions to be answered about the rise of ethnic conflicts and break-up of nation-states, particularly in the world beyond the West, and how they could be prevented. One important insight, offered in different contexts by Chatterjee (1986) and Kahn (1998), is that ethnic conflicts, far from being pre-modern leftovers, are prefigured in the internal contradictions of nationalism, which contains both a particularistic and a universal language. The case studies in section 5 have shown that the global spread of capitalism and liberal democracy sharpens conflict over cultural traditions in many places, instead of, as one might expect, bringing about a homogeneous world culture. The Slovenian writer Slavoj Žižek claims that "irrational fundamentalism" (as found in ethnic, nationalist, or other cultural movements) is an inherent reaction to the universalization of the logic of capital, and stresses the need to "call into question the 'normality' of liberal-democratic capitalism" (Žižek 1994: 220):

> The way to break out of this vicious circle is not to fight the "irrational" nationalist particularism but to invent forms of political practice that contain a dimension of universality beyond Capital; the exemplary case today, of course, is the ecological movement.

This brings us back to the critics of developmentalism, such as Escobar (1995), and their search for "post-development" alternatives (see chapter 3). We can, however, also revisit another "third way" for the excluded which we introduced in chapter 2: the path taken by the Khmer Rouge in Cambodia. In Žižek's view, the Pol Pot regime was not a case of "exotic barbarism"; rather, it represents "a desperate attempt to avoid the imbalance constitutive of capitalism without seeking support in some previous tradition supposed to enable us mastery of this imbalance." The Khmer Rouge had understood correctly, argues Žižek, "the complementary relationship of modernity and tradition: any true return to tradition is today a priori impossible, its role is simply to serve as a shock-absorber for the process of modernization" (Žižek 1994: 224–5) Hence their radical anti-capitalism and endeavor to erase an entire tradition and start from the zero-point.

References

Anderson, B. 1991: *Imagined Communities*. 2nd edition. London: Verso.

Ang, I. and Stratton, J. 1995: The Singapore way of multiculturalism. *Sojourn*, 10 (1), 65–89.

Anthias, F. and Yuval-Davis, N. 1989: Introduction. In N. Yuval-Davis and F. Anthias (eds), *Woman-Nation-State*. London: Macmillan, 1–15.

Ashforth, A. 1996: Of secrecy and the commonplace: witchcraft and power in Soweto. *Social Research*, 63 (4), 1183–234.

Banton, M. 1998: Are there ethnic groups in South Asia? *Ethnic and Racial Studies*, 21 (5), 990–4.

Bhabha, H. 1994: *Locations of Culture*. London: Routledge.

Bolitho, H. 1937: *Royal Progress*. London: B. T. Batsford.

Chabal, P. 1996: The African crisis: context and interpretation. In R. Werbner and T. Ranger (eds), *Postcolonial Identities in Africa*. London: Zed Books, 29–54.

Chatterjee, P. 1986: *Nationalist Thought and the Colonial World. A Derivative Discourse*. London: Zed Books.

Chatterjee, P. 1992: Their own words? An essay for Edward Said. In M. Sprinker (ed.), *Edward Said: A Critical Reader*. Cambridge, MA: Blackwell, 194–220.

Chatterjee, P. 1993: *The Nation and its Fragments. Colonial and Postcolonial Histories*. Princeton: Princeton University Press.

Chow, R. 1994: Where have all the natives gone? In A. Bammer (ed.), *Displacements. Cultural Identities in Question*. Bloomington and Indianapolis: Indiana University Press, 125–51.

Chua, Beng-Huat 1998: Racial Singaporeans: absence after the hyphen. In J. S. Kahn (ed.), *Southeast Asian Identities: Culture and the Politics of Representation in Indonesia, Malaysia, Singapore, and Thailand*. London/New York: I. B. Tauris Publishers. Singapore: Institute of Southeast Asian Studies, 28–50.

Clammer, J. R. 1993: Deconstructing values: the establishment of a national ideology and its implications for Singapore's political future. In G. Rodan (ed.), *Singapore Changes Guard: Social, Political and Economic Directions in the 1990s*. New York: St Martin's Press/Longman Cheshire, 34–51.

Comaroff J. L. 1995: Ethnicity, nationalism and the politics of difference in an age of revolution. In J. L. Comaroff and P. C. Stern (eds), *Perspectives on Nationalism and War*. Yverdon (Switzerland): Gordon and Breach, 243–76.

Concise Oxford Dictionary, 9th edition, 1995. Oxford: Clarendon Press.

Eller, J. D. 1999: *From Culture to Ethnicity to Conflict. An Anthropological Perspective on International Ethnic Conflict*. Ann Arbor: University of Michigan Press.

Fanon, F. 1967:*The Wretched of the Earth*. Translated by Constance Farrington. Harmondsworth: Penguin.

Foucault, M. 1980: *Power/Knowledge: Selected Interviews and Other Writings, 1972–1977*. Ed. Colin Gordon. Brighton: Harvester Press.

Foucault, M. 1986: *The Foucault Reader*. Ed. Paul Rabinow. Harmondsworth: Penguin.

Freeman, M. 1998: Theories of ethnicity, tribalism and nationalism. In K. Christie (ed.), *Ethnic Conflict, Tribal Politics. A Global Perspective*. Richmond, Surrey: Curzon, 15–34.

Gellner, E. 1964: *Thought and Change*. London: Weidenfeld and Nicolson.

Government of India 1982: *Report of the Backward Classes Commission*, Vol. 1. Simla: Government of India Press.

Guha, S. 1998: Lower strata, older races, and Aboriginal peoples: racial anthropology and mythical history past and present. *The Journal of Asian Studies*, 57 (2), 423–41.

Hall, S. 1992: The question of cultural identity. In S. Hall, D. Held, and T. McGrew (eds), *Modernity and its Futures*. Cambridge: Polity in association with The Open University, 273–326.

Hastings, A. 1997: *The Construction of Nationhood, Ethnicity, Religion and Nationalism*. Cambridge: Cambridge University Press.

Hobsbawm, E. 1983: Introduction: inventing traditions. In E. Hobsbawm and T. Ranger (eds), *The Invention of Tradition*. Cambridge: Cambridge University Press, 1–14.

Ignatieff, M. 1993: *Blood and Belonging. Journeys into the New Nationalisms*. London: BBC Books.

Iliffe, J. 1979: *A Modern History of Tanganyika*. Cambridge: Cambridge University Press.

Kahn, J. S. 1998: Southeast Asian identities: introduction. In J. S. Kahn (ed.), *Southeast Asian Identities: Culture and the Politics of Representation in Indonesia, Malaysia, Singapore, and Thailand*. London/New York: I. B. Tauris Publishers. Singapore: Institute of Southeast Asian Studies, 1–27.

Kaplan, M. 1995: *Neither Cargo nor Cult: Ritual Politics and the Colonial Imagination in Fiji*. Durham, NC: Duke University Press.

Kohnert, D. 1996: Magic and witchcraft: implications for democratization and poverty-alleviating aid in Africa. *World Development*, 24 (8), 1347–55.

Lerner, D. 1968: Modernization. In *International Encyclopedia of the Social Sciences*, Vol. 10. New York: Macmillan/Free Press.

Lowe, L. and Lloyd, D. 1997: Introduction. In L. Lowe and D. Lloyd (eds), *The Politics of Culture in the Shadow of Capital*. Durham, NC: Duke University Press, 1–32.

Malkki, Liisa H. 1995: *Purity and Exile: Violence, Memory, and National Cosmology among Hutu Refugees in Tanzania*. Chicago: University of Chicago Press.

Mani, L. 1987: Contentious traditions: The debate on *sati* in colonial India. *Cultural Critique*, 7, 119–56.

Maybury-Lewis, D. 1992: *Millennium. Tribal Wisdom and the Modern World*. New York: Viking.

Narayan, U. 1997: *Dislocating Cultures. Identities, Traditions and Third World Feminism*. New York: Routledge.

Norval, A. J. 1999: Rethinking ethnicity: identification, hybridity and democracy. In P. Yeros (ed.), *Ethnicity and Nationalism in Africa. Constructivist Reflections and Contemporary Politics*. Basingstoke: Macmillan, 81–100.

Ranger, T. 1983: The invention of tradition in colonial Africa. In E. Hobsbawm and T. Ranger (eds), *The Invention of Tradition*. Cambridge: Cambridge University Press, 211–62.

Ranger, T. 1993: The invention of tradition revisited: the case of colonial Africa. In T. Ranger and O. Vaughan (eds), *Legitimacy and the State in Twentieth-century Africa*. Basingstoke: Macmillan in association with St Anthony's College, Oxford, 62–111.

Ranger, T. 1996: Postscript: colonial and postcolonial identities. In R. Werbner and T. Ranger (eds), *Postcolonial Identities in Africa*. London: Zed Books, 271–81.

Ranger, T. 1999: Concluding comments. In P. Yeros (ed.), *Ethnicity and Nationalism in Africa. Constructivist Reflections and Contemporary Politics*. Basingstoke: Macmillan, 133–44.

Rao, N. 1994: Interpreting silences: symbol and history in the case of Ram Janmabhoomi/ Babri Masjid. In G. C. Bond and A. Gilliam (eds), *Social Construction of the Past. Representation as Power*. London: Routledge, 154–64.

Reynolds, C. J. 1998: Globalization and cultural nationalism in modern Thailand. In J. S. Kahn (ed.), *Southeast Asian Identities: Culture and the Politics of Representation in Indonesia, Malaysia, Singapore, and Thailand*. London/New York: I. B. Tauris Publishers. Singapore: Institute of Southeast Asian Studies, 115–45.

Robins, K. 1991: Tradition and translation: national culture in its global context. In J. Corner and S. Harvey (eds), *Enterprise and Heritage: Crosscurrents of National Culture*. London: Routledge, 21–44.

Roy Burman, B. K. 1979: Challenges and responses in tribal India. In M. S. A. Rao (ed.), *Social Movements in India, Volume II: Sectarian, Tribal and Women's Movements*. New Delhi: Manohar, 101–22.

Said, E. W. 1990: Third World intellectuals and metropolitan culture. *Raritan*, Winter, 27–50.

Smith, A. 1991: *National Identity*. London: Penguin.

Smith, A. 1995: *Nations and Nationalism*. Cambridge: Polity.

Stewart, F. with Basu, A. 1995: Structural adjustment policies and the poor in Africa: an analysis of the 1980s. In F. Stewart (ed.), *Adjustment and Poverty. Options and Choices*. London: Routledge, 138–70.

Sunindyo, S. 1998: When the earth is female and the nation is mother: gender, the armed forces and nationalism in Indonesia. *Feminist Review*, 58, Spring, 1–21.

Watts, M. 1992: The shock of modernity: petroleum, protest, and fast capitalism in an industrializing society. In M. Watts and A. Pred, *Reworking Modernity. Capitalisms and Symbolic Discontent*. New Brunswick: Rutgers University Press, 22–58.

Werbner, R. and Ranger, T. (eds) 1996: *Postcolonial Identities in Africa*. London: Zed Books.

Williams, R. 1988: *Keywords: A Vocabulary of Culture and Society*. Revised and expanded edition. London: Fontana Press.

Yeros, P. 1999: Introduction: on the uses and implications of constructivism. In P. Yeros (ed.), *Ethnicity and Nationalism in Africa. Constructivist Reflections and Contemporary Politics*. Basingstoke: Macmillan, 1–14.

Young, C. 1993: The dialectics of cultural pluralism: concept and reality. In C. Young (ed.), *The Rising Tide of Cultural Pluralism*. Madison, WI: The University of Wisconsin Press, 3–35.

Young, C. 1994: Evolving modes of consciousness and ideology: nationalism and ethnicity. In D. E. Apter and C. G. Rosberg (eds), *Political Development and the New Realism in Sub-Saharan Africa*. London and Charlottesville, VA: University of Virginia Press, 61–86.

Yuval-Davis, N. 1997: *Gender & Nation*. London: Sage Publications.

Žižek, S. 1994: *Tarrying with the Negative. Kant, Hegel, and the Critique of Ideology*. Durham, NC: Duke University Press.

6 Human Rights, Cultural Difference, and Globalization

Contents

1 Introduction

Human rights is a key theme through which the old and the new ways of thinking about development and culture have been played out in international debates. Since the 1980s human rights have played an increasingly important role in development policies, North–South relations, and globalization. The first document that outlines human rights as a multifaceted and universal set of rights to which humans are born is the Universal Declaration of Human Rights (United Nations 1948). Two subsequent international and legally binding instruments, the International Covenant on Economic, Social and Cultural Rights (United Nations 1966a) and the International Covenant on Civil and Political Rights (United Nations 1966b), focus in greater detail on different and sometimes conflicting aspects of human rights. Several other documents have also emerged under the auspices of the United Nations (UN) to address the rights of particular groups, e.g. children and women (figure 6.1). While development discourse has always claimed universal validity, human rights only became an integral part of development policies when relations between the capitalist West and the communist East began to warm, and the Cold War to ease. In this chapter we explore how contemporary debates over human rights and their relevance to developing countries in many ways epitomize the debates over culture and development we traced in the earlier chapters of this book. Is the surge of

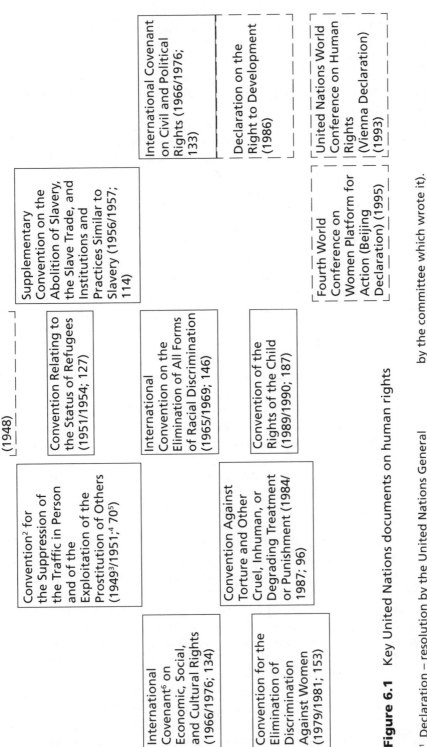

Figure 6.1 Key United Nations documents on human rights

[1] Declaration – resolution by the United Nations General Assembly.

[2] Convention – a legally binding international agreement between states or countries that provides standards of conduct for governments to fulfill. Conventions may also be called treaties, covenants, or pacts.

[3] Year of adoption (approval of the final text of the convention by the committee which wrote it).

[4] Year of entry into force (a convention enters into force after it has acquired a specified number of ratifications).

[5] Number of countries which had ratified the convention by mid-1977 (and thus agreed to be legally bound by its provisions).

[6] Covenant – see footnote 2 on Convention.

interest in human rights an indication for the degree to which the nations and societies of this globe have come to share principles and values concerning the relations between individuals, governments, and institutions? Or does it indicate a crisis of the very notion of universal human rights? A crisis which has been brought about by critiques of Western philosophical and political thought posing as universal truth, and by political challenges to Western political and cultural supremacy.

Contemporary debates about human rights characteristically revolve around one or both of two sets of dichotomies, that of universalism versus particularism, and that of individualism versus collectivism/communalism. What human rights advocates highlight as the main virtue of the concept – that human rights by definition apply to human beings everywhere and at all times – is criticized by a range of critics as its main fault; the claim to universal application ignores the fact that rights are based on cultural traditions and may vary from society to society. Other critics pay more attention to the ways in which human rights tend to focus on the individual, and argue that this artificially separates individuals from their communities, and underplays the importance of duties and sacrifice for the greater good. Another strand of criticism holds that human rights' focus on the individual fails to recognize the common oppression which large groups of individuals experience in many societies. According to these critics the notion of rights vested in the sovereign individual are of little help to women, ethnic minorities, or the economic disadvantaged, who would be better advised to pursue their collective interests. Furthermore, there has been a long-standing debate over which human rights are the most relevant in a particular place and a particular time. In this debate, social and economic rights are often set against civil and political rights, based on arguments that draw on the other two dichotomies, and also on the political antagonism between socialist and capitalist perspectives.

In the context of development discourse, these three debates sometimes overlap and become projected onto the perceived cultural divide between the West and the non-West. A common view is that human rights are "grounded in the Western, natural rights philosophy" which was "first mooted by the Graeco-Roman philosophers and subsequently refined, during the Middle Ages, by Christian philosophers and theologians," until it "ripened during the Enlightenment" into the idea of "the rights of man" to life, liberty, and the pursuit of happiness (Carmen 1996: 178). Critics argue that therefore, their application to non-Western societies can be opposed on the grounds that they do not form part of the cultural and political heritage of these societies, and their enforcement worldwide is another expression of Western cultural imperialism. Singled out among the human rights not suitable to non-Western countries, at least while they are struggling to develop, are civil and political rights. However, other scholars, speaking both from Western and Third World positions, have pointed out that the radical liberal thought underpinning the concept of human rights has been very useful in justifying anticolonial struggles, and maintain relevance for the new social movements mushrooming across the world today. Some have argued that the concept of human rights has roots in all of the major world religions (Ishay 1997), and that the West can claim neither sole parentage nor that it has been a particularly rigorous foster parent.

We begin this chapter by asking what explains the heightened interest in human rights precisely at a time when notions of progress, modernization, and development are under attack. In subsequent sections, we examine the implications of the debates over human rights for three different policy areas, focusing particularly on the points where they intersect with discourses of development and culture. This involves, first, exploring the debate over civil and political rights versus social and economic rights, a debate which sometimes is simplified as one between human rights versus the right to development. In using the issue of child labor in developing countries to bring this debate into sharper focus, we acknowledge that child labor was the subject of human rights debates during the European industrialization in the nineteenth century, and has recently been identified as a human rights concern in many Third World countries by international institutions and national governments. The issue of child labor brings out several contentious questions within the broader human rights debate, from the question of what constitutes childhood in different historical and cultural settings, to the question of whether a child's right to a childhood should take precedence over a child's right to a basic standard of living. It also opens up questions over development policies and globalization processes, as the struggle to defend children's basic human rights sits uneasily with wider issues of economic restructuring, and the "conversion" of many developing countries to market economies. It can be argued that these processes have increased the use of children as workers in a world where increasing numbers of poor families have nothing but their labor to sell in order to survive. The issue of child labor therefore appears to reveal the contradictions between the social and economic rights of the Human Rights Declaration, and basic civil rights of children, within a context of global and local power relations that shape individuals' ability to satisfy their basic needs.

Second, in looking at the ways in which the human rights debate is argued out in relation to the rights of women, we focus on cultural difference versus universal rights. When and why do claims that women suffer from similar rights violations across the globe work to undermine the role and status of particular groups of women, as well as imposing Western concepts of femininity on them? How, on the other hand, can an insistence on differences between women and their specific cultural heritage have similar effects? This extends the arguments in chapter 4 on the politics of difference.

Perhaps the most contentious dispute over human rights since the Second World War is over collective rights. The right to self-determination is therefore the focus of our third policy theme. As we have discussed in chapter 5, the right of nations to determine their own government gave political legitimation to anticolonial struggles for independence, despite its origin in the European Enlightenment. In recent decades the right to self-determination is claimed mainly by ethnic minority groups and indigenous peoples (many of whom refer to themselves as First Nations), and is sometimes violently pursued by them, and fiercely resisted by the "nation-states" which govern them. Practices of genocide and "ethnic cleansing," which occurred in the 1990s in countries as different as Rwanda and Bosnia, take the right of an ethnic group to self-government to its extreme, and deny individuals not belonging to that group the right to live in the same territory, or indeed to live at all. Genocide also demonstrates the importance of balancing seemingly contradictory human rights; it denies humanness to one group in order to implement the right to self-determination of another (Malkki 1995; see chapter 5). On the other hand, many of today's governments do not respect the human rights of all their subjects, and many ethnic minorities face systemic discrimination by their governments. Should ethnic minorities and indigenous peoples whose human rights are not being protected by their governments be able to count on international assistance in their quest for self-determination? Or is self-determination something that only the individual and her/his collective group can assert on their own, rather than an established principle, as suggested in the UN Declaration of Human Rights.

2   The human rights discourse and the discourse of development

The Universal Declaration of Human Rights was proclaimed by the General Assembly of the UN in 1948. Its preface states that "disregard and contempt for human rights have resulted in barbarous acts which have outraged the conscience of mankind," indicating the historical moment at which it was drafted (United Nations 1948). Only three years earlier, the Second World War had ended in fascist Germany's defeat, which began to reveal the crimes against humanity committed by the German government and its many helpers. The UN Charter, which established the United Nations only weeks after the end of the war, was an immediate response to it. It pledges the intention of the initial member governments of the UN "to save succeeding generations from the scourge of war" and "to reaffirm faith in fundamental human rights" (United Nations Charter 1945). The terms "universal" and "fundamental" in these charters were important. They leave no doubt that these human rights are intended to apply to each and every human being, regardless of any difference. This is reaffirmed in Article 2 of the Universal Declaration of Human Rights, which states that:

> Everyone is entitled to all the rights and freedoms set forth in this Declaration, without distinction of any kind, such as race, color, sex, language, religion, political and other opinion, national or social origin, property, birth or other status.

The final article of the Universal Declaration (Article 30) asserts the permanence of these rights and freedoms which no state, group, or person would be permitted to destroy. Across the globe governments and people accept that the principle of human rights must be defended, but, as Steven Lukes (1993) points out, at the same time human rights are also violated virtually everywhere. Lukes argues that these violations are less an expression of well-founded challenges and criticisms of human rights – which we discuss below – than of hypocritical governments failing to uphold them because it may not be in their own interest. However, it is also possible that the human rights to material well-being, for example, are beyond the capability of some Third World governments. The Universal Declaration's Article 28 thus recognizes the need for "a social and international order in which the rights and freedoms set forth in this Declaration can be fully realized." Is the increase in official documents and the rise in awareness about human rights in the last two decades a sign that we are moving toward an international order that is better suited to the respect of human rights?

Clearly, colonialism did not constitute an appropriate international order for the realization of human rights. At the same time as the major European powers and the United States prided themselves on their universal human rights charters and bills of rights, these rights were denied to their colonized subjects, as well as to women and other marginalized groups in the colonial motherlands. French philosopher Jean-Paul Sartre (1967: 8) captured the growing realization of the colonized that the West's human rights discourse was only lip service, and did not apply to them. While at first the colonized patiently tried to explain to the West "your humanism claims we are at one with the rest of humanity but your racist methods set us apart," a more belligerent position emerged in the 1950s when colonized people turned their backs on the West and "its universal rights of man":

> Leave this Europe where they are never done talking of Man, yet murder men everywhere they find them, at the corner of every one of their own streets, in all the corners of the globe.

The accusation of Western hypocrisy regarding universal human rights endures even after most colonies have gained their independence. In the postwar decades the Cold War power struggle between the capitalist and the communist sectors of the world often operated as a shield for widespread human rights violations. As Immanuel Wallerstein (1995: 157) points out, between 1945 and 1970 human rights

> were conspicuous by their absence or diminished role everywhere. From the purge trials in Eastern Europe to various forms of dictatorship in Third World countries ... it was scarcely an era of the triumph of human rights. But even more significantly, it was not a period in which there was very much rhetorical concern with human rights by the world's political movements. Advocates of human rights causes everywhere were seen as threatening national unity in the cold war struggle.

The United States' support of brutal dictatorships in Latin America and Africa from the 1950s to the 1970s is one example; the lack of protest over the killings of hundreds of thousands of Indonesian civilians during the military coup in 1965 is another. In contrast, the killing of six Indonesian student protesters in May 1998 by the Indonesian armed forces evoked an avalanche of protests across the world (e.g. Landler 1998; Shenon 1998). Since the mid-1970s, the higher international profile of human rights, and the accumulating treaties and declarations on human rights indicate a gradual shift toward an international climate that is more favorable to the universal pursuit of human rights. But the rosy images of a global world of nation-states working in partnership toward common goals conflict with the reality of widening economic disparities between the most highly and the least developed countries.

Hence, the Declaration on the Right to Development, adopted by the UN General Assembly in 1986, sought to give more prominence to the Third World countries' concerns with improving well-being through development. It stresses equality of opportunity as the main principle relating to both individuals and nations, and declares that states should cooperate with each other in ensuring development and eliminating the obstacles to development. However, the lack of support for the Declaration by some of the most important donor countries, including the United States, Britain, Germany, Japan, Sweden, and Denmark, reveals their resistance to establishing development in general, and development aid in particular, as a right which states can call upon (Tomasevski 1993a).

Worse, the policies which Western-dominated international institutions such as the International Monetary Fund and the World Bank formulated in the 1980s to address the economic problems of Third World countries often resulted in basic human rights being undermined. As Katarina Tomasevski (1993a: 4), a researcher at the Danish Center of Human Rights, highlights

> The definition of "development" in the late 1980s did not leave much room for human rights. While human rights necessitate that governments create conditions for the realization of human rights, particularly in education, nutrition and employment promotion, the precepts of the time insisted on decreased public spending and diminishing the public sector.

Tomasevski (1993a: 5) thus calls "paradoxical" the prominence of human rights in the 1990s: global free markets as the dominant recipe for development remains, but Third World governments are now also requested to become more accountable to their citizens through free elections. "Some inherent link," she claims, "is assumed therein where free elections produce free markets, and free markets lead to free elections." While the right to own property in the Universal Declaration of Human Rights may be considered as a justification for a free-market approach, critics argue that it does not enshrine the free market as the only acceptable economic system, and should not overrule the right of people to decide over how they wish to organize their economy. Nevertheless, development assistance from Western donor countries and international agencies has increasingly been made dependent on the receiving country adopt-

An article in the *Guardian Weekly* describes as a yearly propaganda war the mutual human rights accusations between the United States and China (Gittings 1999). The article is illustrated with a table, which demonstrates clearly the long-standing debate over civil and political versus economic and social rights (see table 6.1).

Table 6.1   How the US sees China – how China sees the US

How the US sees China	How China sees the US
How rights have deteriorated sharply with a crackdown on organized political dissent.	Poor, disabled, elderly, blacks suffer human rights abuses.
Prison conditions are harsh; numerous executions follow summary trials.	Huge prison population includes 200,000 mental patients.
Websites are blocked and some foreign broadcasts blocked.	Temperatures in Texas death row cells are unbearably high.
Force is used to compel abortion or sterilization.	Voter turnout is the lowest among all developed countries.
Subversive Muslim activity in Xinjiang is the subject of a crackdown.	Richest 1 percent of Americans own more than 90 percent of the wealth.
There are up to 10 million sex workers in China.	41.7 million Americans lack medical insurance.
Reports of female infanticide are credible.	The United States is an abyss of racial discrimination, especially in the jobs market place.
Independent trade unions are illegal and activists jailed.	Only 10 percent of members of the US Congress are female.
Controls over Tibetan monasteries are tight and Tibetan schools are closed down.	

Source: Gittings (1999). (Statistics from US State Department; China Country Report on Human Rights Practices 1998; Xinhua; Human Rights Records in the US; Ren Yanshi.)

ing a free-market approach, *and* advancing their citizens' civil and political rights, mainly by taking steps toward free and democratic elections.

The recent prominence of human rights in development policy revives one of the most enduring debates over human rights – the question whether the right to material well-being has precedence over other human rights, such as that to participate in one's country's government, or the freedom of expression. Some Third World governments have argued that social and economic development is their most urgent task, and that "human rights begin with breakfast!" In order to satisfy their citizens' basic needs, in a world of skewed power relations, unequal trade, and uneven development, it may be necessary to trade off other human rights, particularly those that are considered to be shaped by the Western tradition of liberalism. How is this trade-off justified between social and economic rights on the one hand, and civil and political rights on the other?

3   Human needs and human rights – a trade-off?

It was in the nineteenth century that social and economic rights emerged on political agendas in Europe. As Ishay (1997) points out, socialist thinkers challenged the unlimited pursuit of property rights, and argued that it precluded the universal political equality advocated by liberals: "They thus embraced rights that were not secured at the time by capitalism: the prohibition of child labor, the establishment of factory health and safety measures, and universal voting rights (including women's right to vote)" (Ishay 1997: xxv). Other so-called second-generation rights, such as the rights to a fair wage, social security, and equal pay, became later enshrined in several articles of the Universal Declaration of Human Rights (see table 6.2). When the Declaration was drawn up, the United States, Britain, and France and their allies wanted an emphasis on civil and political rights, while the Soviet Union and its socialist allies wanted to see a greater commitment to the right to a decent standard of living. The resulting document reflects the greater influence of the Western countries at the time, with only one article referring to the right not to be poor. As Nikki van der Gaag (1998) points out, after the demise of the Soviet empire it is now the countries of the "Majority World" which defend the right to material well-being as being more relevant than the other human rights spelled out in the Universal Declaration. This so called "liberty trade-off" (Donnelly 1989: 165) is based on the assumption that the exercise of civil and political rights might threaten development plans, lead to short-term thinking geared to winning elections, and render governments incapable of insisting on unpopular but necessary sacrifices for development. Particularly in the 1970s and 1980s, some Western scholars sympathized with this view, and argued that "a more liberal political system may be incapable of producing and sustaining the reorientation in the economy necessary for these types of success" in satisfying basic needs, as shown in socialist Cuba and China (Stewart 1985, quoted in Donnelly 1989: 164), or in capitalist South Korea.

Table 6.2   The various types of rights in the Universal Declaration of Human Rights

Major aspects of human rights	Articles of the Universal Declaration of Human Rights
basic civil rights	**Article 1**: "All human beings are born free and equal in dignity and rights." **Article 2**: "Everyone is entitled to all the rights and freedoms . . ." **Article 3**: "Everyone has the right to life, liberty and the security of person." **Article 4**: "No one shall be held in slavery or servitude." **Article 12**: Right to protection of privacy, family home, correspondence, and honor and reputation. **Article 13**: "Everyone has the right to freedom of movement . . ."
political rights	**Article 21**: "Everyone has the right to take part in the Government of his country."
rule of law	**Article 5**: "No one shall be subjected to torture." **Article 6**: "Everyone has the right to recognition everywhere as a person before the law." **Article 7**: "All are equal before the law." **Article 8**: "Everyone has the right to an effective remedy by the competent national tribunals . . ." **Article 9**: "No one shall be subjected to arbitrary arrest, detention or exile." **Article 10**: "Everyone is entitled to full equality to a fair and public hearing . . ." **Article 11**: Right to be presumed innocent until proved guilty. **Article 14**: Right to asylum from prosecution.
freedom of expression and association	**Article 19**: "Everyone has the right to freedom of opinion and expression . . ." **Article 20**: "Everyone has the right to freedom of peaceful assembly and association."
equality of opportunity	**Article 16**: Equal right to marry and to found a family. **Article 23**: Right to work, equal pay for equal work, just and favorable remuneration, and right to form and join trade unions. **Article 26**: "Everyone has the right to education."

Table 6.2 *contd.*

Major aspects of human rights	*Articles of the Universal Declaration of Human Rights*
material well-being	**Article 17**: "Everyone has the right to own property . . ."
	Article 22: "Everyone, as a member of society, has the right to social security . . ."
	Article 24: "Everyone has the right to rest and leisure . . ."
	Article 25: "Everyone has the right to a standard of living adequate for the health and wellbeing of himself and of his family."
cultural rights	**Article 15**: "Everyone has the right to a nationality."
	Article 18: "Everyone has the right to freedom of thought, conscience and religion . . ."
	Article 27: "Everyone has the right to freely participate in the cultural life of the community."
	Article 29: "Everyone has duties to the community," including the duty to respect the rights and freedoms of others.

Source: United Nations (1948).

One particular manifestation of this position is found in some East Asian government leaders, e.g. Malaysian Prime Minister, Dr Mahathir Mohamed, and former Prime Minister of Singapore, Lee Kuan Yew, who have used the concept of "Asian values" to signal their countries' adherence to principles that are different from universal human rights. An important place among "Asian values" is the right to economic development. Another "Asian value," the willing subordination of the individual to the community and to higher authorities, tends to be interpreted by Western onlookers as a lack of civil and political liberties. Some Asian leaders have spoken out strongly against Western interference. They argue that Western countries use their preferred human rights – mainly civil and political rights – as a pretext to justify cutting aid and restricting trade with developing countries, in order to bolster their own economic dominance and keep the rest of the world poor. In this way, Western countries violate the right of poor people in developing countries to survive and to attain a decent standard of living.

It is not only conservative Asian leaders who make such allegations. Radical Indian author Winin Pereira has also come to the conclusion that Western powers use human rights as a political tool to "shore up oppression against the peoples of the Majority World" (van der Gaag 1998: 8). One way to respond to these criticisms is to give more equal emphasis to the two kinds of rights, social and economic on the one hand, and civil and political on the other, and to stress their mutual connection. Van der Gaag (1998) sees such a shift occurring in a speech in 1997 by the High Commissioner for Human Rights, Mary Robinson, who stated that poverty was the source of numerous basic human rights violations. Others maintain that it was the World Conference on Human Rights in Vienna in 1993, when the world's governments (185 states were represented) reaffirmed that all human rights were interrelated and interdependent, and pledged to promote the universal respect for, and observance and protection of, all human rights. If the Vienna World Conference can be seen to reflect the participating governments' perspectives, then it indicates that there is universal agreement about the universality and the indivisibility of human rights. One right should not be traded off against another.

In practice, however, human rights often conflict with each other. One example where such conflict is evident is in the debate over child labor in the Third World.

3.1   Child labor and human rights

The images of young children cleaning shoes or selling sexual services in city streets, or working in coal mines, carpet factories, or as soldiers, rarely fail to evoke feelings of outrage among most observers, yet many children, particularly but not only in Third World countries, must work in order to survive. The International Labor Organization estimates the number of child workers under the age of 15 at 250 million, with the majority found in Asia. However, due to its smaller overall population, Africa is the continent of child labor – in some countries of sub-Saharan Africa, as many as half of all children between 10 and 14 are working (International Labor Organization 1997). The nature of their work is extremely varied, as a picture of just one city in the relatively prosperous state of Gujarat in India reveals (table 6.3). In this place, children are employed to clean cement bags (for recycling), cut diamonds, assist in shops, do domestic work, and many other types of activities (Swaminathan 1998). What is the problem with children working? Why the outrage?

The case for abolishing child labor

One objection to child labor is that it frequently involves violating the human rights of child workers. Children (defined by UNICEF and the ILO as persons under the age of 16) are entitled to basic human rights under international law, and while they do not have the same rights as adults (e.g. the right to participate in their government), this is compensated by an acknowledgment that children have special needs with regard to care and protection. Some types of child labor, e.g. where the child is "sold" to an employer to repay the debts of

Table 6.3   Distribution of child workers in Bhavnagar (India) by occupation and gender, 1995

Occupation	Boys	%	Girls	%	All	%
Clean cement bags	332	10.6	708	28.2	1,040	18.5
Plastic rope plaiting	111	3.6	129	5.1	240	4.3
Diamond cutting	439	14.1	151	6.0	560	10.5
Family shops	104	3.3	30	1.2	134	2.4
Waste collection	172	5.5	125	4.9	297	5.3
Animal husbandry	130	4.2	148	5.9	278	4.9
Trades[1]	120	3.8	155	6.2	275	4.9
Manual labor	82	2.6	53	2.1	135	2.4
Factory worker[2]	226	7.2	169	6.7	395	7.0
Construction	84	2.7	157	6.2	241	4.3
Domestic chores[3]	13	0.4	144	5.7	157	2.8
Domestic service	12	0.4	277	11.0	289	5.1
Shop assistant[4]	465	14.9	130	5.2	595	10.6
Tea stalls and hotels	508	16.3	13	0.5	521	9.2
Conservancy work[5]	16	0.5	30	1.2	46	0.8
Household production[6]	80	2.6	61	2.4	141	2.5
Ship-breaking[7]	106	3.4	19	0.7	125	2.2
Garage worker	102	3.3	2	0.1	104	1.8
Beggar	16	0.5	5	0.2	21	0.4
No response	5	0.2	2	0.1	7	0.1
Total	3,123	100	2,509	100	5,631	100

Source: Swaminathan (1998: 1518).

[1] Trades refers to skills like potters, cobblers, tailors.
[2] Factory work refers to a range of factories including iron smelting, cotton spinning and weaving, chemical, rubber, and engineering units, biscuit making and bakeries.
[3] Domestic chores refers to unpaid domestic service for the family.
[4] Shop assistants include vendors, and helpers in different types of establishments.
[5] Conservancy work refers to cleaning and sweeping for the municipality (public spaces) and for offices and factories.
[6] Household production includes cottage manufacture, such as *bidi* (local type of cigarette) rolling.
[7] Ship-breaking refers to the dismantling and recycling of ships.

his or her parents, or in the cases of child trafficking and child prostitution, violate the basic human right to life, liberty, and the security of person (Article 3) and the right not be held in slavery or servitude (Article 4).

In most cases, child labor infringes the right to education (Article 26), as it

Deterring child labor in export garment factories in Bangladesh

One example of Western opposition to child labor is the "Child Labor Deterrence Act," introduced as a bill to the United States' Senate by Senator Tom Harkin in 1992. In an article in the *New Internationalist*, Shahidul Alam (1997) reports that the intended beneficiaries, the children working in the garment factories of Bangladesh, feel they are worse off now:

> According to a press release by the garment employers in October 1994: "50,000 children lost their jobs because of the Harkin Bill." A UNICEF worker confirms "the jobs went overnight." . . . A senior International Labour Organization (ILO) official has no doubt that the original bill was put forward "primarily to protect US trade interests" – Tom Harkin is sponsored by a key US trade union, and cheap imports from the Third World were seen as undercutting American workers' jobs. "When we all objected to this aspect of the Bill," says the ILO official, "which included a lot of resistance in the US, the Bill was amended, the trading aspect was toned down, and it was given a humanitarian look." It was when it was reintroduced after these amendments in 1993 that the Bill had its devastating impact in Bangladesh.
>
> The child workers themselves find it particularly hard to interpret the US approach as one of "humanitarian concern." When asked why the buyers have been exerting such pressure against child labour, Moyna, a ten-year-old orphan who has just lost her job, comments: "They loathe us, don't they? We are poor and not well educated, so they simply despise us. That is why they shut the factories down." Moyna's job had supported her and her grandmother but now they must both depend on relatives. Other children have had no alternative but to seek new kinds of work. When UNICEF and the ILO made a series of follow-up visits they found that the children displaced from the garment factories were working at stone-crushing and street hustling – more hazardous and exploitative activities than their factory job. . . .
>
> [Factory o]wners see Tom Harkin as a well-meaning soul with little clue about the realities of garment workers' lives. "As a student, I too hailed the Bill," says Sohel, the production manager at Captex Garments. "I was happy that someone was fighting for children's rights. But now that I work in a factory and have to turn away these children who need jobs, I see things differently. Sometimes I take risks and, if a child is really in a bad way, I let them work, but it is dangerous."
>
> The notion that a garment employer might be helping children by allowing them to work may seem very strange to people in the West. But in a country where the majority of people live in villages where children work in the home and the fields as part of growing up, there are no romantic notions of childhood as an age of innocence. Though children are cared for, childhood is seen as a period for learning employable skills. Children have always helped out with family duties. When this evolves into a paid job in the city neither children nor their families see it as anything unusual. In poor families it is simply understood that everyone has to work.

hampers the child's opportunity to go to school and develop skills, knowledge, and other human capabilities. Connected to this argument is an understanding of children as being entitled to a particular way of life which corresponds to their status as children – the entitlement to a childhood which is protected from the concerns of the adult world.

A second strand of argument pursued by opponents to child labor is based on economic considerations. It is argued that the tasks children are asked to do can jeopardize their health, welfare, and safety; that working conditions are often poor and unregulated, and pay is generally much lower than for adults. Children are usually not in a position to defend their rights as workers, and are therefore more easily exploited by employers than adult workers. Child labor undermines efforts to achieve development in Third World countries because it tends to lower wage levels, fosters a poorly educated labor force, and imposes future costs on society as a result of impairing workers' health through inappropriate work at a young age. Furthermore, in the view of some Western countries, a soft line on child labor in many Third World countries encourages migration of labor-intensive low-skilled industries to these countries, with the result of reducing employment opportunities in Western countries which take a harder line. This perspective has inspired controversial campaigns against child labor in the West – controversial because they seem to be fueled mainly by partisan economic interests, rather than a concern for the rights and well-being of children (see box). As Ben White (1996: 6) points out, well-publicized initiatives such as the Harkin Bill in the United States, and the campaigns to boycott products made with child labor, mainly focus on the export sector in Third World countries, "which represents a very small percentage of child employment in most countries, and with some exceptions (the South Asian carpet industry may be one) is not the sector in which the worst working conditions and abuse of children are found."

The case for regulating child labor

In 1989, the UN adopted the Convention on the Rights of the Child, which specifies a wide range of rights to which children are entitled under international law. Among the long list of articles, one (Article 32) stipulates the right to protection from work that threatens the child's health, education, physical, mental, spiritual, moral, or social development, and requests governments to set a minimum age of employment and to regulate working conditions. However, this does not rule out child labor as such, and other articles can be interpreted to legitimize certain acceptable kinds of child labor. For example, Article 3 states that the best interests of the child must be the primary consideration, and Article 27 confirms the right of a child to an adequate standard of living.

Another position, taken by some development organizations, governments, and children's representatives, therefore maintains that child labor should be regulated, rather than simply prohibited. Poor children should be given the opportunity to earn an income through safe and non-exploitative work, at the same time as being provided educational opportunities. In defending a regulationist viewpoint on child labor, some refer to the history of European development, and point out that every industrializing society goes through a period where cheap labor – including that of children – is exploited. Others take a cultural angle at the issue and argue that the prevailing ideas of child-hood in many non-Western societies are different from those of the West, in that they perceive childhood as an "apprenticeship for adulthood," during which children learn useful skills for later life, and contribute to family in-comes. This view is shared by many of the child workers who attended a Conference on Child Labor in Amsterdam in 1996 as representatives of the emerging child workers' movements in various parts of the Third World. Find-ing himself in conflict with the abolitionist policy of the adult trade union movement and the International Labor Organization, one Peruvian child workers' representative, Vidal Cocoa Mamani, stressed the pride and sense of responsibility which child workers feel when they are able to contribute to family incomes. Thus the right to work should not be restricted to adults (Swift 1997: 21). The 1989 UN Convention on the Rights of the Child makes space for such a possibility, with articles on children's rights to freedom of expres-sion and association (Articles 12 and 15), suggesting a redefinition of children as "capable social actors" (Ennew 1995: 23–4, quoted in White 1996: 7).

The regulationist perspective, with its many facets, requires that a distinc-tion be made between "child work" – the more acceptable forms of children's work which may be beneficial – and "child labor" – the exploitative forms of

Figure 6.2   Children washing clothes at the lake in Udaipur, India

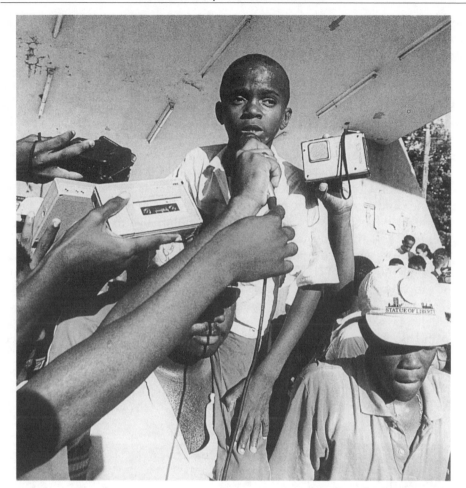

Figure 6.3   A child addresses an election rally in Haiti

children's work. Such a line, however, is not easy to define, and, as White (1996: 10) suggests, "[t]he term 'child labour' itself has over the years become laden with such emotional connotations, and with such long institutional history, that it might be best to scrap it completely from future discussions." Instead, he suggests that we think of child work along a continuum from intolerable on one end of the spectrum, through detrimental and neutral to beneficial on the other end. This would enable policy makers and society more generally to focus on the removal of children from the intolerable, exploitative types of work, while otherwise aiming to transform children's employment from detrimental to neutral or beneficial types of work.

But there are other problems with taking a regulationist perspective. One is that regulations already exist in many countries, but are not always effectively enforced. Where laws on child labor have been tightened up and more actively enforced, the employment of children tends to become more hidden and less easy to count and regulate – take, for example, domestic work, child prostitution, or family workshops. There is little information available about the situation of children working in small workshops or family establishments, although 75–85 percent of all child workers in Asia, for example, are to be found within family activity in rural areas alone (Falkus, Blackburn, Brasted, Kaur, and Wright, 1997), which is often unpaid and sometimes highly exploitative. The lack of attention to these forms of child labor is partly based on the assumption that "working for one's parents, at home, without pay is more acceptable than working for others, outside the home, for money" (White 1996: 5). However, cultural constructions of the family as a caring and nurturing environment for children do not always correspond with reality, and therefore, as White (1996) argues, many children prefer work in factories to work at home.

4   Gender, cultural difference, and the universality of human rights

The debate over whether human rights are universal, or culturally specific constructs of the West, has waged for almost two decades now (Pollis 1996; Narayan 1998), but originates with the birth of the Universal Declaration (Preis 1996). In a nutshell,

> cultural relativists see the Universal Declaration of Human Rights as enumerating rights and freedoms which are culturally, ideologically, and politically nonuniversal. They argue that current human rights norms possess a distinctively "Western" or "Judeo-Christian" bias, and hence, are an "ethno-centric" construct with limited applicability. Conversely, universalists assert that human rights are special entitlements of all persons. They are grounded in human nature and as such, are inalienable. (Preis 1996: 288)

A cursory look at the texts included in the *Human Rights Reader* (Ishay 1997) suggests an almost pure Western, or Judeo-Christian, intellectual heritage of human rights, especially since the Enlightenment period. One way of interpreting this situation, from a universalist stance, is to point out that the European Enlightenment and subsequent emergence of industrial capitalism put the West in a position to transcend the limitations of local experience, reflect on universal human morality, and establish state legal and administrative systems to implement rights. Human rights are based in European liberalism only because Europe was the first region to modernize. Some Western human rights scholars thus take an evolutionist approach, similar to the "stages of development" view of the modernization school of development (see chapter 2), and suggest that people choose "which aspects of a 'new' culture they wish to adopt and which aspects of the 'old' they wish to retain" (Donnelly and Howard 1987, quoted in Preis 1996: 296). The implication is that as societies modernize, cultures also modernize and become more in tune with the liberal doctrine of human rights.

However, cultural relativists – both scholars and politicians – have long argued that in many non-Western societies, the liberal doctrine of human rights does not resonate with people's views of the world and of social relations, and that notions of rights will continue to vary from one culture to another (Pollis 1996). East Asian societies are often cited as evidence for the claim that particularly in highly developed non-Western societies, culturally specific values and social principles – such as the so-called "Asian values" – are vehemently defended by their leaders against claims of human rights' universal validity (see chapter 2). Whether the leaders of non-Western countries faithfully reflect their society's cultural traditions or redefine them in selective – and politically advantageous – ways is a question which has also raised discussion (e.g. Narayan 1998; Pollis 1996), and will be considered below.

Paradoxically, both sides of the universalist–relativist divide have drawn support for their arguments from discussions on gender and human rights. Supporting the notion of universality, Ernesto Laclau (1995: 106) points out

> When Mary Wollstonecraft, in the wake of the French Revolution, defended the rights of women, she did not present the exclusion of women from the declaration of rights of man and citizen as a proof that the latter are intrinsically male rights, but tried, on the contrary, to deepen the democratic revolution by showing the incoherence of establishing universal rights which were restricted to particular sectors of the population.

On the other hand, feminists and non-feminists have resisted claims that human rights are universal, with the argument that many human rights-based interventions into cultural practices affecting Third World women smack of colonialism, and reflect a Western lack of understanding for non-Western cultures and femininities. The debate about *sati* (whereby a widow is burnt on her husband's funeral pyre) in India is one example where these arguments have been heard (see chapter 5).

4.1   Cultural relativism and the notion of culture

Over the past two decades, several developments have bolstered the arguments of cultural relativists. Postmodernist critics of the Enlightenment project claim that its premise of the universality of reason and science is without basis. As McGrew (1992: 97) explains, postmodernism "denies the possibility of universal reasoning and accounts of the social life which claim universal validity," and instead views the human world as pluralistic and incoherent, refusing any attempt "to impose order on it through totalizing and universal theoretical discourses." In claiming that there is no such thing as a universal truth, or a universally applicable theory, postmodernism leads to a relativist stance on human rights.

Further support for the relativist position comes from some aspects of postcolonial critiques which brand universal rights as a Eurocentric invention, relevant only to the dominant sectors of nineteenth-century Europe. In an excellent discussion of the relationship between universalism and particularism, Laclau (1995) argues that European culture of the nineteenth century indeed considered itself as the incarnation of the universal. Pre-modern Europe held on to Christianity's conception of the universal being comprehensible only to God, who can choose to convey it to humans through irrational events, such as miracles, or by giving it a particular body, such as in the incarnation of God in Jesus. The Enlightenment sought to replace God with universal reason.

> European universalism had precisely constructed its identity through the cancellation of the logic of incarnation and, as a result, of the universalization of its own particularism. So, European imperialist expansion had to be presented in terms of a universal civilizing function, modernization and so forth. The resistances of other cultures were, as a result, presented not as struggles between particular identities and cultures, but as part of an all-embracing and epochal struggle between universality and particularisms – the notion of peoples without history expressing precisely their incapacity to represent the universal. (Laclau 1995: 97)

Thus Europe, by assuming that it represented, for a time at least, the universal, set itself up as superior to other cultures, and in effect legitimized inequality – based on class, race, culture, gender – by claiming to be the privileged agent of universal reason (see chapter 1). In some critics' view, this presents ample reason for taking a cautious or even hostile approach to human rights' alleged universal applicability. Laclau himself, however, argues that the link between Eurocentrism and universalism should not lead to the rejection of universalism; rather, the universal principles Europeans were the first to advocate should be decentered, separated from social agents, and expanded to become more inclusive.

Besides such philosophical arguments, the main source of support for cultural relativism comes from the anthropological tradition. As we pointed out in chapter 1, anthropological theories of culture have stressed cultural difference between the West and the non-West or Third World, depicting it as a gulf not only of lifestyle and belief systems, but also of time. Among the earliest rejections of the Universal Declaration of Human Rights was that of the American Anthropological Association, on the grounds that "the rights of Man in the Twentieth Century cannot be circumscribed by the standards of any single culture" (Herskovits 1947: 543, quoted in Preis 1996: 286–7).

In recent years, however, the theory of cultural relativism, so dominant for the first sixty years of the twentieth century, has lost its relevance within anthropology. Under the impact of decolonization, globalization, and postmodernism, anthropologists have gradually abandoned the conception of culture as a homogeneous, integral, and coherent unity (see chapter 1). A growing number of anthropologists no longer subscribe to the "peoples and cultures" view underpinning cultural relativism, which assumes that the world consists of separate societies, each with its own distinctive culture, radically different from others. Gupta and Ferguson (1997) point out two lines of anthropological critique emerging since the 1950s. One line, influenced by dependency theory and Marxist analyses of the capitalist world system, argues that ideas of cultural separateness and isolation have been made redundant by powerful regional and global forms of connectedness – economic as well as cultural. The other, more recent line focuses on the critique of representation (e.g. Clifford and Marcus 1986), revealing "[t]he apparent boundedness and coherence of culture as something made rather than found" (Gupta and Ferguson 1997: 2). In particular, the postcolonial experiences of social marginality, brought about by colonial domination, diaspora, displacement, have shattered "[t]he natural(ized), unifying discourse of 'nation,' 'peoples,' or authentic 'folk' tradition, those embedded myths of culture's particularity" (Bhabha 1994: 172). This shift in anthropological thinking about culture should help in re-evaluating the contemporary relevance of the universality–relativity debate.

Perhaps more important than these theoretical developments, at least for the practice of human rights, are the ways in which human rights values are interpreted and appropriated at the local, everyday level. Notwithstanding their European origins, human rights have become a vehicle for articulating a multitude of concerns all over the globe (Preis 1996: 289), often revealing deep social divisions and conflicts over cultural traditions in Third World countries. The fact that "remote" indigenous peoples in Australia, local women's groups in Vanuatu, and child workers in India draw on human rights in order to advance their particular interests may seem paradoxical, but becomes less so if we remind ourselves of the work of Stacey Pigg (1996) and others, described in chapter 3. In researching how universal discourses, such as development or human rights, are interpreted on the ground, Pigg (1996) points out that the local is not simply a homogeneous and spatially delineated place dominated by traditional culture, but rather "comes into being through engagement with the wider systems of many beyonds" (Pigg 1996: 192). In terms of our examples, if indigenous peoples, local women, and child workers came into their contemporary being through the wider systems of colonialism, patriarchy, and capitalism, then why should now the universal discourse on human rights be irrelevant to them?

In the next section, we explore these arguments in relation to the debates on gender and human rights. As we indicate in chapter 4, cultural relativist arguments are also invoked in discussing the question whether development – and, more specifically, international development assistance – should aim toward achieving equality between women and men. The relativist–universalist dichotomy thus re-emerges in Martha Nussbaum's (1995a: 4) question, "whether . . . we should seek a universal measure or measures of quality of life for all men and women, or defer, instead, to the many different norms that traditional cultures have selected."

4.2   Male bias, cultural essentialism, and women's human rights

Over the past two decades, local and international campaigns on women's human rights have gathered momentum, marked by strong representations at recent UN conferences on human rights (in Vienna in 1993) and on women (in Beijing in 1995). What explains the push for women's human rights to be recognized and protected? Based on the assessment there is no country in the world where women's quality of life is equal to that of men (Nussbaum 1995a), and that "the unequal status of women . . . results from gender discrimination" (Tomasevski 1993b: ix), human rights activists and some feminist scholars argue that the concept of "human" in human rights be expanded to include women. According to this perspective, two key factors have hampered the recognition of women's rights as human rights. First, male bias in the early formulations of human rights as the "Rights of Men" has been carried into the Universal Declaration of Human Rights, both in terms of language (the frequent use of "his" and "he"), and in its tendency to view human rights as rights exercised by male heads of households against each other, and against their government. Susan Moller Okin (1998: 34–5) elaborates on the need to rethink human rights in the light of women's experiences:

> A growing body of feminist human rights literature argues that the male bias of human rights thinking and its priorities had to change for women's rights to be fully recognized as human rights. The problem is not so much that men's claims to rights A, B and C have been recognized, whereas women's claims to these exact same rights have not – which is not to say that this never happens. The problem is that existing theories, compilations, and prioritizations of human rights have been constructed after a male model. When women's life experiences are taken equally into account, these theories, compilations, and prioritizations change significantly. Examples of issues that come to the fore, instead of being virtually ignored, include rape . . ., domestic violence, reproductive freedom, the valuation of childcare and other domestic labor as work, and unequal opportunity for women and girls in education, employment, housing, credit, and health care.

By reading the reality of women's lives into the gaps between the abstract formulations in the key human rights conventions, a reprioritized and retheorized catalogue of human rights emerges in which women's difference from men is acknowledged and incorporated (Brems 1997).

A different approach would prefer to see a truly universal human being emerging from a revised concept of human rights. Martha Nussbaum believes that our concern for women's rights and needs requires that we "focus on what is common to all, rather than on differences," i.e., "the capabilities and needs that join all humans, across barriers of gender and class and race and nation" (Nussbaum 1995b: 63, 61). In what is at the same time a universalist and an anti-essentialist argument, Nussbaum strongly argues against defining women's capabilities differently from men's, on the grounds that gender-specific spheres and norms often involve female spheres and norms being devalued, and that "in the present gender-divided state of things we cannot get beneath culture reliably enough to get the necessary evidence about basic capabilities" (Nussbaum 1995b: 102). With this view that gender is culturally and socially constructed, Nussbaum is able to circumvent both patriarchal and feminist claims to women's essential difference which have, in different ways, underpinned arguments about the irrelevance of human rights to women. Male bias in the earlier human rights documents is a reflection of the society that produced these documents, and more recent declarations and conventions have made significant steps toward widening the definition of human rights to include women (Okin 1998). The Convention for the Elimination of All Forms of Discrimination Against Women (CEDAW) (United Nations 1979) was one such step, and the Vienna Declaration (United Nations 1993) and the Beijing Platform for Action (United Nations 1995) constituted further progress along this path.

The second factor which, human rights activists and some feminists argue, has undermined the application of human rights to women is related to culture. They point out that discrimination on the grounds of sex, despite being prohibited in the Universal Declaration of Human Rights, is "frequently justified as being in accordance with many of the cultures – including religious aspects of these cultures – practiced in the world today" (Okin 1998: 33). A large number even of those governments that have ratified the CEDAW are either unable or unwilling to enforce its provisions. This indicates that many governments adopt a cultural relativist position on human rights which does not go as far as rejecting altogether the relevance of human rights to their female citizens, but which allows them to reject specific rights, or to reject the interpretation of specific aspects of rights. Even more subtly, some cultural relativists might accept a right with all its components and with its general interpretation, but reject the classification of a particular cultural practice as a violation of that right. The interpretation of female circumcision as a legitimate cultural practice, rather than as cruel, inhuman, or degrading treatment under the Convention for the Abolition of Torture, is one frequently cited example (Brems 1997: 144; Okin 1998: 38).

In the eyes of those who want women's rights to be recognized as human rights, "'respecting cultural differences' has increasingly become a euphemism for restricting or denying women's human rights" (Okin 1998: 36). The link between cultural difference and gender difference is such that Martha Nussbaum argues for a choice to be made between "the voice of tradition and a critical universalism" (that is, a universalism able to critically examine the basis of its own assumptions), on the grounds that "many traditional norms do not make full equality in the many functions of life a goal for females" (Nussbaum 1995a: 4). In the lead-up to the UN Conference on Human Rights in Vienna (United Nations 1993), feminist human rights campaigners successfully lobbied at the local, governmental, and international levels for women's human rights to be recognized as prevailing over the rights of communities to practice their culture. The final document of the Vienna Conference spells defeat for the cultural relativist cause, stating that

> While the significance of national and regional particularities and various historical, cultural and religious backgrounds must be borne in mind, it is the duty of States, regardless of their political, economic and cultural systems, to promote

and protect all human rights and fundamental freedoms. (Vienna Declaration, quoted in Brems 1997: 151)

Two years later, the UN's Fourth International Conference on Women in Beijing again reasserted the universality of human rights, this time making direct reference to the conflict between women's rights and cultural rights. In the Beijing Declaration and Platform for Action, which emerged from the conference as an international guideline for women's policies, we read

Any harmful aspect of certain traditional, customary or modern practices that violates the rights of women should be prohibited and eliminated (Beijing Declaration 1995: 112, quoted in Okin 1998: 46)

While these developments are celebrated as a victory by feminist human rights activists, they also have raised concern among other groups, as we discuss below. First, however, we should consider two issues that contributed in bringing together the critiques of male bias and cultural relativism. One is the realization that the private sphere of the household has been the site where the human rights of women are most vulnerable to abuse, while at the same time being perceived by many nationalists as the "inner sanctum" of a country's culture (Chatterjee 1993: 121; see chapter 5). As Okin (1998) points out, the individual's right to privacy in "his" personal and family life (Universal Declaration of Human Rights, Article 12) may hide, and even legitimize, the abuse of women's human rights. At the same time, the family home, and particularly its female inhabitants, has been heralded as an important site for protecting and nurturing cultural traditions. Opening up the notion of human rights to include violations not only *of* the private sphere but *in* the private sphere thus brings together feminist critiques of male bias and universalist critiques of cultural particularism.

Globalization is the second issue that has promoted the convergence of these two strands of critique. There is widespread evidence of global capital undermining women's human rights to equal pay for equal work, just remuneration, and the right to form and join trade unions across the world, taking advantage of local cultural practices which render women more vulnerable to such violations (see chapter 4). Multinational companies and local businesses alike can hide their exploitation of women's work, while at the same time claiming to respect cultural traditions. In order for women and men to get fair treatment and equal opportunities in a global capitalist labor market, international labor and human rights must be enforced everywhere.

Some problems with the universalist stance on women's human rights

Despite the support which the campaign for women's human rights has received among human rights activists, feminists, and governments across the North–South divide, the debate over cultural and gender difference has not been laid to rest. Within feminism, dissenting voices argue that the notion of "women's human rights" invites inappropriate generalizations about women's experiences, and assumes that these experiences differ from men's in some fundamental or essential way. Even where this difference is subsumed within an expanded notion of the human individual, as in Nussbaum's (1995) approach, some feminist scholars remain suspicious. As Judith Butler (1992: 7) argues, "[t]o establish a set of norms that are beyond power or force is itself a powerful and forceful conceptual practice that sublimates, disguises and extends its own power play through recourse to tropes of normative universality." In other words, extending the notion of universal human rights to women inevitably shores up the power of the norms underpinning it. Both the critique of gender essentialism and of universalism are frequently linked with a concern about Western cultural imperialism. However, as Uma Narayan (1998: 89; see also chapter 4) points out, this conflation "ignores the degree to which cultural imperialism often proceeds by means of an 'insistence on Difference,' by a projection of imaginary 'differences' that constitute one's Others as Other, rather than via an 'insistence on Sameness.'" The assumption that cultural imperialism operated to level cultural differences around a Western norm leads many feminists into another trap – that of cultural relativism based on essentialist pictures of "national culture and traditions."

It can be argued that essentialist views of culture are not only found among those who are concerned that political demands for justice, equality, rights, or democracy are symptoms of the "cultural corruption" wrought by "Western ideas" (Narayan 1998: 91), whether they be postmodern feminists or conservative fundamentalists. They arguably also underpin Martha Nussbaum's (1995a) dichotomy between universal rights and cultural traditions, which suggests that cultural traditions – particularly in the Third World – are the key obstacle to women's social and economic advancement. Okin's (1998: 39) suggestion that "ethnic and religious groups, too, can develop the same distaste for being seen as condoning serious harms done to women," while indicating that views can change, nevertheless assumes that ethnic and religious groups tend to condone the violation of women's human rights. It also begs the question, "the same distaste as whose?" Hers? The West's?

Narayan argues that the temptation to polarize "Western" and "non-Western" values should be resisted. It hides the degree to which Western and non-Western elites collaborate in eroding the rights and quality of life for many citizens in both Western and Third World contexts. Instead of uncritically accepting the essentialist picture of a culture, we should inquire how this picture has been put together (see chapter 5). As she points out, "those with social power conveniently designate certain changes in values and practices as consonant with 'cultural presentation' while designating other changes as 'cultural loss' or 'cultural betrayal'" (Narayan 1998: 95). A final nail in the coffin of the cultural essentialism thesis is the fact that in most societies we find dissenting views about cultural practices and their meaning and relevance, and therefore no perspective should be granted "the status of being the sole authentic representative of the views and values of a particular culture" (Narayan 1998: 102).

Situating women's human rights

The literature we have discussed thus far has kept us at a highly abstract level, which is emphasized rather than mitigated by the use of some highly emotive examples of human rights abuses. Little information is offered about the non-Western cultures in the arguments on either side of the universalist–relativist divide. Ann-Belinda Preis (1996: 315) suggests that by exploring the "unpredictable, fragmentary and partial nature of human rights" in the everyday life of social actors, it may be possible to move beyond the impasse of the debate. Bearing in mind that cultures are made, not simply inherited, and that the construction of culture is laden with conflicts, the question whether human rights are "recognized" or "rejected" in any particular cultural context becomes more difficult to answer.

One example of such an exploration is found in Margaret Jolly's (1996) article on the Vanuatu Women's Center's engagement with domestic violence. At the center of her discussion is the question whether culture and tradition, referred to as *kastom* in Vanuatu, is "only to be seen as impediments to the realization of women's natural rights?" (Jolly 1996: 171). Jolly explains that *kastom* is the selective retrieval, during Vanuatu's transition to independence, of traditional values and practices which had been modified and adapted under colonial and missionary influence from the nineteenth century onwards. As *kastom* is tied up with Vanuatu citizens' self-understanding as an independent nation, it is important that the Vanuatu Women's Center, an indigenous non-governmental organization, locates itself on the side of *kastom* in its fight against domestic violence. Failing to do so could jeopardize the women's ability to influence indigenous men, especially as the Center's funding through overseas sources could "lay them open to the charges of undue foreign influence and, worse, a betrayal of *kastom*" (Jolly 1996: 180). During a Conference on Violence and the Family sponsored by the Vanuatu Women's Center in 1994, the judiciary was represented mainly by white men who took the view that violence against women was often exacerbated by *kastom* practices. In contrast, many of the women represented at the conference did not want to see their culture denigrated as inherently violent, or set themselves apart as "modern" women in opposition to "tradition" and to their men. In their own arguments against domestic violence, the women endeavored to tread a fine balance between *kastom* and Christian views of the family, and a human rights position on women's rights to education and empowerment, by demanding newly created traditions and collective values which are non-violent and respectful of human rights.

5 Human rights of ethnic minority groups

In this final section, we address some of the questions raised by the application of human rights to culturally distinctive groups such as ethnic minorities or indigenous peoples. The last decade, in particular, has put "ethnic nationalisms" in East and Central Europe, and indigenous rights movements in many parts of the First and Third Worlds, firmly on a map that already featured longer-standing "communalisms" in Asia and "tribalisms" in Africa (Kahn 1998: 1). While chapter 5 discussed some of the reasons for this alleged resurgence of cultural politics, several important issues have remained under-researched, particularly in relation to human rights.

"Ethnocultural minorities around the world," claims Will Kymlicka (1996: 22), "are demanding various forms of recognition and protection, often in the language of 'group rights.'" This is regarded by many commentators with a weary eye, as a new trend that could threaten the international consensus on the importance of the individual rights laid down in the Universal Declaration. They warn that group (or collective) rights may lead to the imposition of group identity on individuals, and subordination of individual rights to the interests of the group (e.g. Lukes 1993). Some point out that legitimizing group rights based on ethnic identity "promises to entrench rather than to erase existing forms of disadvantage and disempowerment" (Comaroff 1995: 264). However, others dispute that there is a chasm between individual and group rights, claiming instead that it is precisely these so-called individual rights which form the basis for many claims raised by minority groups. We explore this debate over individual versus group rights against the background of a growing number of indigenous and ethnic rights movements, using examples from both First and Third World contexts.

Even broader, and at the same time more complex, is the question whether the human rights that emerged from a particular context – European liberal democratic tradition – are "sufficient to accommodate the legitimate interests which people have in virtue of their ethnic identity" (Kymlicka and Shapiro 1997: 4), often in a rather different historical, economic, political, and social context. The proliferation of "cultural politics," of movements claiming to represent particular group interests on the one hand, and of international covenants and declarations on specific rights issues (such as indigenous rights, children's rights, etc.) on the other, suggests that existing instruments are not adequate. Indigenous peoples' demands for land rights, for example, cannot be easily read into the Universal Declaration's "right to own property." Indeed, the individualistic definition of property in the European tradition has often been used to justify their expropriation, as in the case of Australia being declared an "empty land" by colonial settlers.

An equally valid argument, however, could be made for the case that further elaborations of human rights in the light of group interests will do little to improve their enforcement. One reason is that human rights are mainly to be enforced by governments within their national territories, but these are becoming less and less able to do so. Global flows of communication, capital, finance, etc. are "eating away" (Comaroff 1995: 253) at the boundaries of the nation-state, and thus undermining the sovereignty and power to act of governments. The nation-state is also being challenged from within its own boundaries, by the very movements that contribute to the "explosion of cultural politics" (Comaroff

1995: 259). Many of these movements can be seen as a reaction against the effects of globalization, and the national governments' inability or refusal to take the basic human needs of its citizens seriously. Another reason against the establishment of group rights brings us back to the changing ways of thinking about culture. If primordial explanations of ethnic and indigenous identities are rejected as outmoded or false, and constructionist perspectives adopted instead, then such cultural identities cannot be possessed by individuals or groups. Instead, cultural identity is a "mobile, often unstable relation of difference" (Gupta and Ferguson 1997: 13).

5.1   Ethnic minority group rights versus individual rights

The debate over ethnic minority group rights overlaps to some extent with the relativism–universalism debate discussed in the previous section. Underlying both debates is a view of human rights doctrines as being based on the idea of the inherent dignity and equality of all individuals, and focuses mainly on the rights which individuals hold against each other, and against their government (Okin 1998). While those in favor of recognizing the rights of ethnic groups see this as an obstacle, critics fear that a strengthening of group rights would lead to a dangerous undermining of already precarious basic civil rights. Let us examine the case for ethnic group rights first.

Defining indigeneity

The term "indigenous" can relate to individuals, communities, peoples, and nations. One frequently used definition is by Martinez Cobo, which identifies as "indigenous" a group which has historical continuity with pre-invasion and precolonial society, and considers itself distinct from the now dominant sector of society. Indigenous groups "are determined to preserve, develop and transmit to future generations their ancestral territories, and their ethnic identity, as the basis of their continued existence as peoples, in accordance with their own cultural patterns, social institutions and level systems" (United Nations 1986/7, quoted in Pritchard 1998: 43). However, in practice, as well as in its Draft Declaration on the Rights of Indigenous Peoples, the Working Group on Indigenous Populations leaves the task of defining who is indigenous to indigenous peoples themselves.

Proponents of group rights argue that most nation-states are ethnically heterogeneous, a situation which results in some degree of "tension between promoting the identity of a particular community and encouraging integration into the majority group that controls the state" (Phillips 1993: 7). These tensions can develop into violent conflict and involve serious abuses of the human rights of members, particularly of minority groups. Examples range from bombing raids on Kurdish settlements in Iraq and Turkey, to arson attacks on Muslim Indians in the "communal" riots in Mumbai, or on Pakistani British citizens by racist gangs in London, to the forcible separation of indigenous children from their families so as to integrate them into mainstream society in Australia. People suffer such human rights violations not so much as individuals, but rather on the grounds of their group belonging, and the assertion of their human rights therefore requires that their group identity be protected and promoted.

Minority rights are signaled in Article 27 of the UN Covenant on Civil and Political Rights, which declares:

> In those states in which ethnic, religious or linguistic minorities exist persons belonging to such minorities shall not be denied the right, in community with the other members of their group, to enjoy their own culture, to profess and practice their own religion, or to use their own language.

This right, however, is contingent on being recognized as a minority group, that is, as having a group identity which is different from others. Furthermore, it has a number of ramifications which are not immediately obvious; for example, an indigenous group's culture, religion, and language may be so closely linked to a particular way of life and resource base that modernization and the development of this resource base by a dominant center effectively undermines the group's right under Article 27. In response, the group may seek self-government, or even independence, which would allow it to "enjoy their own culture" and consolidate their resource base (Eide 1993). For the Working Group on Indigenous Populations, set up in 1982 to address the "limited relevance of UN activities to the situation of Indigenous peoples" (Pritchard 1998: 40), the right to self-determination is both a crucial and controversial issue: "While Indigenous participants [in the Working Group] oppose any restriction upon their right of self-determination, most governments continue to call for some qualification" (Pritchard 1998: 46). The 1994 Draft Declaration on the Rights of Indigenous Peoples (Working Group on Indigenous Populations 1994) recognizes indigenous peoples' right of self-determination, but it remains to be seen what kinds of changes it will undergo as it advances through the UN system.

Native tongues refuse to be silenced in Australia

In 1998, the Northern Territory government, in the north of Australia, decided to abolish the bilingual education programs in seventeen mainly Aboriginal-controlled schools. In an angry newspaper article in

The Australian, Maria Ceresa (1998) argues that this decision flies in the face of Article 14 of the draft declaration of the UN Rights of Indigenous Peoples, affirming their right to be educated in their own languages. It also indicates that the government is inconsistent in supporting this right for indigenous people in the Third World but not Australia's own. She writes:

Jeannie Nungarrayi Herbert will never forget her school days on the remote Warlpiri Aboriginal community of Lajamanu in the Tanami Desert, 800 km south-west of Darwin. Now 46, she remembers being "flogged with a cane until black and blue" for speaking her mother tongue in the classroom. This strategy did not wipe out her Warlpiri. Today, this Batchelor College graduate [Northern Territory, Australia] is a passionate advocate for Aboriginal-controlled bilingual education. . . .

The philosophy of transitional bilingual education is that indigenous children learn first in their own language and later switch to English. It is supplemented by English as a second language programs. It has resulted in community control of the school curriculum, increased retention rates and unassailable pride in language and culture. The bilingual programs also have started to address the chronic shortage of interpreters in Aboriginal languages, so vital in healthcare and the justice system.

English literacy rates among indigenous children in the Northern Territory remain a national disgrace. . . . [A] 1996 study found indigenous children in remote areas were seven years behind other Australian children in literacy. This is hardly surprising, considering 79 per cent of Aboriginal people in the Northern Territory speak an indigenous language. For many, English is their second, third, fourth and sometimes fifth language. . . .

In response to claims that results in English attained under bilingual schools are "at best inconclusive," [the Education Minister] scraps the bilingual programs. . . . Nevertheless, the Government does see merit in supporting bilingual programs for other nations' indigenous people: in Papua New Guinea and Vietnam, for example.

Other countries treat their indigenous languages as national treasures. The survival of the Welsh language has depended on crucial support from Westminster. This year the Brazilian Government moved to revive hundreds of Indian languages in the Amazon for the first time since Brazil's colonisation by the Portuguese 500 years ago.

In Australia we are dealing with survival, not revival. According to a 1990 study, *The loss of Australia's Aboriginal language heritage* by linguist Annette Schmidt, two-thirds of the original 250 Aboriginal languages are extinct. Of the 90 surviving languages, 20 are in a relatively healthy state. But Schmidt predicts that during the next 30 to 40 years, the number of surviving languages will be fewer than 10.

Meanwhile, like many ethnic groups, the Darwin Greek Orthodox School receives a government subsidy to run language and cultural classes. In a multicultural society that is fair enough, but if that funding were withdrawn tomorrow, the sons and daughters of our Greek-born Australians would have the opportunity to return "home" to learn the language of their forefathers. No such option exists for Herbert's relatives.

Many proponents of group rights refer to examples of indigenous peoples in order to support their argument. However, there are also several other types of minority groups: migrants who are culturally different from the dominant society; and ethno-nationalists who seek a share in state power, or to dominate a heterogeneous society, or to secede from it (Eide 1993). Expansionist, exclusivist, and secessionist modes of ethno-nationalism are a threat to international order and human rights protection and should be counteracted, argues Eide (1993: 12). This should be done not through repression of ethnic groups, but through "an appropriate and effective policy of minority or group protection." The UN Declaration on the Rights of Persons Belonging to National or Ethnic, Religious and Linguistic Minorities (United Nations 1992) is one step in this direction, calling on states to protect and promote the identity of minorities and to ensure that they do not suffer any form of discrimination in the larger society. At the same time, however, the rights of ethnic groups should not prejudice the human rights and fundamental freedoms enjoyed by all, or "sovereign equality, territorial integrity and political independence of States," according to Article 8 of the Declaration on Minorities.

Critics argue that this balance is difficult to strike. Measures aimed at promoting group identities may involve positive discrimination, such as the reservation of certain jobs and educational opportunities for members of minority groups in India. Similarly, the right of minorities to run their own institutions may prejudice the human right of all citizens to be treated equally, and may limit the basic human freedom of minority group members who deviate from

Figure 6.4 Pro-independence demonstration in Dili, East Timor, just moments before the 1991 massacre

group norms and values. As Rhonda Howard (1992) explains, individual and group rights are incompatible because the individual rights are held against state and society, while group rights can only be exercised by those who belong to a group. Some governments have justified their failure to promote minority rights and identities by pointing out that this might lead to ethnic and racial conflict. Third World governments are concerned about threats to national integrity and political stability, and the negative impact they may have on the development process. For example, granting land rights to indigenous peoples could strengthen their resistance to economic developments, such as mining on these lands, from which all citizens could benefit.

A third position in the debate over group rights and individual rights holds that they are closely related, rather than opposed to each other. To live your own life, argues Lukes (1993: 30), you do not only need rights as an individual; social and cultural preconditions must also exist, and this "may well involve the protection and even fostering of collective goods," such as institutions, education, and culture. As Kymlicka and Shapiro (1997: 4) point out, "many of the claims raised by ethnocultural groups seem to fall on the 'individual' side of the ledger." Mick Dodson, the former Aboriginal and Torres Strait Islander Social Justice Commissioner, sees the strengthening of indigenous rights as a way of seeking "justice from a higher authority" in the face of governments' "consistent failure to deliver justice" (Dodson 1998: 19), rather than conferring special rights on indigenous peoples. Referring to Australia, he reminds us of:

> The 20,000 Aboriginal people without adequate water, the 5,000 homeless Indigenous families, the 14,000 Aboriginal people in Western Australia who live without proper sewerage systems, power sources, or other essential services. These people, along with the children who don't get pre-school, let alone secondary or higher education, could all find suitable provisions under the [International Covenant on Economic, Social and Cultural Rights and the Convention on Racial Discrimination]. (Dodson 1998: 28–9)

In Dodson's view, the Draft Declaration on the Rights of Indigenous Peoples seeks to ensure that "the body of international law does what it set out to do: protect and promote the rights of all peoples" (Dodson 1998: 21). It makes indigenous peoples visible, enables them to claim their rights, and thus enhances their status in domestic power struggles (Wilder 1997). Referring to ethnic groups in Nigeria, Eghosa Osaghae (1996: 177) takes the view that group rights are integral to a human rights approach: "without redressing inequalities, the entrenchment of individual human rights would be meaningless to members of disadvantaged groups." Nigeria's federal system tends to favor the dominant ethnic groups in each state, and the right to non-discrimination in the country's constitution has not been able to protect the basic rights of ethnic minorities. In order to be able to "enjoy the same rights that others enjoy," the right of ethnic minorities to exist, preserve their culture, share power and resources, etc., have to be recognized (Osaghae 1996: 186).

5.2   Globalization and human rights

Surrounding the debate over the relationship between group rights and human rights are changes in the ways we think about culture which have shifted our understanding of key concepts involved in the debate. As is already evident from the definitions of "indigenous" and "ethnic" (see box), the beneficiaries of group rights are difficult to identify clearly. This is in part due to the theoretical shift from a primordialist view of ethnic/indigenous identity as a consequence of birth, to a conception of ethnicity as a historical construction, something that evolves and changes. Globalization has played its role in this theoretical shift, and has shaped the global context within which ethnicities, nations, and indigenous communities exist.

In discussing "the world-historical context of recent identity politics," Comaroff (1995: 251) stresses that "the signs and practices of ethnicity and nationality are *always* products of a dialectic of forces local and global." But the "gathering momentum" of globalization in recent times, characterized by an unprecedented growth in global institutions, people movements, communication flows, etc. (Comaroff 1995: 252; see also chapters 1 and 3), poses questions of identity-based rights more starkly. At the same time as rights-based social movements and identity politics are claiming center stage, "the language of rights and obligations, so central to the modern myth of a people, has become increasingly inadequate to describe the condition of many populations, such as the migrant, diasporic, and refugee populations" (Bhabha 1994: 175). The spatially bounded concept of culture, which dominated social sciences in the first part of the twentieth century (Gupta and Ferguson 1997) and still haunts the human rights articulations, is being pulled apart. As Comaroff asks, "where now does, say, Turkish 'society' begin and end? At the borders of Turkey? Or does it take in Berlin?" (Comaroff 1995: 255). It is conceivable, indeed likely, that being Turkish may mean different things in different places, and give rise to different rights claims.

Another paradox raised by processes of globalization relates to the enforcement of human rights. While the state retains the key responsibility for ensuring that all human rights are observed, the deconstruction of state boundaries through global currency, trade, capital, and labor flows undermines the state's ability, even if it wanted, to ensure its citizens' social and economic needs are met and to regulate violence. Comaroff (1995: 259) suggests that globalization and the "crisis of the nation-state" leads to two simultaneous processes, one being the defensive and sometimes oppressive assertion of sovereignty and control by the state, the other an "explosion of identity politics within the national community." As he points out,

> nothing is as likely to ensure that humans will assert (or invent) their differences than being made aware . . . of the *in*difference of the state to their predicament. . . . Nor is it hard to understand why, when faced with such indifference, subordinated groups stress their *cultural* distinctiveness in agitating against their disempowerment. (Comaroff 1995: 261)

Take, for example, the upsurge in indigenous movements in Mexico, highlighted by the "Zapatista Rebellion," which began in the southern state of Chiapas on January 1, 1994, the day that the North Atlantic Free Trade Agreement went into effect. The guerillas' declaration of war identified them as the "original descendants" of Mexico, and called on all Mexicans to join them in opposing the government:

> Today we say enough is enough! To the people of Mexico: Mexican brothers and sisters: We are a product of 500 years of struggle: first against slavery, then during the War of Independence against Spain led by insurgents, then to promulgate our constitution and expel the French empire from our soil, and later [when] the dictatorship of Porfirio Diaz denied us the just application of the Reform laws and the people rebelled and [revolutionary] leaders like [Pancho] Villa and [Emiliano] Zapata emerged, poor men just like us. We have been denied the most elemental education so that others can use us as cannon fodder and pillage the wealth of our country. They don't care that we have nothing, absolutely nothing; not even a decent roof over our heads, nor land, nor work, nor health care, no food, and no education. Nor are we able freely and democratically to elect our political representatives, nor is there independence from foreigners, nor is there peace nor justice for ourselves and our children. (Comandancia General del EZLN, quoted in Collier and Quarantiello 1994: 2)

Mexico's inclusion in NAFTA made the situation worse, with cheap corn imports from neighboring USA threatening the meager livelihood of the small rural producers (*The Economist* 1994: 19) who constitute the majority of Mexico's estimated nine million indigenous people. In other parts of the country, too, indigenous Mexicans have started to demand the right to self-determination for their communities (e.g. Payne 1996).

Comaroff (1995: 264) is skeptical about the promise of group rights helping to "erase existing forms of disadvantage and disempowerment," arguing that oppressive structures based on the triangulation of race, class, and gender are unlikely to be dismantled through a politics of group rights, advantages, or entitlements. As Laclau (1995) points out, inversion of the particular relation of oppression – e.g. by granting special rights to a particular group – would leave the form of oppression unchanged. What needs to be inverted is the *form* of oppression – with its universal reference to oppressors and oppressed – and that would radically change the identities of both. This kind of argument, against the background of processes of globalization, throws us back on universalist conceptions of human rights, whereby the universal becomes a "symbol of missing fullness," rather than a concrete list of rights. As Laclau (1995: 103) explains, considering the universal in this manner implies that "no particularity can be constituted except by maintaining an internal reference to universality as that which is missing." If we apply Laclau's viewpoint to our previous example, the Zapatistas' definition of their indigeneity is inextricably linked with the human rights missing from their lives – the rights to life, health, work, education, and to participate in their government – and which other, more privileged, Mexicans have long been able to enjoy.

6 Summary

This chapter has focused on human rights as a component of the contemporary debates over the meaning of development. The recent prominence of human rights as a development issue has been described as paradoxical by a number of writers, because human rights, while ostensibly important to Western civilization and international development policy, have been accorded a marginal role in the practice of development. The reasons why human rights have had such rhetorical prominence in recent years are linked to the impact of social movements, such as postcolonial struggles and the women's movement; the reconfiguration of global politics following the demise of the Soviet empire; and an increasingly vocal intellectual and political critique of the discursive dominance of Western knowledge.

The three key areas on which the chapter focuses bring out different aspects of the old and new ways of thinking about development and culture. The discussion of child labor sheds light on the age-old debate about human needs versus human rights – which comes first, freedom from poverty, or civil and political freedom? Cultural constructions of childhood and the family are essential in determining the position one takes regarding prohibition or regulation of child labor, and the broader issue of the rights of the child.

The question of cultural relativism discussed in chapter 4 is also central to the debates over the universality of human rights. As the discussion on the rights of women indicates, there are no simple answers. There are strong arguments for supporting both the universalist and the relativist stance on women's human rights. One possibility in overcoming this impasse is to recognize the constructedness of culture, and to pay more attention to how the universal principles are understood and interpreted in local contexts.

The weakening and fragmentation of the nation-state, discussed in chapter 5, has accentuated the contradictions between collective and individual rights, as the tensions between majorities and minorities become acute, and increasingly articulated in terms of primordial identities. Indigenous claims to self-determination further complicate the debate over collective versus individual rights. However, as Laclau points out, the arguments for specific group rights do not necessarily address the causes of these conflicts. Simply asserting group rights over other kinds of rights does little to change the forms of oppression. The example of apartheid South Africa stands out as a case where the recognition of group rights underpinned a racist political economy.

References

Alam, S. 1997: Thank you, Mr Harkin, sir! *New Internationalist*, 292, 12–14.

Banton, M. 1998: Are there ethnic groups in South Asia? *Ethnic and Racial Studies*, 21 (5), 990–4.

Bhabha, H. 1994: *The Location of Culture*. London: Routledge.

Brems, E. 1997: Enemies or allies? Feminism and cultural relativism as dissident voices in human rights discourse. *Human Rights Quarterly*, 19, 136–64.

Butler, J. 1992: Contingent foundations: feminism and the question of "postmodernism." In J. Butler and J. Scott (eds), *Feminists Theorize the Political*. London: Routledge, 3–21.

Carmen, R. 1996: *Autonomous Development. Humanizing the Landscape*. London: Zed Books.

Ceresa, M. 1998: Stilling the voices of Koori culture. Native tongues refuse to be silenced. *The Australian*, December 21, p. 11.

Chatterjee, P. 1993: *The Nation and its Fragments. Colonial and Postcolonial Histories*. Princeton: Princeton University Press.

Clifford, J. and Marcus, G. E. (eds) 1986: *Writing Culture: The Poetics and Politics of Ethnography*. Berkeley: University of California Press.

Collier, G. A. and Quarantiello, E. L. 1994: *BASTA! Land and the Zapatista Rebellion in Chiapas*. Oakland, CA: The Institute for Food and Development Policy.

Comaroff, J. L. 1995: Ethnicity, nationalism and the politics of difference in an age of revolution. In J. L. Comaroff and P. C. Stern (eds), *Perspectives on Nationalism and War*. Iverson: Gordon and Breach, 243–76.

Dodson, M. 1998: Linking international standards with contemporary concerns of Aboriginal and Torres Strait Islander peoples. In S. Pritchard (ed.), *Indigenous Peoples, the United Nations and Human Rights*. London/Leichhardt: Zed Books/The Federation Press, 18–29.

Donnelly, J. 1989: *Universal Human Rights in Theory and Practice*. Ithaca, NY: Cornell University Press.

Donnelly, J. and Howard, R. (eds) 1987: *International Handbook of Human Rights*. New York: Greenwood Press.

The Economist 1994: The revolution continues. *The Economist*, January 22, 1994, 19–21. (no author)

Eide, A. 1993: *New Approaches to Minority Protection*. Manchester: Manchester University Press/Minority Rights Group International.

Ennew, J. 1995: NATS (working children and adolescents): historical emergence of a category. *NATs Working Children and Adolescents International Review*, 0, 19–26.

Falkus, M., Blackburn, S., Brasted, H., Kaur, A., and Wright, D. 1997: *Child Labour in Asia: Some Perspectives on Selected Countries*. International Development Issues 49. Canberra: Australian Agency for International Development.

Gaag, N. van der 1998: No hiding place. *New Internationalist*, 298, 7–11.

Gittings, J. 1999: US and China trade rights charges. *Guardian Weekly*, 160 (10), March 7, 1999, p. 4.

Gupta, A. and Ferguson, J. 1997: Culture, power, place: ethnography at the end of an era. In A. Gupta and J. Ferguson (eds), *Culture, Power, Place. Explorations in Critical Anthropology*. Durham, NC: Duke University Press, 1–29.

Herskovits, M. 1947: Statement on human rights. *American Anthropologist*, 49, 539–43.

Howard, R. 1992: Dignity, community, and human rights. In A. A. An-Na'im (ed.), *Human Rights in Cross-cultural Perspectives: A Quest for Consensus*. Philadelphia: University of Pennsylvania Press, 81–102.

International Labor Organization 1997: *Targeting the Intolerable*. Geneva: ILO.

International Women's Tribune Center 1998: *Rights of Women. A Guide to the Most Important United Nations Treaties on Women's Human Rights.* New York: International Women's Tribune Center.

Ishay, M. R. 1997: Introduction. In M. Ishay (ed.), *The Human Rights Reader.* London: Routledge.

Jolly, M. 1996: Woman ikat raet long human raet o no? Women's rights, human rights and domestic violence in Vanuatu. *Feminist Review*, 52, 169–90.

Kahn, J. S. 1998: Southeast Asian identities: introduction. In J. S. Kahn (ed.), *Southeast Asian Identities: Culture and the Politics of Representation in Indonesia, Malaysia, Singapore, and Thailand.* London/New York: I. B. Tauris Publishers. Singapore: Institute of Southeast Asian Studies, 1–27.

Kymlicka, W. 1996: The good, the bad and the intolerable. Minority group rights. *Dissent*, 43, Summer, 22–30.

Kymlicka, W. and Shapiro, I. 1997: Introduction. In I. Shapiro and W. Kymlicka (eds), *Ethnicity and Group Rights.* New York and London: New York University Press, 3–21.

Laclau, E. 1995: Universalism, particularism and the question of identity. In J. Rajchman (ed.), *The Identity in Question.* London: Routledge, 93–108.

Landler, M. 1998: Indonesian riot police open fire at protests, killing six students. *New York Times*, May 13, 1998, Section A, p. 1.

Lukes, S. 1993: Five fables about human rights. In S. Shute and S. Hurley (eds), *On Human Rights: Oxford Amnesty Lectures.* New York: Basic Books, 19–40.

McGrew, A. 1992: A global society? In S. Hall, D. Held, and T. McGrew (eds), *Modernity and its Futures.* Cambridge: Polity in association with the Open University, 61–116.

McLennan, G. 1992: The enlightenment project revisited. In S. Hall, D. Held, and T. McGrew (eds), *Modernity and its Futures.* Cambridge: Polity in association with the Open University, 327–77.

Narayan, U. 1998: Essence of culture and a sense of history: a feminist critique of cultural essentialism. *Hypatia*, 13 (2), 86–106.

Nussbaum, M. C. 1995a: Introduction. In M. C. Nussbaum and J. Glover (eds), *Women, Culture and Development.* Oxford: Clarendon Press, 1–34.

Nussbaum, M. C. 1995b: Human capabilities, female human beings. In M. C. Nussbaum and J. Glover (eds), *Women, Culture and Development.* Oxford: Clarendon Press, 61–104.

Okin, S. M. 1998: Feminism, women's human rights, and cultural differences. *Hypatia*, 13 (2), 32–52.

Osaghae, E. E. 1996: Human rights and ethnic conflict management: the case of Nigeria. *Journal of Peace Research*, 33 (2), 171–88.

Payne, D. W. 1996: Between home and history. Mexico's Indians refuse to disappear. *Dissent*, 43, Summer, 61–6.

Pereira, W. 1997: *Inhuman Rights – The Western System and Global Human Rights Abuse.* The Other India Press/Apex Press/Third World Network.

Phillips, A. 1993: Introduction. In A. Eide (ed.), *New Approaches to Minority Protection.* Manchester: Manchester University Press/Minority Rights Group International, 5–8.

Pigg, S. L. 1996: The credible and the credulous: the question of "villagers' beliefs" in Nepal. *Cultural Anthropology*, 11 (2), 160–201.

Pollis, A. 1996: Cultural relativism revisited: through a state prism. *Human Rights Quarterly*, 18 (2), 316–44.

Preis, A.-B. 1996: Human rights as cultural practice: an anthropological critique. *Human Rights Quarterly*, 18 (2), 286–315.

Pritchard, S. 1998: Working Group on Indigenous Populations: mandate, standard-setting activities and future perspectives. In S. Pritchard (ed.), *Indigenous Peoples, the United Nations and Human Rights*. London/Leichhardt: Zed Books/The Federation Press, 40–64.

Sartre, J.-P. 1967: Preface. In F. Fanon, *The Wretched of the Earth*. Translated by Constance Farrington. Harmondsworth: Penguin, 7–26.

Schmidt, A. 1990: *The loss of Australia's Aboriginal Language Heritage*. Canberra: Aboriginal Studies Press.

Shenon, P. 1998: U.S. to appeal to Indonesian military to stop crackdown. *New York Times*, May 14, 1998, Section A, p. 6.

Swaminathan, M. 1998: Economic growth and the persistence of child labor: evidence from an Indian city. *World Development*, 26 (8), 1513–28.

Swift, A. 1997: Let us work. *New Internationalist*, 292, 21–3.

Tomasevski, K. 1993a: *Development Aid and Human Rights Revisited*. London: Pinter Publishers.

Tomasevski, K. 1993b: *Women and Human Rights*. London: Zed Books.

United Nations 1948: Universal Declaration of Human Rights. A/RES/217 A (III), December 10, 1948.

United Nations 1965: International Convention on the Elimination of All Forms of Racial Discrimination. A/RES/2106 A (XX), December 21, 1965.

United Nations 1966a: International Covenant on Economic, Social and Cultural Rights. A/RES/2200 A (XXI), December 16, 1966.

United Nations 1966b: International Covenant on Civil and Political Rights. A/RES/2200 A (XXI), December 16, 1966.

United Nations 1979: Convention for the Elimination of All Forms of Discrimination Against Women. A/RES/34/180, December 18, 1979.

United Nations 1986: Declaration on the Right to Development. A/RES/41/128, December 4, 1986.

United Nations 1986/7: Study of the Problem Against Indigenous Populations, Vol. 5. Conclusions, Proposals and Recommendations. Special Rapporteur Martinez Cobo. UN Doc E/CN/4/Sub2/1986/7 Add 4 para 379.

United Nations 1989: Convention on the Rights of the Child. A/RES/44/25, November 20, 1989.

United Nations 1993: Vienna Declaration and Programme of Action adopted at the World Conference on Human Rights. A/CONF.157/24, June 25, 1993.

United Nations Fourth World Conference on Women 1995: Beijing Declaration and Platform for Action. Report of the Fourth World Conference on Women, Beijing, September 4–15. United Nations Publication.

Wallerstein, I. 1995: *After Liberalism*. New York: New Press.

White, B. 1996: *Globalization and the Child Labour Problem*. Working Paper Series No. 221. The Hague: Institute of Social Studies.

Wilder, L. 1997: Local futures? From denunciation to revalorization of the Indigenous Other. In G. Teubner (ed.), *Global Law Without a State*. Dartmouth: Aldershot, 215–56.

Working Group on Indigenous Populations 1994: Report of the Working Group on Indigenous Populations on its Twelfth Session. UN Doc E/CN/4/Sub2/1994/30.

7 Culture, Development, and the Information Revolution

1   Introduction

In chapter 3 we looked at globalization as a term describing a range of economic, political, and cultural processes shaping the contemporary world with particular intensity as the twenty-first century begins. In particular, we considered the arguments about whether globalization is a homogenizing force toward one "world culture," or whether greater diversity might not be one of its consequences. The case studies examined in chapter 3 suggested that globalization is a very complex set of phenomena in terms of development and the "Third World." The local and the global engage each other, not necessarily on equivalent terms, but nevertheless in ways which do not straightforwardly lead to a homogeneity based on the imposition of a globalizing Western culture, or on a heterogeneity based on some authentic preservation or strengthening of local particularities. In terms of development, one of the consequences of globalization appears to be, on the one hand, an expansion of the "reach" of orthodox development discourse, caught in Western trajectories of knowledge and power, while, on the other, out of the complex dynamic between global and local contexts, a plurality of meanings of "development" are produced. The outcome is a relativization of mainstream "development" as one among many possible visions of progress and change, albeit the only one global in its scope and reach. "Development" is revealed as a contested term in ways which undermine the taken-for-grantedness of its emancipatory claims to progress, as arguments emerge about "counter-development" and "post-development."

In this chapter, we revisit these issues with a different slant. Most of us are probably familiar with the hype surrounding the so-called "information revolution" over the last few years in the press, and in at least some national and international policy settings. Many, if not most, of the readers of this book will in some way or other be users of the technology constituting this "revolution," whether facsimiles, mobile phones, cable and satellite television, or the quintessential "superhighway," the internet. What is revolutionary about these technologies is the way they variously enable the flexible and rapid transfer of information in a variety of forms. Microprocessors and optic fiber now make possible global circuits of knowledge exchange and data processing, perhaps most spectacularly in the finance sector, where vast sums of money are rapidly transferred at the behest of investors responding to an endless flow of data on economic indicators. National borders and the bounds of distance collapse as capital ebbs and flows on a global scale in an endless search for bigger profits. Large corporations are now able to fine-tune their production processes such that "[t]he global economy combines instantaneous electronic transactions with the accelerated distribution of physical goods through 'just-in-time' delivery systems" (Robins 1997: 24). Benetton, the multinational clothing manufacturer and retailer, pioneered such a system, linking every cash register in its far-flung retail empire directly to the small-scale enterprises which manufactured its clothing, enabling it to dispense with a costly labor- and capital-intensive stock-holding system (Braham 1997).

Culturally too, the "information revolution" is generally seen to have major implications. On the one hand, Bill Gates, the head of the giant Microsoft corporation, forecasts that "[t]he information highway is going to break down barriers and may promote a world culture, or at least a sharing of cultural activities and values" (quoted in Hedley 1998: 205). On the other, in what Shohat and Stam (1996: 147) refer to as the "dystopian" view of globalization, Hedley describes a more negative process. "Rather than producing physical products in a technically neutral fashion, it will involve rapid and widespread transmission of information in a culture-laden, asymmetrical way" (Hedley 1998: 204). Yet other commentators point to the progressive potential of the internet especially, to rework notions of community, civil society, and democracy as individuals connect with one another in "virtual space" in ways which overcome the constraints of formal politics in most contemporary large-scale societies. As Cronin and McKim point out, "[a] defining feature of the Internet is that no one person, company, government or organisation has ultimate control" (Cronin and McKim 1997: 241). Economically, socially, and politically, the new forms of communication technologies are much more difficult for national governments to control and deploy for their own purposes, as satellite and digital technologies ignore the constraints of terrestrial borders. Other commentators point out that behind all the hype about "revolution" gross inequalities still lurk: "By the year 2000, as the rest of us gaze in wonder at millennium celebrations and ponder the luxuries of the digital future, about a billion people will be living in absolute poverty" (Golding and Harris 1997: 3).

Table 7.1 Selected indicators of information and telecommunications penetration by country income level

Group	Telephone main lines per 1,000 people, 1995	Personal computers per 1,000 people, 1995	Internet users per 1,000 people, 1996
Low-income economies	25.7	1.6	0.01
Lower-middle-income economies	94.5	10.0	0.7
Upper-middle-income economies	130.1	24.2	3.5
Newly industrializing economies (NIEs)	448.4	114.8	12.9
High-income economies	546.1	199.3	111.0

Source: World Bank (1999: 63).

   The potential benefits and drawbacks of the "information revolution" are now at the center of debates over development. The World Bank's 1998/99 *World Development Report* (1999) sees the information revolution as a powerful new tool with which to fight poverty and realize "development" of the Third World. Others are more cautious about this new focus on knowledge and information technologies. "What comes first? Clean water or communication technologies?" (Panos Institute 1998: 2). Thabo Mbeki, Vice-President of South Africa, pointed out that "Over half of humankind has never dialled a phone number. There are more telephone lines in Manhattan than in the whole of Sub-Saharan Africa" (quoted in Lynch 1997: 253) (table 7.1 and figure 7.1). Nevertheless, as the global economy becomes more and more based on access to and exchange of information, development seems to hinge on successful participation in this new economy of knowledge. Failure to access and utilize the new forms of technology and information implies an even greater marginalization from the world economy, and a widening of the gap between those in the know and those who are not.
   It is not only mainstream development organizations like the World Bank who see the "information revolution" as a potentially transformatory tool for the Third World and development. Many progressive non-governmental organizations (NGOs) and social movements in the Third World are utilizing such technologies as the fax, modem, and internet to facilitate networking and information exchange across political and geographic boundaries (Coeur de Roy 1997; Hornik

Figure 7.1   A communications center in Mumbai, India

1988). Advocacy groups are able to project their points of view directly to the peak policy organizations through email and on-line discussion, such as the one set up by the Panos Institute and the World Bank to discuss the 1998/1999 report on *Knowledge for Development* (World Bank 1999). Given a basic PC and internet link, development workers and activists from diverse regions of the globe were brought into direct communication with each other, and with the Bank's experts, in a free exchange of comment and criticism. New transnational communities are being forged as groups geographically disparate are brought into direct communication with each other through the use of email.

Thus the new technologies appear to offer new opportunities for empowerment and emancipation on the part of the poor and dispossessed of the Third World in ways which resist and transform the orthodoxies of mainstream development, and flout the constraints of oppressive governments. However, another side to the "information revolution" is the way in which it can operate to consolidate existing hegemonies at the cultural level. Global television, through satellite and cable, encourages a diversity and access to "other" ways of living and being, while at the same time it imposes a uniformity of genre and style. Latin American "soaps" may well compete effectively alongside North American shows in many parts of the Third World, but they are still "soaps." As such they conform to a narrativization of everyday life which has more to do with the mentalities of US corporate media cultures than to Mexican or Brazilian ways of narrating life. From this perspective, much of the hype about the new information technologies simply disguises new forms of a very old cultural imperialism, entrenching Western cultural logics ever more deeply at the expense of indigenous and local perspectives.

This chapter explores these and related issues in order to arrive at some tentative conclusions about the consequences of the new information technologies and globalization in terms of culture, development, and global inequality. The information revolution is still only in its infancy, but the linkages between globalization and media technologies are not. In the next section we look briefly at the ways in which the media and modernity are connected, before considering the ways in which the contemporary processes of globalization and technological innovations are challenging established ways of thinking about those connections in terms of the Third World, culture, and development. Subsequent sections explore the ways in which communication technologies are being constructed within development discourse, and the ways in which those same technologies are being harnessed to counter the orthodoxies of development.

2   Media and modernity

Technologies of communication are more than just the nuts and bolts – or chips and bites – that constitute the apparatus they involve. Communication lies at the heart of sociality. It is the means by which symbolic knowledge is conveyed, stored, and circulated. Through communication people create connections between each other and construct communities of identity and belonging. Changes in the form and scope of communication therefore impact on the nature of social interaction and the circulation of symbols, values, and cultural knowledge. As Thompson contends (1995: 4)

> the use of communication media involves the creation of new forms of action and interaction in the social world, new kinds of social relationship and new ways of relating to others and to oneself. . . . In a fundamental way, the use of communication media transforms the spatial and temporal organization of social life, creating new forms of action and interaction, and new modes of exercising power, which are no longer linked to the sharing of a common locale.

For most of human history, communication was possible only in face-to-face interactions, between people inhabiting the same space and time. Social relations were small-scale and isolated within the bounds of the village. Where a broader sense of community emerged, as in medieval European Christendom, "the figuring of imagined reality was overwhelmingly visual and aural. Christendom assumed its universal form through a myriad of specificities and particularities," including images of Christ as a Burgundian peasant or Mary as a local merchant's daughter (Anderson 1991: 22–3). The universal was imagined in the form of the local, and relied on the immediate translation of the symbolic image by an elite interlocutor, such as the local priest. In this sense, symbolic knowledge remained tied to an immediate physical and temporal proximity.

The coming of modernity disrupted this homology between space, place, and time. It tore "space away from place by fostering relations between 'absent' others, locationally distant from any given situation of face-to-face interaction" (Giddens 1990: 18). Crucially, the local was no longer largely self-contained but "thoroughly penetrated by and shaped in terms of social influences quite distant from them" (Giddens 1990: 19). Central to this disruption and transformation of non-modern ways of being were innovations in communications technologies, starting with the invention of the printing press in the fifteenth century and the concomitant growth of a reading public, a market for new kinds of written texts in vernacular languages, such as novels, instruction manuals, and newspapers. These new forms of mediated communication encouraged new kinds of social relationships and institutions. The aural and visual cultures of the medieval world were giving way to print cultures in which "writers could now address themselves to an invisible public; face-to-face relationships were giving way to public cultural forms of a more anonymous sort" (Landes 1988: 52). Benedict Anderson (1991) argues that this "print capitalism" was a necessary precondition for the emergence of that quintessentially modern "imagined community," the nation, in which a spatially dispersed and anonymous population are able to refigure connectedness through time and space in a notion of "simultaneity" that fosters a sense of national community. Take the example of the newspaper:

> We know that particular morning and evening editions will overwhelmingly be consumed between this hour and that, only on this day, not that. . . . The significance of this mass ceremony – Hegel observed that newspapers serve modern man as a substitute for morning prayers – is paradoxical. It is performed in silent privacy, in the lair of the skull. Yet each communicant is well aware that the ceremony he performs is being replicated simultaneously by thousands (or millions) of others of whose existence he is confident, yet of whose identity he is not. (Anderson 1991: 35)

Thus, Thompson (1995: 10) argues, "the development of the media has transformed the nature of symbolic production and exchange in the modern world," and has mirrored the characteristic institutional features of modernity, such that symbolic knowledge is produced on an ever-expanding scale as commodities in the market place, and hence accessible across space and time by individuals (figure 7.2). "Mass media" refers to this capacity of the technologies of printing, radio, television, and the like, to be available to many recipients at once. Hence the media assumes an institutional distinctiveness in modern societies, wielding "symbolic power" in terms of "the capacity to intervene in the course of events, to influence the actions of others and indeed to create events, by means of the production and transmission of symbolic forms" (Thompson 1995: 17). This power attained a greater significance with the development of telecommunications in the second part of the nineteenth century. The telegraph and telephone fundamentally altered people's experience of time and space. The two were no longer necessarily contiguous; the same time no longer meant the same place, as telecommunications facilitated an awareness of "now" which went beyond a particular locale. With the advent of radio and television and telecommunications on a global scale, it is now commonplace to register one's own sense of time and place through reference to events and people spatially remote, illustrated in such questions as "what were you doing when . . . John F. Kennedy was assassinated? The wall came down in Berlin? Princess Diana died?" Combined with the development of rapid mass transport, this generates the compression of space and time, as in the ways an Australian telecommunications advertisement is able to urge people to "go home" on the telephone, encouraging a migrant constituency to use the telephone to collapse the barriers of distance emigration engenders, with poignant images of the immediacy of emotion and connection enabled by the telephone link between Italy, Britain, Greece, and Australia. As Thompson (1995: 34) points out, the world seems smaller and more familiar. "So profound is the extent to which our sense of the world is shaped by media products today that, when we travel to distant parts of the world as a visitor or tourist, our lived experience is often preceded by a set of images and expectations acquired through extended exposure to media products." At the same time, these symbolic forms are increasingly the material with which individuals forge understandings of themselves and others. Appropriation of media messages becomes one means of self-fashioning in a modern world severed from the constraints of face-to-face contact.

The innovations of the last twenty years in communication technologies have intensified many of these features of modernity. The computer network, satellite communication systems, and their manifestations in the internet and global television networks have compressed time and space even further. Messages

Figure 7.2   Global features on the landscape of the Mongolian plain

and images flash around the globe instantly, drawing people from many different locations and cultural systems into new flows of symbolic knowledge and information. The tight coordination of Kurdish protests around the world on the arrest of the leader of the Kurdish Workers' Party, Abdullah Ocalan, by the Turkish authorities in February 1999 was one manifestation of this. The synchronized feature of the protests transformed a local struggle for autonomy into a global issue as governments as far apart as Sydney, Moscow, Athens, London, and Berlin, to name only some, were forced to confront the issue in their own jurisdictions (Cypel 1999; *Guardian Weekly* 1999). Another, of a very different ilk, was the global reach of the public mourning on the death of Princess Diana in 1997 (Ang, Barcan, Grace, Lally, Lloyd, and Sofoulis 1997). Arjun Appadurai has charted the complex and contradictory nature of these "scapes," as we discussed in chapter 3. Some social scientists have extended such arguments further to argue that the overall impact of these technological innovations is a major factor in a shift to a qualitatively different kind of social system. Manuel Castells has developed this theme most comprehensively in his thesis that the information revolution is marking a shift from an industrial system to an "informational" system or "network society" (Castells 1996a; 1996b; 1997; 1998). In the industrial system the basis of wealth and power was control over the production process of material goods. Knowledge and information were tools to this end. In the informational society, information is both the primary raw material and major outcome: "because information and knowledge are deeply embedded in the culture of societies, culture and symbol processing become direct productive forces in the new society" (Castells 1996a: 16). "Culture as the source of power, and power as the source of capital, underlie the new social hierarchy of the Information Age" (Castells 1998: 348). While cultural battles are fought by the media, it is not the media which is the power-holder, but rather the networks of information exchange and symbolic information.

The relevance of Castells's argument here is the scenario he draws of the effects of this shift in terms of global and local inequalities. In the industrial system, it was plentiful raw materials and cheap labor which drew the peripheral societies into its circuits of production and accumulation, albeit in dependent forms. For some, as in the newly industrializing countries (NICs) of East and Southeast Asia, this lopsided integration led eventually to a degree of successful integration into dominant circuits of productive power and capital accumulation. The informational society, however, generates a different structure of development and dependency, around three "rules," as Castells terms them:

1   "the ability to use (and to some extent to produce) information technologies has become a fundamental tool of development."

2   "the whole world becomes interconnected in its economic functions through information and communication flows." Without access to these flows, societies cannot participate in the global economy.

3   "the informational economy, while connecting the whole planet in a series
    of networks of flows, does so selectively." Significant parts of the world,
    deficient in the knowledge and information valued as the productive mo-
    tor of the new system, become irrelevant to the global informational economy
    (Castells 1996a: 27).

These faultlines of marginality will not necessarily follow the current divide
between North and South, as the example of India's burgeoning importance as
a software producer suggests (D'Souza 1996). However, it is difficult to see
societies where institutions such as education are grossly underdeveloped and
the basic technical infrastructure such as electricity are inadequate and unreli-
able, closing the gap between themselves and those societies already at the
core of the information revolution, as both producers and users. Instead, Castells
draws a complicated picture of inequality whose axes are global/local rather
than North/South. While whole societies may well be excluded from the new
system, another pattern is the "dualization of dependent societies," in which
segments of society are integrated into the global informational economy and
culture, while the bulk of the population remains largely outside it (Castells
1996a: 28). The Indian case seems to bear this out, where abject poverty, illit-
eracy, and lack of the most basic accouterments of modernity exist alongside a
sophisticated participation in the global informational society as both producers and consumers.

    The consequences of this are complicated by another faultline running
through the information revolution between increasing globalization and
growing individualization. On the one hand, satellite communications and
television networks span the globe, drawing more and more people into global networks of information and images. On the other, there is a process of
segmentation as those same technologies allow for greater targeting of audiences and markets, extending to the individualizing of reception permitted
by the use of VCRs and walkmans. Increasingly, with the use of multimedia
computer networks, there is the possibility of "individualized, self-program-
mable image representation and perception, that will increasingly disconnect
individuals from the mass media, while connecting the individualized communication expressions to the individuals' mental world" (Castells 1996a: 20).
The result, Castells suggests, may well be a socially fragmented and divided
world "made out of the fundamental opposition between the *net* and the *self*"
(Castells 1996a: 31). The overarching social institutions of work, education,
mass media, and the like, which currently form the webs of connection within
social life, would be replaced by segmented networks or flows involving their
participants in a constant process of reinvention of self in order to manage a
social system predicated on innovation, flexibility, and unpredictability
(Castells 1996a: 34). For those excluded from or resistant to these new forms
of cooption and sociality, the temptation would be to construct autonomous
identities external to the organizing principles of the network society, what
Castells terms "the rise of tribes" in movements such as religious fundamen-

talism, ethnic separatism, or localism (Castells 1998: 351–352); or by establishing what he calls "perverse connections" to the global economy through criminal activities such as drug trading or arms smuggling (Castells 1996a: 28). The experience of Afghanistan is suggestive here, where a very marginal society in terms of globalization and the information revolution turns to fundamentalism or outlaw activities, such as the trade in heroin, to sustain a sense of identity and agency.

Castells's rather gloomy depiction of the consequences of the information revolution hinges in part on the disconnection of culture from experience in the "culture of real virtuality":

> On the one hand, dominant functions and values in society are organized in simultaneity without contiguity; that is, in flows of information that escape from the experience embodied in any locale. On the other hand, dominant values and interests are constructed without reference to either past or future, in the timeless landscape of computer networks and electronic media, where all expressions are either instantaneous, or without predictable sequencing. All expressions from all times and from all spaces are mixed in the same hypertext, constantly rearranged, and communicated at any time, anywhere, depending on the interests of senders and the moods of receivers. This virtuality is our reality because it is within the framework of these timeless, placeless, symbolic systems that we construct the categories, and evoke the images, that shape behaviour, induce politics, nurture dreams, and trigger nightmares. (Castells 1998: 350)

In many ways Castells's arguments are insightful, at this early stage of the "revolution," and offer early warning of the potential dangers it holds if social systems are not flexible in adapting to the new demands of global circuits of information. However, his depiction of the "informational society" is remarkably static for such a dynamic new system. There is relatively little weight given to the process of reception and intervention, such that those who form part of the (implicitly more powerful) networks of information and symbolic production are assumed to fairly unproblematically conform to the demands of that particular generalizing cultural form. Those who are marginal or resistant to incorporation are depicted as external to the forms of communication forming the core of the revolution. Little of the dynamic and contradictory nature of Appadurai's model of flows and scapes seeps into Castells's scenario. In this respect, he seems to owe more to the structural certainties of dependency theory than is perhaps initially apparent. Ultimately, the ability of the core to continually strengthen its control over the key productive capacities and wealth-creating aspects of the global system, whether industrial or informational, appears unassailable unless optimal conditions pertain, as Castells outlines in *End of Millennium* (1998: 360). If all the people in the world are informed, if business is socially responsible, if belief in democracy is restored, if there is harmony with nature, among humans and with the self, then things will turn out all right! In this sense, most people, particularly the poor and marginal, remain victims in this vision, powerless to participate in or coopt the new informational age for their own purposes. This bears close resemblance to the major theoretical frame-

work that has, to date, analyzed the impact of media technologies and globalization on the Third World – cultural imperialism. In the next section we shall
consider the ways in which this theory is being revised, as a prelude to looking
at the ways in which the information revolution is being treated in mainstream
development discourse and in non-mainstream development contexts.

3   Cultural imperialism revisited

The central thesis of the cultural imperialism perspective as applied to communication and media is that the post-Second World War development of a global
mass media has essentially constituted a process of Americanization of the rest
of the world. The combination of US-based transnational corporate activity with
American leadership in the development of communication technology and
expertise forged an invincible global dominance such that the American model
of commercial media became the normative model for the development of media
systems the world over. As one of the earliest advocates of this thesis, Herbert
Schiller, put it, an "electronic invasion" threatened to subvert and overwhelm
the traditions and cultural inheritance of all those societies less advanced in the
ways of the media (Thompson 1995: 166). Recently, however, a number of commentators have begun to query the assumptions of the cultural imperialism
thesis, pointing to a much more complex picture of the economic, political, and
cultural consequences of the global development of media and communication. We can summarize these under three headings.

3.1   American dominance

The thesis tends to conflate economic power with cultural power (Golding and
Harris 1997: 5). Thompson points out that even in the heyday of American
economic might, there were other ideoscapes effectively competing for the hearts
and minds of the world's people than that of American consumerism, not least
communism, exemplified in the duel of the radiowaves between the Voice of
America and Radio Moscow. Over the last two decades, with the major economic and political restructuring of the world order, "new forms of symbolic
power, in some cases linked to the resurgence of nationalism and fundamentalist religious beliefs, have emerged in different parts of the world" (Thompson
1995: 167). American movies and programs do not always displace local products. The serialization of the Hindu epic, the *Mahabharata*, won 90 percent of
domestic viewers in a three-year run on the state-owned station Doordarshan,
in the late 1980s (Shapiro 1992, cited in Shohat and Stam 1996: 149). Its translation into a "religious soap opera" on the small screen, however, gave the ancient myth a new and vibrant intimacy as millions of viewers tuned in week
after week to watch their favorite characters. Didactic mythology became familiar and domestic, as religion and television combined to reinscribe the myth
in the costumes, language, and geography of northern India. In the process,

Ananda Mitra argues, "Doordarshan was able to establish the necessary links between the production of a national image and the Hindu religion" entrenching in popular culture "the residual connection between Bharat, as the Hindu state of the time of the Mahabharat, and Bharat, as the Hindu state poised on the brink of the twenty-first century" (Mitra 1994: 153). Other ways of being Indian, by faith, region, language, and dress, were implicitly marginalized, while the "advanced" patina of television reinforced a connection already being made in the political arena between Hindu nationalism and progress, which has seriously compromised the communal balance in contemporary Indian society (Mitra 1994). The Indian example illustrates the complexities of the relation between communication technologies and culture missed in the simplistic attribution of overwhelming power to American (or Western) media, either as technology or content. In this case, the specific qualities of television as a technology of communication, its intimate, domestic reception and the demands of serialization, combined to particular local effect.

A Turkish case study adds an ironic twist to the imperialism thesis. In their study of global media and cultural identity in Turkey, Sahin and Aksoy (1993) point out that access to global media technologies, particularly satellite television, has made Turkey one of the largest transnational broadcasters in the world. What originally began as a way of broadcasting "home culture" to Turks living in Germany became a broader project of pan-Turkish revivalism as the fall of the Soviet Union opened up the Turkic audiences in the new republics of Central Asia. A new state-owned television channel advertises the Turkish model of development, "to show them how a Muslim population can be successful if it follows the Western model. . . . This was to be a step toward the cultural unity of the Turkish-speaking people around the globe" (Sahin and Aksoy 1993: 39). In this example, the time–space compression achieved by the new media and communication technologies works to facilitate other dreams of cultural expansionism apart from that of "cocacolaization"!

3.2 Authenticity of Third World cultures

The theory works with an implicit dualism between an "authentic" culture besieged by the all-consuming juggernaut of global media corporations peddling Hollywood commercialism. Local "culture" is seen as some kind of hermetically sealed entity pitched against the overwhelming might of a similarly sealed "dominant culture" (Ang 1996: 152). As Sreberny-Mohammadi (1997) points out, this ignores the history of colonialism and imperialism which predates both American dominance and electronic mass media, and which precludes any claim to "authenticity" by West or non-West alike. "Most forms of culture in the world today are, to varying extents, hybrid cultures in which different values, beliefs and practices have become deeply entwined" (Thompson 1995: 170). Changes in the Chinese television and movie industries in Hong Kong illustrate this point:

> In the 1950s, Cantonese movies dominated the Hong Kong market, drawing on
> traditional Cantonese cultural forms. . . . Their popularity declined in the 1960s
> and early 1970s, when Hollywood films consistently outgrossed locally produced
> Chinese films. By the 1980s, however, the most popular film genres in Hong Kong
> were once again locally produced, in the Cantonese language, but evincing defi-
> nite elements of "indigenization" of the Western action adventure movie format.
> (Ang 1996:154)

Bruce Lee's emergence as a star of Hollywood-produced "Kung Fu" movies
further illustrates the cultural cross-overs and hybrid qualities of much "global" media.

   Nevertheless, it is certainly the case that American media products have a
universal and normative status, and that the main flow of media images is
from the West to the Third World. Shohat and Stam (1996: 148) cite the fact that
most films are in fact produced outside the West, with India producing the
most fiction films in the world today, and yet the Oscar ceremonies "inscribe
Hollywood's arrogant provincialism: the audience is global, yet the product
promoted is almost always American, the 'rest of the world' being corralled
into the restricted category of the 'foreign film.'" Even in-flight movies on Third
World airlines assume a film such as *Honey, I Shrunk the Kids* is universal fare
for a clientele of Sikhs, Muslims, and Hindus flying from Thailand to India
(Shohat and Stam 1996: 149).

3.3   Passivity of the audience

The "hypodermic needle" theory, as Shohat and Stam (1996: 149) term it, assumes a direct and unmediated reception of the message of American media
products by Third World audiences. However, a number of studies have shown
that the process of reception, interpretation, and appropriation of the symbolic
content of media products is a complex process of active negotiation on the
part of the audience. People are not empty receptacles into which the media
pours its messages; they already have existing contexts, frameworks, and
motivations they "view" with. In this sense, the space–time compression of
globalization theory does not hold, as Ang notes:

> the spatial dimension cannot be discounted when it comes to what happens to
> those images once they arrive in specific locations. At this cultural level, at once
> more mundane and more fluid local realities can themselves present an unpre-
> dictable interpretive screen through which the intruding electronic screen images
> are filtered . . . global media do affect, but cannot control local meanings. (Ang
> 1996: 151)

An illustration of this is the ways in which the villagers of upper Egypt made
sense of the American and Egyptian soaps, in Lila Abu-Lughod's (1995) study,
discussed in chapter 3. The villagers contextualized the programs in terms of
their own locations and understandings of life, as marginal and poor participants in Egyptian modernity. Another example is the way in which Trinidadians

interpreted the American soap opera *The Young and the Restless* in terms of the Trinidadian concept of *bacchanal*, a term which refers to the confusion, disorder, and fluidity of everyday life in a society on the periphery of, yet constantly buffeted by, the global order (Miller 1992, cited in Ang, 1996: 160). "The fact that, in the late 1980s, an American soap opera became a key instrument for forging a highly specific sense of Trinidadian culture reveals the way in which the local can construct its syncretic, postmodern brand of cultural identity through consumption of the global" (Miller 1992, quoted in Ang 1996: 160).

Thompson argues that a new "symbolic axis" has been created of "globalized diffusion and localized appropriation," which is increasing in importance as the circulation of information and communication becomes ever more global in character. He traces the effects of this in terms of the process of appropriation around three themes.

(1) *The use and significance of media messages depends on the context of their recipients.*
He cites a study of the role of communication media in the Iranian revolution. In the struggle against the Shah in the 1970s, religious imagery and language were deployed to articulate resistance as a struggle between Islamic traditionalism and decadent Western modernity. This did not stop the religious opposition utilizing the modern technology of audio cassettes to surreptitiously circulate the exiled Ayatollah Khomeini's speeches widely inside Iran. In the post-revolutionary era, a reversal occurred. Videos of Western movies and music circulated underground, forming a subversive popular cultural space against what many perceived as the oppressive nature of the Islamic regime (Sreberny-Mohammadi and Mohammadi 1994, cited in Thompson 1995: 174–5).

(2) *Symbolic distancing from everyday life.*
Appropriation of global media products and their symbolic content exposes people to other ways of living and being. Familiar local ways of living become relativized in ways that can sometimes feed into a more critical reception of dominant local political hegemonies. In China, for instance, as access to television increased dramatically in the 1980s, people gained a picture of the West which did not necessarily match the anti-Western rhetoric of the communist government: "when we look at the TV programs we can see that the West is not so bad" (Lull 1991, cited in Thompson 1995: 176). On the other hand, a more ambiguous consequence of this relativization process resulted in Turkey, where it has, at least in part, fed into a pan-Turkish sentiment which may reinforce dominant nationalist politics, which in turn fuels internal oppressions such as the Kurdish struggle for cultural autonomy in southeast Turkey (Sahin and Aksoy 1993).

(3) *Source of tension and conflict.*
Global media images and messages can conflict with local beliefs and ways of life, instigating tensions and even overt conflict. Young Bedouin women in the Western Desert love Egyptian soap operas because they present very different

and appealing lifestyles, where marrying for love and independent living are possible, in contrast to Bedouin norms and practices (Abu-Lughod 1989, cited in Thompson 1995: 175). James Lull argues that the greater access to global media in China in the 1980s was one important contributor to the democracy movement which peaked tragically in the Tian An Men Square massacre. The media provided a pool of alternative ways of thinking and living, acting as a resource with which to query the official line and imagine alternatives (Lull 1991, cited in Thompson 1995: 178).

To summarize, the cultural imperialism thesis overstates the power of the "global" as a straightforward extension of American/Western economic, political, and cultural dominance; and understates the ways in which the "local" interacts with the global. In order to grasp the subtle complexities of the "information revolution," a more refined understanding of the workings of both globalization and media technologies is required. While acknowledging the "persistent asymmetry between centre and periphery, and to the very substantial Americanness of much of the 'global' media" (Ang 1996: 161), an explanatory model needs to recognize the fluidity of the interplay between the two, such that no one coherent global culture gels.

4   Communication technologies, knowledge, and development discourse

The implications of the information revolution are being evaluated somewhat differently within mainstream development discourse. The World Bank's Report *Knowledge for Development* acknowledges the risks inherent in the application of these new technologies, particularly in terms of inequality of access "where a fortunate few surf the World Wide Web while others remain illiterate" (World Bank 1999: 14). But it nevertheless sees enormous benefits flowing from their application in developing countries, ranging from new income opportunities for the poor, to improved governance as electronic networking facilitates the exchange of information between institutions involved in the policy process. The existing "knowledge gaps" between developed and less-developed societies can be solved through "development" of the institutions and organizations of poor countries. Moreover, poor countries can "leapfrog" from underdeveloped communication technologies to the most advanced forms, thus closing the technological gap more quickly.

An example is the installation of digital telephone networks. Countries such as Botswana, Gambia, and Jamaica have gone from small or non-existent nondigital systems to fully digitalized networks, while wealthy industrialized nations such as Germany and Japan are still struggling to make the transfer from their established non-digital systems (figure 7.3). Mobile phone use is much higher in the Philippines and Thailand than it is in France or Canada, where wire-based networks still dominate (World Bank 1999: 59).

**Some developing economies have
leapfrogged over the richer industrial ones
and installed fully digital networks.**

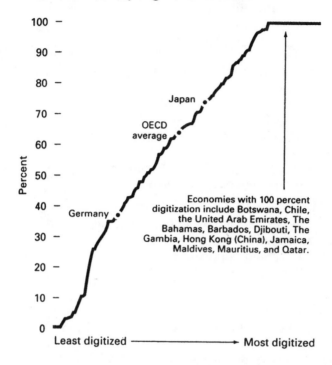

Note: Data are for 1993 for 164 economies worldwide. Source:
International Telecommunication Union data.

Figure 7.3   Economies ranked by share of the telephone network digitized

Few if any of the cautions expressed by Castells or the cultural imperialist perspective are shared by the World Bank, and while it acknowledges the task is not necessarily easy, there is little of the sense of complexity conveyed in the work of those revising the cultural imperialism thesis. Narrowing the knowledge gap is a matter of following a three-step plan (see box), coupled with institution building designed to address information problems that negatively affect the operation of the market, by "establishing recognized standards and enforcing contracts, thus making possible transactions that would otherwise not occur" (World Bank 1999: 3). This must also involve "addressing information problems that hurt the poor," by "taking time to learn about their needs and concerns, so that society can then offer them useful information and assist them in devising ways to reduce their isolation from markets and to improve their access to formal institutions" (World Bank 1999: 3). This inclusive market-centered model of successful adaptation to, and adoption of, the new information technologies, derives its optimism and programmatic clarity in large part from the ways in which mainstream development discourse has long constructed the relationship between media technologies and development through the lens of modernization theory.

Three steps to narrowing the knowledge gap (adapted from World Bank 1999: 2–3)

1 Acquiring knowledge by
   - accessing existing knowledge from elsewhere through a free and open market
   - developing local knowledge through research and development
   - building on indigenous knowledge

2 Absorbing knowledge by
   - extending universal basic education to all, including previously disadvantaged groups, such as girls
   - lifelong learning opportunities
   - supporting tertiary education, especially science and engineering

3 Communicating knowledge by
   - taking advantage of new information technology – through increased competition, private sector provision, and appropriate regulation
   - ensuring the poor have access

---

5 Communicating modernization

In the1960s and 1970s the new information technology then galvanizing development theorists and policy makers was the transistor radio, which brought mass communications media to the poor in a cheap, simple, and portable format:

> [O]n a worldwide scale it is the medium of radio that has been man's most potent communication innovation since the development of writing. The large-scale manufacture of cheap, battery operated transistor radios has been the breakthrough responsible for putting most of the world's people into an international communication network. (Jamison and McAnany 1978: 9)

The poor majority could now be reached en masse by governments and other development agencies to motivate, educate, and instruct them in the ways of development and modernization. As Daniel Lerner put it, communication had taught people in developing countries to expect progress and a better life; now it could be used to teach them how to get it (Lerner 1967: 314). Wilbur Schramm, writing in the same volume, maintained that communication's role was to "implant and extend the idea of change, to raise the aspirations of . . . people so that they will want a larger economy and a modernized society" (Schramm 1967: 18). Radio's one-way, centralized mode of communicating and dispersing information was ideally suited to this top-down approach typical of modernization theory, which sought to teach Third World people "to take part in planning and governing; to tighten their belts, harden their muscles, work longer, and wait for their rewards" (Schramm 1967: 19). Essentially, this model of communication assumed a modernizing elite at the national level (themselves previously informed by the "modern" experts of the West) who would cajole, exhort, and educate the backward and traditional masses to follow their path of modernization. Nominal participation in the development process was accorded certain groups through such avenues as the radio forums experimented with in India: "a group of farmer-leaders meet once a week to hear a radio talk by an expert, then they discuss what to do about the suggestions he [sic] makes" under the guidance of a village community worker (Schramm 1967: 13). As Schech and Vas Dev (1999: 7) observe, "[t]he modernization school saw development as a global process mediated by mass communication at the national level." Mass communication's particular function was to "focus the attention of millions of diverse individuals upon the same object at the same time," and thus create a "climate for development" in any given society (Lerner 1967: 124).

In the 1990s a more inclusive language dominates the World Bank Report (1999). There is less talk of "modernizing elites" and much more emphasis on aspiring to close the "information gaps" within developing societies by bringing the poor in. Communication as "a two-way street" is facilitated by the new technologies, which allow "the flow of information from those who have much of it to those who have less" (World Bank 1999: 13), at the same time as they "hold potential for teaching government and institutions about the poor, for designing programs that benefit them, and for enhancing their participation and empowerment" (World Bank 1999: 60). The emphasis in the Report is on the ways in which information technology can give disadvantaged and remote groups of Third World people instantaneous and relatively inexpensive access to the global market place, which the World Bank views as holding the key to sustainable poverty alleviation. As examples of ways in which poor Third World producers benefit from the new communication technologies, the World Bank (1999: 60–1) cites:

- Women in Panama post pictures of their handicrafts to the World Wide Web and gain access to the world market.
- Subsistence farmers in the Philippines become pineapple specialists, using telex and fax machines to communicate directly with researchers and market representatives.
- Farmers in Côte d'Ivoire use cellular phones to get international cocoa price quotations direct from Abidjan.

A more cautious note is sounded, however, by one development worker based in Ecuador:

> In the information economy, the Internet is a means of transporting goods to market and a means of creating markets through advertising. The goods are information, not Nicaraguan coffee, Sri Lankan tea or sweaters from Ecuador. We could end up with a situation in which the Internet provides the infrastructure for a global economy in which we all import Microsoft products and try to sell handicrafts. (Bruce Girard of Pulsar, Ecuador, cited in Panos Institute 1998: 11).

6   Knowledge and development

In other ways not much has changed between the top-down certainties of the 1960s modernizers and the switched-on fervor of the World Bank's approach in the late 1990s. Both operate with a deficit model of the Third World and knowledge. Knowledge, especially knowledge for and about development and modernity, is something the West has and the Rest needs to get – from the West. In particular, it is the poor who are lacking the appropriate knowledge and information to address their own needs, as the opening paragraph of the *Development Report* evocatively illustrates:

> Knowledge is like light. Weightless and intangible, it can easily travel the world, enlightening the lives of people everywhere. Yet billions of people still live in the darkness of poverty – unnecessarily. Knowledge about how to treat such a simple ailment as diarrhoea has existed for centuries – but millions of children continue to die from it because their parents do not know how to save them. (World Bank 1999: 1)

The connections between the Enlightenment, progress, and development discourse, discussed in chapter 1, "shine" through here. Echoes of the "civilizing mission" of colonialism and missionary tropes of benevolence are strong, as the opening sentences evoke images of a wonderful "white" light of Western knowledge beaming into the dark minds of the poor masses of the Third World. The final sad statement begs the questions, "what knowledge?" and "why do some have it and others not?" as the poor are depicted as guilty perpetrators of their own plight. Ignorance, not economic, political, and social inequality, is the cause of poverty, and the burden is on the poor to educate and uplift themselves, albeit with the help of newfangled machines which will "plug" them into the necessary circuits of information and markets. Despite the rhetoric of inclusion, participation, and empowerment, the dominant image of the poor is one of ignorant lack, requiring external knowledge and assistance.

It is important to acknowledge the ways in which information technologies can be, and indeed are, harnessed by individuals, organizations, and institutions in the Third World in ways which contribute to human development. This is seen, perhaps most successfully to date, in health services, where, as a former Ugandan Health Minister commented, "[i]nformation poverty is one of the most serious obstacles facing health professionals in the developing world" (quoted in Panos Institute 1998: 14). Computer networking has facilitated data collection and dissemination, collaborations and consultations between medical professionals, and invaluable access to on-line medical libraries and current research (Panos Institute 1998). But there is an ironic edge to the depiction of the poor of the Third World as knowledge deficient, at a time when the knowledges of indigenous peoples, mainly poor and from the Third World, are being recognized and drawn on more than ever before as vital resources for "development."

The World Bank Report acknowledges the importance of local and indigenous knowledges, but it does so in a very narrow way, which reflects its limited and contentious use of the term "knowledge." The "knowledge" it depicts as "enlightening" is the knowledge of the market. While it recognizes there are many kinds of knowledge, it concentrates on two types (World Bank 1999: 1):

- Knowledge about technology – "know-how" about nutrition, birth control, software engineering, accountancy, which is unequally distributed between rich and poor – as nations and as people.
- Knowledge about attributes – "such as the quality of product, the diligence of a worker, or the creditworthiness of a firm – all crucial to effective markets."

The knowledge the Report focuses on is technical knowledge or skill, highly specialized and specific in its focus. It also sees knowledge as a commodity, something that can be both bought and sold on the market. This view of knowledge as a commodity is also what underlies the regulatory frameworks common in advanced capitalist societies, of patent and copyright laws, or intellectual property rights (IPRs), by which a person or (more common these days) a corporation can legally define ownership of an idea or invention. Such legal frameworks developed in Western Europe and North America in tandem with the industrial revolution and capitalism. Today, the notion of property rights has been expanded by the innovations in biotechnology to include genetic materials from plants and even people (Christie 1995: 73, cited in Gray 1997: 60). As globalization and information technologies combine to expand the importance of knowledge as the "raw material" of the global economy (Castells 1996a: 16), developed countries have moved to extend and formalize the existing global framework for intellectual property rights. A new agreement on trade-related intellectual property rights (TRIPs), effective from 1996, strengthened intellectual property rights for members of the World Trade Organization, while giving developing countries a transition period to 2006 to bring their national IPR frameworks into line with the world standard (World Bank 1999: 33–4). As the World Bank Report acknowledges, the overall effect of this move is likely to benefit the producers of knowledge, primarily based in the developed countries, and increase the information gap (World Bank 1999: 35).

The strengthening of a global regulatory system for IPR has particular consequences for indigenous communities, as it is their knowledge and biological resources which are the latest frontier of commercialization. Breakthroughs in biotechnology and pharmaceuticals in particular have "increased scientific and commercial interest in the genetic resources of indigenous people and their land, and their traditional knowledge of such resources" (Gray 1997: 60). Multinational corporations are able to make use of this knowledge commercially, without in any way acknowledging or compensating the indigenous people from whose knowledge and resources the commercial application was developed. One example is the illegal reproduction of Aboriginal paintings onto fabric or carpets. In the so-called Carpet Case, a lawsuit revealed how the work of eight Aboriginal artists was illegally copied for the designs of carpets, which were manufactured in Vietnam and then reimported to Australia for sale (Johnson 1996). Or another example in which the Western Australian government has made an agreement with a pharmaceutical company ensuring their access to the Smokebush plant, which the company is investigating for possible application in the fight against Acquired Immune Deficiency Syndrome (AIDS). There is no recognition of, or benefits accorded to, the indigenous peoples on whose land the plant grows, and who have long used it medicinally. Stephen Gray (1997: 61) notes that:

> The Patents Act 1990 (Cth) reflects the primarily economic focus of Australian intellectual property law, refusing to protect mere knowledge or "discoveries" until they are turned into economically valuable "inventions." The practical consequence of this for Aboriginal people is that non-Aboriginal scientific or commercial interests are frequently able to exploit Aboriginal genetic resources, or knowledge gained from these resources, with the protection of Australian patent law.

The World Bank Report itself cites the example of the rose periwinkle plant, unique to Madagascar, from which a pharmaceutical multinational developed successful anti-cancer drugs worth over US$100 million in sales. Madagascar received nothing (World Bank 1999: 35, Box 2.6). If the US government is successful in its application for patent claims over the genetic material from indigenous people in Panama, Papua New Guinea, and the Solomon Islands, then the very bodily substances of indigenous people will legally be alienated from them. Without a direct economic application, indigenous knowledge and resources count for nothing in the knowledge market. The Report sees the main issue in all this as a question of finding an appropriate mode of compensation for local communities when their indigenous knowledge is patented by, usually First World, corporations. It cites a Costa Rican case where a contract was struck between the national biodiversity institute and a multinational corporation for a share of royalties in any commercial applications that might result in exchange for access to extensive biomedical extracts, as the model solution (World Bank 1999: 35). The well-known British cosmetics company, The Body Shop, pioneered the negotiation model of accessing indigenous knowledge and materials, indeed shaping its marketing image around its benevolent "green capitalism" (Roddick 1991).

However, this ignores the much more fundamental issue of how knowledge is being constructed in such a system. The very idea of divorcing "knowledge" from context, and breaking it up into specialized bits which can be exploited and exchanged on the market, is deeply alien to indigenous ways of thinking about knowledge.

For indigenous peoples, life is a common property which cannot be owned, commercialized, or monopolized by individuals. Based on this world view, indigenous peoples find it difficult to relate intellectual property rights issues to their daily lives. Accordingly, the patenting of any life forms and processes is unacceptable to indigenous peoples (Asian Consultation Workshop: 1995).

To indigenous communities around the world, the issue is not one of establishing a property right in intellectual knowledge on the basis of economic application, but an issue of self-determination (see chapter 6).

Extract from Jalayinbul Statement on Indigenous Intellectual Property Rights (1993)

Indigenous Peoples and Nations share a unique spiritual and cultural relationship with Mother Earth which recognises the inter-dependence of the total environment and is governed by the natural laws which determine our perceptions of intellectual property.

Inherent in these laws and integral to that relationship is the right of Indigenous Peoples and Nations to continue to live within and protect, care for, and control the use of that environment and of their knowledge.

Within the context of this statement Indigenous Peoples and Nations to [sic] reaffirm their right to define for themselves their own intellectual property, acknowledging their own self-determination and the uniqueness of their own particular heritage.

Within the context of this statement Indigenous Peoples and Nations also declare that we are capable of managing our intellectual property ourselves, but are willing to *share* it with all humanity provided that our fundamental rights to define and control this property are recognised by the international community. [emphasis in original]

The generous sentiments expressed in the final paragraph of the Jalayinbul Statement sit uneasily alongside the World Bank's relentlessly narrow view of knowledge as that which is useful for the market and will realize its "owners" a profit. From an indigenous perspective the "knowledge" being communicated by such mainstream development institutions hardly rates as such. It remains to be seen what the outcomes will be of indigenous challenges to the IPR regime, although it is already becoming much more difficult for scientific establishments and corporate interests to simply appropriate the knowledge and biological resources of indigenous peoples and their land, as the World Bank acknowledges (1999: 35, Box 2.6). Interestingly, the very ability of indigenous communities to network globally and place the issue of indigenous knowledge and self-determination on the international political agenda has been in large measure due to their effective use of those same information technologies which have also accelerated the scientific and commercial exploitation of their knowledge and land, a point we shall explore in the final section below.

7   Wired for change

At this early stage of the "revolution" it is difficult to forecast which, if any, of the prognoses about the information revolution's impact on development will bear the test of time in the new century, as globalization and technological change proceed apace. In other words, we do not know as yet whether the pessimistic scenarios of marginalized, "switched off" islands or digitized cultural imperialism will be proven right, or the more optimistic perspectives of cultural pluralism and inclusive modernization. However, there is already evidence that the new information technologies are being appropriated in ways which confound the underlying premises of some, if not all, of the four approaches to the "revolution" outlined thus far in this chapter.

Many NGOs, including progressive Southern-based ones, are as positive about the benefits of electronic communication and digitalization as the World Bank, and are delighted with the willingness of donor organizations to fund IT applications. Dorothy Grace Guerrero (1997) writes passionately of the potential of IT, especially electronic mail, to pitch the grassroots people-controlled alternative development movement to a global interconnectedness with each other. Echoing a large number of writers who see the horizontal connections and publicity of the internet as evidence of its democratic potential, she identifies a slow movement among voluntary associations, NGOs, and the like to build "processes of transnational democratization" (Bello 1995, cited in Guerrero 1997: 83). She cites a number of examples of the progressive use of the new technologies, including the Zapatistas of Chiapas, Mexico, who "have mastered the use of the cyberspace in popularizing their struggle and exposing the dark side of NAFTA" (Guerrero 1997: 79; see also Castells 1997). On a more cautious note, others acknowledge such instances, but also warn of the dangers of cooption as NGOs find themselves at the mercy of mainstream donors for the technical back-up and continued funding necessary to keep up with the pace of change in IT. As well:

> Having decided to connect to the World Wide Web as a means of retrieving information and establishing communication more effectively, NGOs may face the danger of becoming dependent ... to that kind of knowledge and communication supplied by the Internet. In doing this they may risk undervaluing those

more indigenous and culturally specific forms of knowledge. (Vas Dev and Schech 1999)

At the same time, some indigenous communities appear to be able to appropriate the new technologies for their own cultural purposes. Remote Australian Aboriginal communities have been at the forefront of pioneering the use of communication technologies as a means of cultural maintenance. A fascinating study by the anthropologist Eric Michaels of one such community's initial exposure to Hollywood videos in the 1980s is suggestive of the intricacies involved. Michaels noted that the Warlpiri people, an isolated community in the central desert region of Australia, found electronic media much more accessible and attractive than print or literacy. On the basis of his observations, he refuted the view that "the introduction of imported video and television programs [meant] the destruction of Aboriginal culture. Such a claim can only be made in ignorance of the strong traditions and preferences in graphics, the selectivity of media and contents, and the strength of interpretation of the Warlpiri" (Michaels 1994: 96, cited in Ang 1996: 159). Rather, he argued that video might be more compatible with Warlpiri culture and its graphic system than print media. Such a hypothesis calls into question the assumption that indigenous knowledge systems might be incompatible with the latest information technologies, and puts a new spin on the old binary of tradition/modernity, when the non-modern might actually find the "postmodern" world of virtuality more compatible than its creators!

Another case study raising similar issues is Diane Nelson's ethnographic account of the ways in which Mayan activists are using IT to sustain cultural survival in Guatemala. Their starting point is that the "decolonization of the Maya begins with knowing how to use technology and not being used by it" (ALMG 1990: 42, cited in Nelson 1996: 292). To this end they make use of literacy (in Spanish), desktop publishing, the radio, and computers. In Guatemala, however, to be indigenous meant to be non-literate, uneducated, and "traditional." Mayans who achieved an education, spoke Spanish, and worked in white-collar jobs were automatically defined as Ladino (the dominant non-indigenous identity), and hence denied their indigenous identity: "in Guatemala . . . you cannot be both Indian and modern" (Nelson 1996: 288). Thus by insisting on appropriating the trappings of modernity to assert their cultural rights to indigeneity, the Maya "are decoding and reprogramming such familiar binary oppositions as those between past and future, between being rooted in geography and being mobile, between traditional and being modern, . . . between unpaved roads and the information superhighway" (Nelson 1996: 289). The Mayans bring us to a curious and gently ironic full circle. The technology that many commentators insist is the outward manifestation of a revolution that may well take us beyond the "modern" into some kind of "cyberfuture" is being utilized to nurture and sustain the archetypal non-modern identity and knowledge of the "traditional," in ways which make the term "development" even more ambiguous and opaque than it already is.

8 Summary

In this chapter we have canvassed several approaches to the information revolution in terms of culture and development:

1 *Castells's troubled vision of the "informational society,"* which risks a reworking of global and social inequality between the "switched on" and "switched off." Old binaries are reworked in his model around a new tension between the "net and the self." The poor majority of the Third World become irrelevant to, and excluded from, the new society, while resistance seems possible only by remaining outside the "networked."

2 *The cultural imperialism thesis*, which sees a global mass media spearheading the "electronic invasion" of a defenceless Third World, forging an invincible global culture in America's image.

3 *The hybridity thesis*, which offsets cultural imperialism with the agency of Third World people to resist, adapt, and appropriate global media into their own contexts of symbolic knowledge. Although the hegemonic Western cultural influence frames the global context, no one dominant global culture will emerge, but a plurality of vibrant, responsive, and adaptive locals.

4 *New versions of old*: the information revolution as harbinger of a more inclusive vision of modernization, exemplified in the World Bank's perspective on knowledge and development. New information technologies potentially offer the Third World faster and more comprehensive access to the – largely Western – knowledge which will dispel poverty and close the gap between North and South. Essentially, it is a positive mirroring of the cultural imperialism thesis, which is predicated on a channeling of local and indigenous knowledges into the funnel of "market-friendly" Western and capitalist ways.

Regardless of which of the above scenarios is more plausible – and one is tempted to say: all of the above – the informational society clearly places knowledge at the forefront of struggles over the meaning and outcomes of development. The evidence surveyed in this chapter supports the conclusions reached at other points in this book. On the one hand, global capital and its ways of knowing harness information technologies to extend its hegemony, yet even capital is increasingly diverse in its spatial and cultural qualities. This is most clearly demonstrated in the claims that East Asia offers a qualitatively different kind of capitalism based on its cultural distinctiveness (see chapter 2). On the other hand, the same technologies are being consumed and used in a variety of complex local ways to reimagine "authentic" identities and to re-establish cultural autonomy in ways that sometimes actively resist the discursive dominance of the West. The contradictions over power and knowledge raised in the discussion of information technologies in this chapter echo the primary point the book as a whole seeks to make about the relationship between culture and development. By drawing on cultural studies, specifically the notion of discourse, and the idea of culture as a network of representations rather than a bounded entity, we have been able to show how dominant conceptions of development are implicated in relations of knowledge and power, which in turn underpin the reproduction of global inequality. At the same time, the uneven complexity of globalization produces not uniformity, but diversity and hybridity. The effect is that development as discourse, process, and practice is caught in the ambiguities of complicity and resistance. The dominant model of development is relativized and revealed as one particularly powerful, but not necessarily successful, local imagining, challenged even in its own center by alternative models of green ecology. The singular vision of modernity embedded in development discourse is belied by the plurality of modernities being forged out of the crucible of the "development experience" of the last fifty years, as Pigg's (1992) ethnography of *bikas* in Nepal discussed (see chapter 3). Paradoxically, new information technologies may offer the potential to reconfigure development studies by enabling new syntheses to emerge from the plethora of local experiences of development. The horizontal linkages made possible by ICTs are already bringing local knowledges and experiences to global audiences, particularly through the informational and activist networks on the World Wide Web. It is at least conceivable that out of this "global babble" new frameworks for imagining development may emerge.

References

ALMG (Academia de Lenguas Mayas de Guatamala) 1990: *Documentos del Seminario: Situacion Actual y Futuro de la ALMG*. Guatemala City: Patrocinio del Ministerio de Cultura y Deportes.

Anderson, B. 1991: *Imagined Communities*. London: Verso. First published 1983. Revised and extended.

Ang, I. 1996: *Living Room Wars. Rethinking Media Audiences for a Postmodern World*. London: Routledge.

Ang, I., Barcan, R., Grace, H., Lally, E., Lloyd, J., and Sofoulis, Z. (eds) 1997: *Planet Diana: Cultural Studies and Global Mourning*. Kingswood, NSW: Research Center in Intercommunal Studies, University of Western Sydney Nepean.

Asian Consultation Workshop on the Protection and Conservation of Indigenous Knowledge, TVRC Tambunan, Sabah, East Malaysia, February 24–7, 1995, mimeo.

Braham, P. 1997: Fashion: unpacking a cultural production. In P. du Gay (ed.), *Production of Culture/Cultures of Production*. London: Sage in association with the Open University, 119–75.

Castells, M. 1996a: The net and the self. Working notes for a critical theory of the informational society. *Critique of Anthropology*, 16 (1), 9–38.

Castells, M. 1996b: *The Rise of the Network Society. The Information Age: Economy, Society and Culture,* Vol. 1. Oxford: Blackwell.

Castells, M. 1997: *The Power of Identity. The Information Age: Economy, Society and Culture,* Vol. 2. Oxford: Blackwell.

Castells, M. 1998: *End of Millennium. The Information Age: Economy, Society and Culture,* Vol. 3. Oxford: Blackwell.

Christie, J. 1995: Biodiversity and intellectual property rights: implications for indigenous peoples. In *Perspectives on Indigenous Peoples' Management of Environment Resources.* Papers delivered at Ecopolitics IX, Darwin, September 1–3, 1995.

Coeur de Roy, O. 1997: The African challenge: internet, networking and connectivity activities in a developing environment. *Third World Quarterly,* 18 (5), 883–98.

Cronin, B. and McKim, G. 1997: The internet. In Y. Courrier and A. Large (eds), *World Information Report 1997/98.* Paris: United Nations Educational, Scientific, and Cultural Organization Publishing, 240–55.

Cypel, S. 1999: L'errance d'Apo, l'indésirable. *Le Monde,* Sélection Hebdomadaire, February 27, 1999, p. 6.

D'Souza, D. 1996: Silicon Valley East. *New Internationalist,* 286, 25.

Giddens, A. 1990: *The Consequences of Modernity.* Cambridge: Polity.

Golding, P. and Harris, P. 1997: Introduction. In P. Golding and P. Harris (eds), *Beyond Cultural Imperialism. Globalization, Communication and the New International Order.* London: Sage, 1–9.

Gray, S. 1997: Vampires round the campfire. Indigenous intellectual property rights and patent laws. *Alternative Law Journal,* 22 (2), 60–7.

Guardian Weekly 1999: Kurd leader captured. *Guardian Weekly,* February 23, 1999, p. 1. (no author)

Guerrero, D. G. M. 1997: From the shadows of the Tigers: Asia's empowering experiences in the Communication Age. *Transnational Associations,* 2, 75–88.

Hedley, R. A. 1998: Technological diffusion or cultural imperialism? Measuring the information revolution. *International Journal of Comparative Sociology,* 39 (2), 198–212.

Hornik, R. C. 1988: *Development Communication, Information, Agriculture, and Nutrition in the Third World.* New York: Longman.

Jamison, D. T. and McAnany, E. G. 1978: *Radio for Education and Development.* London: Sage.

Johnson, V. 1996: *Copyrites. Aboriginal Art in the Age of Reproductive Technologies. Touring Exhibition 1996 Catalogue.* Sydney: National Indigenous Arts Advocacy Association and Macquarie University.

Julayinbul Statement on Indigenous Intellectual Property Rights 1993: *Conference Outcomes, Julayinbul Conference on Intellectual and Cultural Property,* November 27, 1993, Jingarrba.

Landes, J. B. 1988: *Women and the Public Sphere in the Age of the French Revolution.* Ithaca, NY: Cornell University Press.

Lerner, D. 1967: Communication and the prospects of innovative development. In D. Lerner and W. Schramm (eds), *Communication and Change in the Developing Countries.* Honolulu: East–West Center Press, 305–18.

Lull, J. 1991: *China Turned On: Television Reform and Resistance.* London: Routledge.

Lynch, M. D. 1997: Information highways. In Y. Courrier and A. Large (eds), *World Information Report 1997/98.* Paris: United Nations Educational, Scientific, and Cultural Organization Publishing, 285–303.

Michaels, E. 1994: *Bad Aboriginal Art: Tradition, Media and Technological Horizons.* St Leonards, NSW: Allen and Unwin.

Miller, D. 1992: "The young and restless" in Trinidad: a case of the local and the global in mass consumption. In R. Silverstone and E. Hirsch (eds), *Consuming Technologies*. London: Routledge. pp nos.

Mitra, A. 1994: An Indian religious soap opera and the Hindu image. *Media, Culture and Society*, 16, 149–55.

Nelson, D. M. 1996: Maya hackers and the cyberspatialized nation-state: modernity, ethnostalgia, and a lizard queen in Guatemala. *Cultural Anthropology*, 11 (3), 287–308.

Panos Institute 1998: The internet and poverty: real help or real hype? *Panos Briefing* 28, April; http://www.oneworld.org/panos/briefing/interpov.htm.

Robins, K. 1997: What in the world's going on? In P. du Gay (ed.), *Production of Culture/ Cultures of Production*. London: Sage/Open University Press, 11–47.

Roddick, A. 1991: *Body and Soul: Profits with Principles. The Amazing Success Story of Anita Roddick and the Body Shop*. New York: Crown.

Sahin, H. and Aksoy, A. 1993: Global media and cultural identity in Turkey. *Journal of Communication*, 43 (2), Spring, 31–41.

Schech, S. and Vas Dev, S. 1999: Wired in the Third World: the links between communication technologies and development discourses. Unpublished manuscript.

Schramm, W. 1967: Communication and change. In D. Lerner and W. Schramm (eds), *Communication and Change in the Developing Countries*. Honolulu: East–West Center Press, 5–31.

Shohat, E. and Stam, R. 1996: From the imperial family to the transnational imaginary: media spectatorship in the age of globalization. In R. Wilson and W. Dissanayake (eds), *Global/Local. Cultural Production and the Transnational Imaginary*. Durham, NC: Duke University Press, 144–70.

Sreberny-Mohammadi, A. 1997: The many cultural faces of imperialism. In P. Golding and P. Harris (eds), *Beyond Cultural Imperialism. Globalization, Communication and the New International Order*. London: Sage, 49–68.

Sreberny-Mohammadi, A. and Mohammadi, A. 1994: *Small Media, Big Revolution: Communication, Culture and Iranian Revolution*. Minneapolis: University of Minnesota Press.

Thompson, J. B. 1995: *The Media and Modernity. A Social Theory of the Media*. Cambridge: Polity.

Vas Dev, S. and Schech, S. 1999: NGOs and the internet: enslaved to Western style information? Unpublished manuscript.

World Bank 1999: *World Development Report 1998/99. Knowledge for Development*. Oxford: Oxford University Press.

Index